THE SECRET OF

Also by Gregg Braden

Books

The Divine Matrix
The God Code
*The Isaiah Effect**
Secrets of the Lost Mode of Prayer
The Spontaneous Healing of Belief

CD Programs

An Ancient Magical Prayer (with Deepak Chopra)
Awakening the Power of a Modern God
The Divine Matrix (abridged audio book)
The Divine Name (with Jonathan Goldman)
Fractal Time (abridged audio book)
*The Gregg Braden Audio Collection**
Speaking the Lost Language of God
The Spontaneous Healing of Belief (abridged audio book)
Unleashing the Power of the God Code

*All the above are available from Hay House
except items marked with an asterisk

Please visit Hay House UK: **www.hayhouse.co.uk**
Hay House USA: **www.hayhouse.com**
Hay House Australia: **www.hayhouse.com.au**
Hay House South Africa: **www.hayhouse.co.za**
Hay House India: **www.hayhouse.co.in**

THE SECRET OF

AND A NEW WORLD AGE
UNDERSTANDING FRACTAL TIME

GREGG BRADEN

HAY HOUSE

Australia • Canada • Hong Kong • India
South Africa • United Kingdom • United States

Please Note: This book was previously published as *Fractal Time: The Secret of 2012 and a New World Age*. All material is unchanged from the previous edition.

First published and distributed in the United Kingdom by:
Hay House UK Ltd, 292B Kensal Rd, London W10 5BE. Tel.: (44) 20 8962 1230;
Fax: (44) 20 8962 1239. www.hayhouse.co.uk

Published and distributed in the United States of America by:
Hay House, Inc., PO Box 5100, Carlsbad, CA 92018-5100. Tel.: (1) 760 431 7695 or (800)
654 5126; Fax: (1) 760 431 6948 or (800) 650 5115. www.hayhouse.com

Published and distributed in Australia by:
Hay House Australia Ltd, 18/36 Ralph St, Alexandria NSW 2015. Tel.: (61) 2 9669 4299;
Fax: (61) 2 9669 4144. www.hayhouse.com.au

Published and distributed in the Republic of South Africa by:
Hay House SA (Pty), Ltd, PO Box 990, Witkoppen 2068. Tel./Fax: (27) 11 467 8904.
www.hayhouse.co.za

Published and distributed in India by:
Hay House Publishers India, Muskaan Complex, Plot No.3, B-2, Vasant Kunj, New Delhi –
110 070. Tel.: (91) 11 4176 1620; Fax: (91) 11 4176 1630. www.hayhouse.co.in

Distributed in Canada by:
Raincoast, 9050 Shaughnessy St, Vancouver, BC V6P 6E5. Tel.: (1) 604 323 7100;
Fax: (1) 604 323 2600

A catalogue record for this book is available from the British Library.

ISBN 978-1-8485-0222-2

Printed and bound in Great Britain by CPI Bookmarque, Croydon, CR0 4TD.

Editorial consultation: Stephanie Gunning
Editorial supervision: Jill Kramer • *Design:* Tricia Breidenthal

Ancient traditions viewed time as a never-ending dance of cycles—great waves of energy that pulse across the universe, linking the past and the future in their journey. Modern science seems to agree. In the language of physics, time merges with the space it travels through to create <u>space-time,</u> ripples in the quantum ocean that makes the universe possible.

A growing body of evidence suggests that time's waves, and the history within them, repeat as cycles within cycles. As each new cycle begins, it carries the same conditions as the past, but with a greater intensity. It's this <u>fractal time</u> that becomes the events of the universe and life.

Using a code that we're only beginning to understand, the ancient Maya charted fractal time on a series of calendars unlike anything the world has seen since. Because they understood the cycles, they knew that the conditions of the future are also etched into the record of the past. This includes the mysterious end date of the present world-age cycle: December 21, 2012. The key to understanding 2012 and what it means for us today is to know how to read the map of time.

This book is dedicated to our discovery of time as the language of our past, the map to our future, and the world to come.

CONTENTS

INTRODUCTION

---

*"For I dipped into the future, far as human eye could see,
Saw the Vision of the world, and all the wonder
that would be."*

— Alfred, Lord Tennyson (1809–1892), poet

We're living the end of time.

Not the end of the world, but the end of a *world age*—a 5,125-year cycle of time—and the way we've known the world throughout that time. The present world age began in 3114 B.C. and will end in A.D. 2012. Because the end of anything also marks the beginning of what comes next, we're also living the start of what follows the end of time: the next world age, which ancient traditions called the *great cycle*.

From the epic poems of India's Mahabharata to the oral traditions of indigenous Americans and the biblical story of Revelation, those who have come before us knew that the end of time was coming. They knew, because it always does. Every 5,125 years, the earth and our solar system reach a place in their journey through the heavens that marks the end of precisely such a cycle. With that end, a new world age begins. Apparently it's always been this way.

For at least four such cycles (or five, according to the Mesoamerican traditions of the Aztec and the Maya peoples), our ancestors endured the changes in global magnetic fields and climate, diminishing resources, and rising sea levels that come with the end of time. They did so without satellites and the Internet or computer models to help them prepare for such a radical shift.

The fact that they lived to tell the story stands as a powerful testament to an undeniable truth: it tells us beyond any reasonable doubt that the inhabitants of our planet have survived the end of world ages in the past. Beyond simply surviving, our ancestors learned from the difficulties that can accompany the change. In the words of their day, they did their best to tell us what it means to live such a rare moment in history. It's a good thing they did, because such events are few and far between. Only five generations in the last 26,000 years have experienced the shift of world ages. We will be the sixth.

The present world age isn't something that will simply fade away into the sunset of a time that seems to perpetually linger somewhere "out there" in our future. Just the opposite: our world age has an expiration date. It ends at a specific time, with a specific event, on a day that was marked on a calendar more than 2,000 years ago. There is no secret about that date. The Maya who calculated it also inscribed it as a permanent record for future generations. The date is etched into stone monuments that were built to last until the end of time.

Using the format of the ancient *Long Count*

calendar—the system of timekeeping that the Maya developed to track extremely long periods—the last day of the present world age is written as a five-part code. Read from left to right, the parts have unique names that represent decreasing units of time. The leftmost is the *baktun* and represents 144,000 days. Moving right, the *katun* corresponds to 7,200 days; the *tun*, 360 days; the *uinal*, 20 days; and the *kin*, 1 day.[1] With this code in mind, the Mayan calendar places the end date of our age at 13.0.0.0.0 (13 baktun cycles, and 0 cycles for the rest of the units).

When the date is translated to our familiar system of time, the message becomes clear. It tells us that our present world cycle will conclude with the winter solstice that takes place on December 21 in the year 2012. It's on this date that the mysterious Maya identified the astonishing astronomical events that will mark the end of our age . . . and they did so more than two millennia ago.

Time Code 1: We're living the completion of a 5,125-year-long cycle of time—a *world age*—that the ancient Maya calculated would end with the winter solstice on December 21, 2012.

To put into perspective just how rare the ending of such a cycle really is, consider that the last humans to witness the shift from one world age to the next lived in the year 3114 B.C., approximately 1,800 years *before* the time of Moses and the biblical Exodus.

New Meaning to the End of Time

It's only recently that the meaning of a world age has made sense to modern scientists. Although the countdown to the end of time is etched deeply into our unconscious psyche (almost universally, people throughout the world share their sense of a feeling that something is "up"), the conditions that it brings are only now being recognized by scientific disciplines, ranging from geology and oceanography to astronomy and climatology.

The reason scientists seem to be so late in jumping on the bandwagon of 2012 is because of technology, or the lack of it. Only in the last 60 years or so have we had the computers, satellites, and remote-sensing equipment capable of verifying the connection between the end of a world age and the changes it brings to our lives. The global climate, patterns of war and peace, and even our spiritual relationship with God and the universe all appear to be directly influenced by the planetary changes that are being documented now by the best science of today.

Just as we are cautioning future generations about our 20th-century experience of nuclear weapons and global warming, the civilizations of our past cautioned us about their experience of the end of time. Having just lived the end of the last great cycle in their day, Earth's inhabitants did what humans do following an epic event that forever changes the world: they recorded the events for future generations. In doing so, they ensured that we would know what to expect, as well as how to prepare. And our ancestors did it from direct experience.

More than 51 centuries ago, our ancestors did their

best to inform and warn us of what that they knew would be an era of powerful transition in a future that they could only imagine in their dreams. That era is now. To understand their message is to understand our journey through the heavens and time. It's all about cycles.

Time Code 2: Our ancestors recorded their experience of the last "end of time," showing beyond a reasonable doubt that the close of one world age is the beginning of the next, and not the end of the world.

The very nature of a cycle is that it repeats itself. So every time the end of one appears, by definition it's also the beginning of the next. The key here is that to get to the beginning of what's new, the cycle must pass through the end of what exists. While this repeating nature of cycles is obvious on the small scale of things, like seasons of the year and phases of the moon, it's not always so obvious when we're talking about cosmic cycles of solar systems moving through the galaxy.

This is where the message of our Mayan ancestors comes in. They recognized the nature of time's cycles long before science described our journey through the heavens. Their timekeepers preserved what they knew and incorporated their knowledge into stories about the universe and life: nonscientific descriptions of creation and destruction, birth and death, beginnings and endings—descriptions that remain today. While the specifics regarding the end-time vary across traditions, cultures, and religious beliefs, there is a common theme that seems to run through all of them. Almost universally, ancient predictions for our time in history describe an age filled with an epic "darkness."

From the Hindu chronicling of the *yugas* to the Mayan Long Count marking the remaining days of the current great cycle, the close of our age has been anticipated as an era of war, suffering, excess, and inequality. While these descriptions sound ominous, there is a bright side: *although the darkness appears to be necessary, it also appears to be brief.*

The reason: Physically, our solar system is moving through the shortest part of an orbit that looks like a flattened circle, an ellipsis whose far end carries us to the most distant point from the core of our home galaxy, the Milky Way.

The physical effect: Both ancient traditions and modern science tell us that our location in this cyclic orbit determines how we experience the powerful sources of energy, such as the "massive magnetic fields," which radiate from our galaxy's core.[2] Recent studies suggest that it is precisely such cycles that may explain the mysterious patterns of biodiversity—the rise and fall of life on Earth, such as the mass extinctions that happened 250 million and 450 million years ago.[3] Additionally, modern discoveries confirm that Earth's position (orbit, tilt, and wobble) throughout the journey creates the ever-changing cycles that influence everything from temperature and climate to polar ice and the planet's magnetic fields.[4] Details of these effects will be discussed throughout the book.

The emotional/spiritual effect: As we travel farther from our galaxy's core, our distance from the energy located there was described by ancient traditions as the loss of a connection that we sense both spiritually and emotionally. Scientific links between the quality of Earth's magnetic fields, how they're affected by cosmic conditions, and our feeling of well-being seem to precisely support such ancient beliefs.[5]

In the same way that Earth's rotation makes the darkest part of the night appear just before the dawn, our position in the heavens is such that the darkest part of our world age appears right before our heavenly orbit begins the return that brings us closer to our galaxy's core. With that return, we experience relief from the cataclysmic forces of the cycle's darkness. And just as the night must pass in order to get to the new day, the only way to arrive at the light of the next cycle is to finish the darkness of this one.

We all know that dark experiences definitely exist in our world, and we don't need to look far to find them; however, there's also more to life than the suffering that the ancients foresaw—much more. Even in our time of great darkness, the polarities of peace, healing, love, and compassion are alive, well, and abundant.

Our ancestors had an amazingly deep grasp of just what our experience of cosmic cycles means on multiple levels. Somehow they *knew* that Earth's position in the heavens would affect the physical conditions in our world, as well as the emotional and spiritual experiences that we need to embrace them. Through myth, analogy, and metaphor, they reminded us that the farther we travel away from the source of such powerful energy, the deeper we are in darkness and the more out of sync we find ourselves with the fields that influence life here on Earth. From the traditions of the Hopi to the ancient Vedas, it's this experience of separateness that is credited with our sense of being lost as well.

Our ancestors cautioned that at the most distant point in our cycle, we would forget who we are—our connectedness to one another and the earth. They told us that we would forget our past. It's precisely this disconnected feeling that seems to be the consequence of the cyclic journey that carries us to the far end of our galactic orbit. It's also the fear that is spawned by such feelings that has led to the chaos, war, and destruction at the end of cycles past.

At the conclusion of the last two world ages, for example, the Hopi describe the greed and wars that led to the loss of the very things that we cherish the most: our families, our civilization, and ourselves. Archaeological discoveries of an advanced civilization located in the Indus River valley between what is now India and Pakistan seem to support the Hopi myths, as well as those of the 100,000-line epic of the Hindu Mahabharata.[6]

The site has revealed the bodies of humans that appear to be in what the archaeologists called "postures of flight," suggesting that they were fleeing from whatever it was that destroyed their civilization. Students of the Mahabharata suggest that the work describes a great war fought in the valley marking the precise location of the new discoveries. The remains are dated at approximately 10,000 years old, placing them into the time frame of two world ages past.

When we understand what the darkness of our cycle means and why it's necessary, we begin to see the great challenges of our time in a new light. With that light, our moment in history and our response to the changes that come with it take on new meaning. With these ideas in mind, it becomes even clearer that *now is the best time* for us to go through such a cycle.

The reason is that *now is the first time* we have the understanding, the need, and the technology to reach into the realm of all possibilities and choose the kind of future that will arise from the chaos of the present. This is something that would have been impossible even 50 years ago.

If we look closely at the stories and records that have been handed down to us for more than 250 generations, it becomes obvious that those who experienced the end of the last world age worked hard to make sure we know precisely what it means to do so. We find the fruits of their labor preserved for us today in their temples, texts, traditions, and cultures.

The Alignment We've All Been Waiting For

Although the creation stories from ancient civilizations, such as the Hopi, Hindu, and Mayan cultures, differ in specifics, they generally agree when it comes to the cyclic nature of the universe. They state that at least three worlds have existed, and been destroyed, before the one we're living today. While different traditions use different signs to tell us where we are in our world-age cycle, it seems that *all* the signs are essentially telling us the same thing: the shift from our present age into the next is *now*.

What sets the calendar of the Maya apart from the oral traditions, such as the Hopi, is that their timeline for the shift ends on a specific date. While their system of calendars accurately identifies the alignment that marks the shift (a rare astronomical configuration that modern computers have now confirmed), it's what the Maya knew about Earth's journey through the heavens that makes their story even more astounding.

Specifically, they knew that during a zone of time before and after the 2012 winter solstice, Earth and our entire solar system would move into a position that is extraordinary by any standards. It's during this time that we pass an imaginary line that defines the two halves of our disk-shaped galaxy. In just the way the equator of the earth divides the Northern and Southern hemispheres, the equator-like line that we cross in the Milky Way separates the "top" of the galaxy's disk from the "bottom." As the planets of our solar system line up with one another and our sun, our crossing of the galaxy's equator also aligns us with the mysterious source of energy that lies at the heart of the Milky Way. This alignment and the conditions that it creates signal the completion of the great cycle, as indicated by the Mayan calendar.[7]

To be absolutely clear, this is not an event that happens suddenly in a single day. In other words, our crossing of the imaginary line that divides our galaxy does not suggest that we'll all go to bed on December 20, 2012, in one world and wake up the next morning to a radically different world on the 21st. Rather, the winter solstice appears to be the astronomical marker that the Maya chose to designate the center of the transition zone. That zone begins well *before* and ends well *after* 2012.

Because of the size and relative distances of heavenly bodies, to us here on Earth this alignment appears as a slow, gradual shift over a period of time. Our familiar experience of an eclipse is a perfect illustration of how such a gradual shift occurs.

If you've ever watched a lunar eclipse, it probably didn't take long for you to discover that it wasn't going to be over quickly. Once it began, you could duck into the house, fix a cup of tea, make a couple of phone calls, and feed the pets before going back outdoors to observe the eclipse's progress. Even though the earth is hurtling through space at about 65,000 miles per hour, on the night of a lunar eclipse, such an enormous speed isn't obvious. That's the effect of huge objects like planets moving through space at tremendous speeds across vast distances. To us, they look like they're in slow motion.

So in the case of the sun moving into an alignment with the equator of the Milky Way, the winter solstice of 2012 marks a point within the zone of a shift that actually began years ago. In his landmark work identifying the 2012 crossover of the galaxy's equator and its significance, *Maya Cosmogenesis 2012,* John Major Jenkins describes how such a transition is a process rather than an event. Using calculations made by Belgian astronomer Jean Meeus, Jenkins suggests that the progression of the sun across the zone of the Milky Way's equator covers a corresponding zone of time that began in 1980 and ends in 2016.[8] Even with a margin of error of plus or minus a few years, this means that we're already well into the alignment that the Maya predicted more than 2,000 years ago. (While every effort has been made to ensure the accuracy of the information included in this book, new discoveries continue to help us refine our understanding of the 2012 phenomenon. Please see my Website for updates and corrections: **www.greggbraden.com**.)

What does such a rare moment in astronomical history mean in our lives today? The truth is that no one knows for sure. We can't, because no one living today has a direct experience of the last time something like this happened. What we do have, however, are good indicators of what we can expect. We have facts.

When we marry the facts of today's science with the wisdom and the historical records of the past, we find a story that's almost beyond belief. It's the story of a journey—our journey—that began so long ago that it has taken more than 256 generations and five millennia to reach the end. Now that it's doing so, we discover that the end is actually the start of a new journey. Perhaps poet and visionary T. S. Eliot best described the irony of an end being a beginning: "We shall not cease from exploration / And the end of all our exploring / Will be to arrive where we started / And know the place for the first time."[9]

While the story of a shifting world age based in our

planet's orbit through the cosmos may sound like the plot of a *Star Trek* episode, the celestial calculations that our ancestors left us are surprisingly consistent with the scientific findings of today. When we put it all together, they tell the same story. With that story, we suddenly have a new meaning for the greatest mysteries of our past, as well as the clues that tell us what to expect in our future.

Fortunately, our ancestors left us everything we need to meet the challenges of a great world age. It's not only about cycles. It's about our ability to recognize patterns and where we are *within* the cycles.

The Code of Time

In the 1980s, I worked in the defense industry writing software to look for patterns in data. It was during this time that the world experienced one of the most frightening and secretive eras in history: the Cold War. With more than 70,000 nuclear-tipped weapons poised to strike the largest cities in Europe and North America at a moment's notice, I found myself searching for a way to make sense of war within the context of a bigger picture.

Was the Cold War part of a cycle? Could the seemingly random events leading to the wars of the past actually be part of a great, evolving pattern that began long ago? And if such a thing is possible, then do the patterns extend beyond the experience of war into the things that happen in our daily lives, like love and betrayal?

If we were to find that every aspect of our world is

part of an ancient and ongoing cycle, such a discovery would give us a powerful new way to think of ourselves. It would imply that everything from the beginnings and endings of jobs and relationships to the exact years when war is waged and peace is declared is all part of a cycle—a pattern that makes it possible to reveal the *conditions* for the future that we've already experienced in the past. If such a pattern actually exists, then we could even take its meaning one step further.

It would allow us to pinpoint an experience, *any experience*—from romance to hurt—and find that it's part of a pattern that can be known and, more important, be predicted. Such a vantage point would go a long way toward helping us make sense of our world. It would also be of immense value as we embark upon our journey into the 21st century and find ourselves in the uncharted territory of merging the knowledge and ideas of East and West, and ancient wisdom and modern science, to solve the great challenges that threaten our survival.

Well, you've probably guessed that the answer to each of my questions regarding cycles is the same. It's *yes!* The reason for the answer could fill volumes and is the subject of *this* book. The key to such a powerful view of time and history is that we can only understand how cycles relate to life by crossing the fuzzy line that has traditionally separated science from the spiritual traditions of our ancestors.

For example, when we marry the ancient understanding of time's cycles with Nobel Prize–winning physicist Albert Einstein's 20th-century discovery of the unity of time and space, something wonderful begins to happen. Three facts emerge with implications that change everything we've been led to believe about our lives in the world:

Fact 1: Einstein's theory of relativity forever merged our ideas of space and time into the single essence called *space-time*.

Fact 2: The events of everyday life (romances, wars, peace, planetary orbits, stock-market fluctuations, the rises and falls of civilizations, and so on) all happen within space-time.

Fact 3: Things that happen in space-time follow natural rhythms.

These facts carry two powerful implications that lay the foundation for the rest of this book and are summarized below.

Time Code 3: New discoveries show that we can think of time as an essence that follows the same rhythms and cycles that govern everything from particles to galaxies.

Time Code 4: We can think of the *things* that happen in time as *places* within cycles—points that can be measured, calculated, and predicted.

With Time Codes 3 and 4 in mind, we have the reasons and the tools to think of time in a powerful new way. Rather than considering the minutes of each day as nature's way of keeping everything from happening at once, as pioneering physicist John Wheeler once remarked, now we can envision time as a kind of code that connects the past with the future. Just as any other code can be cracked and understood, the message of the ancient Mayan calendar may be deciphered and read like the pages of a book.

For some people, this perspective of time and life is a very different way of thinking about things. For others, while it is certainly unconventional, it also makes perfect sense. The idea is fascinating. The implications are deep, mysterious, and exhilarating. While they challenge much of the way we've been taught to think of the universe, we also find ourselves powerfully drawn to such a possibility. We want to know more. We find ourselves wanting to apply this new understanding of time to the real world to make sense of everything from the tragedies of life to the mysteries of the future. And we can.

Although quantum scientists tell us that we can never predict an exact future, what we *can* predict are probabilities for the future. This is precisely what the existence of repeating cycles of time demonstrates. *Each time a cycle appears, it repeats the general conditions that make something possible, rather than a precise outcome.* Just as the conditions in Earth's atmosphere can create the perfect environment for a tornado without ever actually forming one, time's cycles can bring together all of the circumstances that led to an event in history, without that event occurring again in the present.

The key here is that the ingredients for repetition are present and the situation is "primed." The way those conditions play out, however, is determined by the choices we make in life. Knowing in advance where our choices can have the greatest impact tips the scales in our favor as we complete the cycle that holds our well-being and, ultimately, our survival in the balance.

Time Code 5: If we know where we are in a cycle, then we know what to expect when it repeats.

If we can really think of time in the universe in the same way that we think of the stuff that happens in life—as the *events* that fill it—then the cycles within time can be measured in the same way we measure the stuff that happens. Just as we are able to predict the cyclic return of a comet streaking through the universe, suddenly we can also pinpoint the year when the conditions that led to the rise of a civilization or an act of war will come around again. The beauty of such an understanding is that along with the moments in our time that are ripe for chaos, we can also identify the moments in our future that are ripe for peace.

Because all such cycles are based on natural rhythms, we can use the universal codes that govern everything from the movement of quantum particles to the shape of our galaxy in a formula that takes the guesswork out of finding the places in time we're searching for. That is precisely what we'll do in the chapters that follow.

Once we develop the ideas of time's cycles, we can use our understanding in one of two ways: (1) we can follow the instructions in this book to make our own *Time Code Calculator* that tells us how to find the times in our future when we can expect a repeat of conditions past, or (2) we can use the automated Web-based version that does the same thing for us.

Either way, we'll be able to plug in a specific year, such as the end of the Mayan cycle in 2012, to find the time(s) in the past that tell us what to expect when the cycle returns. In doing so, we give ourselves an unprecedented view into time, and something concrete to anchor our expectations for the end of the present great age.

But the Time Code Calculator is not limited only to major events on a global scale. It works for the things that happen in everyday life as well. It appears that the conditions leading to the pivotal moments we experience—from the joys and crises in our personal lives to the wars and peace between nations—repeat themselves as cycles, large and small, and follow the same natural rhythms. To use the cycles in our lives, we must recognize the patterns: when they begin, how they play out, and how to read their timing.

Time Code 6: The Time Code Calculator shows
us when we can expect the *conditions* of the past to
repeat, not the events themselves.

This is precisely why the Time Code Calculator is
so valuable. Along with the repeating cycles that make
the conditions possible, each cycle also contains *choice
points,* moments when change seems to come easier and
be most effective. So while the themes of global war, personal betrayal, and peace themselves may be set into the
timeline, the outcome for each of these specific themes
is not. As is the case with all of human experience, it's
what we do with the condition presented to us that dic-
tates the next phase of our lives.

In Chapter 1, for example, we'll see how the conditions for a surprise attack on American soil have been
present three times throughout the 20th and 21st centuries. Based on repeating cycles of time, the Time Code
Calculator clearly identifies the two dates when the conditions for such an attack would be present following the
seed event in 1941. But while *we were* attacked on one of
those two dates, on the second we were not. Although
the conditions were present, human choices (which will
be described in Chapter 7) prevented the third attack.

The key to using our choice points is that for us to
affect our future in a conscious way, we must recognize
where we are in the cycle. This all begins with our real-
izing that we're actually living a Time Code of sorts, a
pulsating field of energy that has a beginning, is ever-

expanding, and carries what scientists have called the "forward march of time."

With these ideas in mind, questions arise: What is possible? Does the past really hold a blueprint for the future? What could something that happened a thousand years ago possibly tell us about today? What about the mysterious end date of the Mayan cycles? Is there a way to look backward in time to give us an idea of what may be in store for us come 2012? These are the questions that led to the research for this book. The chapters that follow are their answer.

Why This Book?

There is certainly no shortage of books and media coverage regarding the Mayan calendar and the year 2012. It seems like every month new volumes show up on the bookshelves and in Internet bookstores. As with any topic that strikes a powerful chord within people's hearts and minds, the new books offer very different, often conflicting perspectives. Ranging from scholarly predictions that have taken years to research to stream-of-consciousness dictations claimed to be from off-planet intelligence, all serve a purpose. All add to the collective momentum that appears to be building as we approach the winter solstice of December 21, 2012. The revolutionary insights of philosopher and ethnobotanist Terence McKenna in his books *True Hallucinations* (1993) and *The Invisible Landscape* (1975), and the scholarly work of researchers such as John Major Jenkins, have already explored the mystery and meaning of the 2012 end date . . . and have done so beautifully.

It's precisely because such powerful works already exist that I had to be clear about my contribution to the 2012 literature. What could I possibly say that has not already been said? Perhaps the best way to answer this question is to state explicitly what this book is, what it's not, and what it offers.

In the pages that follow, you will . . .

. . . discover how the conditions for the Mayan end date of A.D. 2012 have already happened in our past as a fractal of what we can expect in our future.

. . . see how nature's "most beautiful numbers" guide us to the places in the past that describe what is to come.

. . . identify the "hot dates" that hold the greatest threats of war and the greatest opportunities for peace in our immediate future.

. . . calculate your own Time Code for the key events and relationships in your life.

. . . discover the personal and collective *choice points* of life and history—moments in time when change seems to come easier than it does at others.

Through the seven concise chapters in this book, I invite you into a powerful and practical way of thinking about your relationship to time, history, and the future. It's important to know up front what you can expect from any new path of self-discovery. For that reason, the following describes precisely what this book is—and what it is not:

— This book *is not* a science publication. Although I will share the leading-edge science that invites us to rethink our relationship to time, this work has not been written to conform to the format or standards of a classroom science text or technical journal.

— This book *is not* a peer-reviewed research paper. Each chapter and every report of research *has not* gone through the lengthy review process of a certified board or selected panel of experts trained to see our world through the eyes of a single field of study, such as physics, math, or psychology.

— This book *is* well researched and well documented. It has been written in a reader-friendly way that describes the experiments, case studies, historical records, and personal experiences that support an empowering way to think of ourselves in the world.

— This book *is* an example of what can be accomplished when we cross the traditional boundaries between science and spirituality. By marrying the 20th-century discoveries of fractal time with the 2,000-year-old Mayan message of cycles and the ancient knowledge of nature's special template for life and balance—*the golden ratio*—we gain a powerful understanding of time as a force and us as explorers of that force, riding time waves through an ocean of never-ending cycles.

The Secret of 2012 & a New World Age is the result of more than 20 years of research and my personal journey to make sense of the repeating cycles of life, love, and war. If you have always sought to answer the questions *Does history repeat itself?* and *How is the future connected with the past?* then you will appreciate this book.

The key to 2012 and our time in history is understanding the language of nature's cycles and using that language today to prepare for the future. Ultimately we may discover that our ability to understand and apply the "rules" of Fractal Time holds the key to our deepest healing, our greatest joy, and our survival as a species.

The Secret of 2012 and a New World Age is written with one purpose in mind: to read the map of the past and apply what we learn as we approach 2012 and the world beyond. In doing so, we give meaning to the past while unlocking the code of life's possibilities in the future—both opportunities that generations to come will have to wait another 26,000 years to see again.

— **Gregg Braden**
Taos, New Mexico, 2009

CHAPTER ONE

THE TIME CODE PROGRAM: FINDING OUR FUTURE IN THE CYCLES OF THE PAST

*"I believe the future is only the past
again, entered through another gate."*

— Sir Arthur Wing Pinero (1855–1934), dramatist

*"Time is an indivisible whole, a great pool
in which all events are eternally embodied . . ."*

— Frank Waters (1902–1995), author and biographer

We live in a universe of cycles.

From the tiny pulses of energy generated by an atom to the rise and fall of enormous magnetic fields within the sun . . . from the constant rhythm of the ocean's tides to the thousands of miles traveled by a tiny hummingbird as it migrates to warmer climates every year, our world is a never-ending dance of nature's repeating cycles. They're part of everything.

Intuitively we know about cycles through direct experience. A woman's menstrual rhythm, for example, is governed by a 28-day cycle that is also linked to the cyclic phases of the moon. Each day our bodies follow the rhythms of a 24-hour period (the circadian cycle of light and dark)—which regulate such things as when we sleep, when we're alert, and when we're hungry. And while the use of 60-watt lightbulbs and the consumption of late-night cappuccinos may have forever changed the way we respond to nature's rhythms, the fact is that the cycles are still there.

When we look a little closer at nature's cycles, we find that each is part of a larger one that unfolds within an even larger one and so on—nested cycles of time and energy that govern the rhythms of the universe and life. The familiar experience of day and night is a perfect illustration of how these nested cycles work. The hours of light and dark that we see daily are due to the way Earth rotates with respect to the sun, a cycle that takes about 24 hours. How long the light and the dark of each day last, in turn, is linked to the way Earth tilts toward or away from the sun while it's orbiting: the cycles that create the seasons of the year. How much our planet tilts is part of an even greater cycle that determines how long the seasons last over thousands of years.

While the experience of day, night, and the seasons offers a clear example of nature's cycles, there's much more to them than the length of a day or when summer begins. In the words of poetry, Ralph Waldo Emerson described our relationship to nature's cycles simply and beautifully: "Our life is an apprenticeship to the truth that around every circle another can be drawn; that there is no end in nature, but every end is a beginning."

Both Emerson's words and our understanding of cycles lead us to the questions that must be asked: *If nature's cycles are everywhere, could it be that everything from our romantic and business relationships to our global relationships, everything from the light of a new birth to the darkness of September 11, 2001, is part of the great cycles that we are just learning to recognize? If so, can we prepare for the future by recognizing the past?*

If such a relationship really exists, it changes everything we've been led to believe about our world and ourselves. We may well discover, for instance, that things as varied as the frequency of our accomplishments and failures, the success of our relationships and careers, and even the length of our lives stem from cycles that we're just beginning to understand. With our new understanding, we may also find that we're no longer the victims of a mysterious fate that we attributed so much of our experience to in the past. To explore such a relationship, however, we must begin by recognizing the patterns that surround us.

The Firefly Code

With my feet dangling just inches above the water, I sat motionless on a log near the stream behind my family's house. In the summer of 1965, I remember breathing the hot, thick Missouri air as the last light of the day faded. Everything changes at night in the woods of America's Midwest. Although I could still see the twilight sky above, the dense growth of moss and vines hanging from the ancient forest blocked the sunset on the ground. I stared into the darkness and waited. Experience had taught me that patience and silence were the keys to studying anything in nature. Over the years I'd gotten very good at both.

At first I saw only one out of the corner of my eye. Then there was another, and another. Suddenly they were all around. It was as if someone had just flipped a switch that said *Now!* and the fireflies of summer were everywhere. Watching them perform their mystical dance of movement and light and then seeing them disappear as suddenly as they appeared was an after-dinner ritual that I looked forward to every year. But for me it was more than simply watching lights flash and vanish. It was about something hidden, something secret and mysterious. It was the rhythm and the cycles. It was the patterns.

As a child, I looked for patterns everywhere. Sometimes they were silly ones, like how many times the lights on our Christmas tree would blink off and on before they went dark and began the next cycle, or how many cars of the same color there were in one row of a grocery-store parking lot. At other times the patterns seemed to call out for someone to find them, like the number of times a firefly would flash its eerie glow before it rested and began again. Surrounded by hundreds of them, I remember thinking that there must be more to the light show than just the random flashes on a summer night.

Maybe the lights were actually a code of some kind,

carrying a message from nature itself. Because insects can't speak, perhaps the lights were the way in which they were communicating, with long and short bursts of light representing the dots and dashes of a language—like nature's Morse code. If I could just count the flashes, *and the time between each pause,* maybe I could "read" the code.

A Universe of Patterns

Well, I never found the "firefly code," at least not in the way I had originally imagined. While the summer light shows *did* turn out to be coded signals of nature, they were part of something even more primal and mysterious than I had suspected. In a high school biology class, I learned that the flashes of light I'd seen on those hot Missouri nights were actually part of a mating ritual of signals—a sex code—from male fireflies looking for their perfect female firefly mates. Sitting on that log, I had placed myself right in the middle of an immense dating ceremony that was driven by the ancient and deeply rooted urge to reproduce.

Although the reality of the firefly code may not have materialized, the idea that time itself could be part of nature's code did. On my seventh birthday, my mother supported my fascination with ancient history and gave me a gift that I would cherish well into my adult life. It was a book by C. W. Ceram describing "lost" civilizations that had been rediscovered in modern times; and featured Greek, Egyptian, Mesopotamian, and South American archaeology. Called *Gods, Graves & Scholars,* it had a profound influence on my way of thinking of the past that continues to this day.[1]

I was especially awed by the fact that powerful civilizations with advanced knowledge, such as the ancient Maya, could have existed so long ago, only to disappear and be lost for centuries. As I studied the glossy photographs showing the tops of their temples rising above the dense Mexican jungles, I wondered what it was that the Maya knew that we'd forgotten, especially when it came to their concept of time. With discoveries that range from new revelations about the Mayan calendar to the profound mathematics of fractal patterns, we can now begin to answer that question today.

As an adult, I recognized that the patterns I'd studied as a child are more than just random oddities. Our world is made of those patterns. Not just chance ones here and there, but patterns within patterns that form order and structure. Many of nature's patterns can be measured and predicted easily—the crescent-shaped dunes of sand that continually drift through the Great Sand Dunes National Park and Preserve high in the mountains of southern Colorado, for instance, or the branching patterns that we see in the veins on an oak leaf or as the water from a garden hose runs downhill. At other times the patterns of nature are not so easy to see, like the invisible winds that move an entire mass of air across a continent, or the psychological forces that drive the world's stock markets.

Whether we see them or not, the patterns of nature

are everywhere. If I really wanted to understand how things work, it was clear that I needed to understand the patterns they're made of. During the last years of the Cold War, I found myself working as a senior computer-systems designer in the defense industry doing precisely that. Perhaps not surprisingly, one of my first assignments was in a specialized area of computer programming known as *pattern recognition.*

One day while I was searching for patterns in nature to use as a model for software to track data, I came across the work of a scientist/philosopher from the early 20th century, R. N. Elliott. Before his death in 1948, Elliott had written a powerful synthesis of how natural laws seem to govern many aspects of everyday life, including nature's cycles. It was that book, modestly titled *The Major Works of R. N. Elliott,* which forever changed the way I thought about the universe, civilization, and, most important, time.[2]

What I found so fascinating about Elliott's work was that he had not only recognized patterns and cycles in nature; he also described ways to apply what he had discovered in the real world. A cornerstone in Elliott's research was one very special number that is found throughout our bodies, our lives, and our world, in ways that I had never been told about when I was in school: the golden ratio. In words that were clear and direct, Elliott showed how it applied to everything from the number of males and females in a natural population to the economies of nations.

It was during the same time that a specialist in stock-market forecasting, Robert R. Prechter, Jr., discovered Elliott's work as well. Recognizing that global economics and the stock market are indicators of the investor community's optimism or pessimism—part of a natural cycle—Prechter took Elliott's ideas one step further and created the most successful market-prediction tool in the history of the New York Stock Exchange. Called the *Elliott Wave Principle,* it is still used today.

The key to the success of the Elliott Wave Principle is found in two basic assumptions:

1. The market will always advance and decline in precise intervals—the "waves" of the Elliott Wave theory.

2. If you know where the advance begins, you can calculate when and how often the declines will occur.

My thinking was that if life and nature follow the patterns of such a code, then it made perfect sense that time itself should do so as well—a time code of sorts. Just like the intervals of the stock market, if we could recognize nature's Time Code, then the cycles it creates could be measured and calculated.

In other words, if we know when a cycle begins and the pattern that it follows, then we also know where and how it will end. Perhaps most important, if we know the *conditions* that a cycle brings, then we also know what to expect each time it reappears. It took many years and many attempts to find a way to apply what I'd learned about cycles to the events of our world. Once I did, there was no turning back.

The reason is because nature's Time Code *works.*

What it reveals is both sobering and astounding. To step back and recognize the patterns we've lived in the past, and are living right now, is perhaps one of the most empowering things we can do as individuals and as a civilization. It's as if our willingness to recognize the interconnectedness of nature's patterns is the gateway to the opportunity of conscious participation in the very cycles that the patterns reveal. In my way of thinking, that's nothing less than the miracle of a second chance.

Perhaps the best way to illustrate how the cycles of time repeat in predictable ways is through an example. What could offer a better one than to find that the defining event for the early 21st century—9/11—is actually part of a larger cycle that began 60 years before the towers of the World Trade Center collapsed?

Could We Have Known?

The sound of the phone jolted me from the bizarre sleep that often follows the 13-plus hours of a flight from Los Angeles to Melbourne, Australia. As I sat up in bed, a stream of nonstop questions flooded my mind: *Where am I? What time is it? Who could possibly be calling me in Australia before the sun has even come up?* In the faint glow of a streetlight shining through a crack in the window shades, I found the phone on the nightstand beside me. Pressing the button that was flashing "Line 1," I didn't have to wait long for the answer to my last question.

Immediately the frantic yet familiar voice of a friend on the other end of the line launched into a barrage of information that made little sense to me. There was no

"Good morning" or "How are you?" or any of the typical greetings that come from friends and family half a world away. The first thing I heard was, "Turn on your television! Now! Something is happening . . . I don't know . . . Oh God!"

Reaching for the TV's remote, I flipped through the channels on the screen suspended from a bracket in the corner of the room. Although the stations weren't familiar, the skyline of the city that they were featuring was. Each channel was showing the same horrible images that looked like something from the finale of a Hollywood thriller. Due to the time difference, while it was dark in Australia, the images I was seeing showed the smoke-filled sky above New York City on the morning of September 11, 2001.

Along with the rest of the world, I was both shocked and mesmerized by what I was seeing. I felt disoriented and uncertain, mystified by the images that were now flowing nonstop on every station. Quickly I dressed and bolted for the hotel lobby. I was not prepared for what I saw. When the elevator doors opened, there were people everywhere, all jammed together, vying for a view of the huge television mounted above the lobby's reception area. Some were red-eyed and crying openly, some were moaning, some were simply standing in the stoic silence that comes from seeing something that makes no sense to us, yet that we know is real.

As I made my way through the crowd onto the street, I could see masses of people in motion everywhere. Although it was early, cafés had opened and appliance stores had turned on every television in their showroom windows so the people on the streets could look on, as

America experienced one of the most horrifying days in its history, which was also a turning point for the world.

I walked briskly along the street past café after café. Everywhere it was the same: confusion, uncertainty, fear, and the nonstop images on the televisions. I found myself asking two questions over and over.

The first was simply *Why?* Why would anyone do something so bizarre, so brutal, so heartless?

The second question was not as simple. It took me back to my childhood inclination to see a world full of patterns. While my mind tried to make sense of what was happening, I suddenly found myself reeling from my own question: *Could we have known?* I heard myself whisper under my breath, "If life and world events really follow patterns and cycles, is today part of a pattern? Is there a way we could have prepared for this day or even prevented it?"

To be absolutely clear, I was *not* asking if we could have known precisely what would happen on that date or how it could have changed the world so much and so fast. And I was *not* suggesting that we could have predicted that someone would use jet planes as lethal weapons to level huge skyscrapers and take the lives of more than 2,000 people. That's not what my questions were about.

At that moment, for me it was about patterns, my need to make sense of something so senseless and to find a place for it to fit in a world of cycles.

Fractal History/Fractal Time

The crowds that filled Melbourne's busy cafés spilled out of the buildings and onto the sidewalks throughout the morning of September 11, 2001. For as far as I could see, there were people everywhere doing their best to go about life as usual. But the morning was anything *but* usual. As office workers and students were going through the motions of the day, it was clear that they were stunned and uncertain. Two times within one city block I'd seen drivers turn into oncoming traffic as if there was no one else on the road, only to be jolted from their driving trance by the sound of the screeching brakes and the horn from the car that was bearing down on them.

In the midst of the confusion, I cautiously crossed from light signal to light signal, making my way back to the hotel. My mind darted between staying aware of the chaos swirling around me and the events I'd witnessed earlier in the day. A single question kept repeating in my mind: *Could the horror of the World Trade Center and the Pentagon attacks be part of something greater?* Beyond terrorists, politics, and conspiracies, *was there a bigger pattern unfolding in front of our eyes, a pattern that could only be seen when we stepped back and looked at the big picture from a different perspective?*

It wouldn't be until 2008 that I would have my answer. In the clarity of that answer, a pattern would emerge that was so obvious that my question changed from *Could we have known?* to *How could we have missed it?*

My thinking was that there must be a very good

reason why ancient mystics, such as the Vedic and Mayan timekeepers, dedicated so much energy and resources to studying time. Because their perspective on history's cycles was so different from our views today, and since both have been found to be so accurate, the two ways of thinking must be part of a greater wisdom. So it would make tremendous sense to combine the wisdom of our past with the best science of today to give us a powerful new way of thinking about life and ourselves.

Merging everything I'd learned while searching for patterns as a computer programmer with what I knew of the ancient Egyptian, Hindu, and Mayan views of cycles, the golden ratio, and nature's fractals, I found a model of time—a Time Code program—that offers a power-ful window into the events of our past as well as our future. The key is that time repeats in cyclic patterns and that each repetition is similar to the last (fractal), with a greater intensity.

The Time Code program can be used in three dif-ferent ways to reveal the cycles of specific events. These are:

- **Mode 1**, which tells us when we can expect the conditions for something that has hap-pened in the past to occur again

- **Mode 2**, which tells us which date in the past holds the conditions we can expect for the future

- **Mode 3**, which tells us when we can expect

the conditions of a personal experience, either
positive or negative, to repeat in our lives

For the events of September 11, 2001, I used Mode
1. For ease of reading, I have placed the description and
specifics of this process in Appendix A. To find the conditions that may have led to a pivotal date in the past,
such as September 11, 2001, or those we can expect for a
date in the future, such as December 21, 2012, I needed
two pieces of information:

1. **The date of the event in question**

    -   This can be a time in the future when we
        want to know what conditions to expect.

    -   This can be a time in the past when the
        seed of an obvious pattern began, exam-
        ined for the purpose of discovering when
        it will repeat in the future.

2. **The total length of the present cycle we're
    exploring:** the 5,125-year-long world-age
    cycle or the larger cycles that define even
    greater ages

To explore September 11, I used the Time Code program to find the seed that may have led to the events
that changed the world. The *first* piece of information
required some research. To discover what pattern September 11 might be a part of, I needed a date that may
have started the cycle *before* the World Trade Center

attack. To have the certainty of a date that could not be questioned, I needed to find one with the same characteristics—the same patterns—that played out on September 11.

Although the controversy and unanswered questions remain in the minds of many people to this day, the one thing that is generally agreed upon regarding September 11, 2001, is that the United States of America was *attacked* on that day. Regardless of how or why it happened, there is a consensus that America and Americans were the target of what can only be described as a vicious attack.

For most people, there wasn't even a hint that something of such magnitude could possibly happen. So it's fair to say that the events of September 11, 2001, took the nation and the world by surprise. As such, the words describing the theme of the seed date I was searching for was one of America being *surprised* and *attacked*.

With the knowledge that past conditions repeat themselves in cycles, a search of history revealed a date that unquestionably matched the criteria. In this case, it even matched the precise words of *surprise* and *attack* used to describe the events of 9/11. The date was December 7, 1941: one that President Franklin D. Roosevelt forever marked in the psyche of the world as the "date which will live in infamy." On that day America's naval base in Pearl Harbor was attacked by surprise, and 2,117 American lives were lost. It was also the day that the United States of America officially entered World War II. After this date was settled on, the year 1941 became the first input point for the Time Code program.

The *second* piece of information—the length of the

cycle within which everything is happening—was easy, because all of recorded human history has happened in essentially the same cycle. Perhaps it's no coincidence that this is the great cycle of 5,125 years described by the Mayan calendar. Although this may sound like an arbitrary choice, there are two facts that make the Mayan calendar unique among the timekeeping systems of the world. While we will explore these facts later in the book, briefly they are:

— **First**, the calendar is the single most accurate system of tracking nature's cycles of galaxies, planets, and our relationship to the sun known until the 20th century.

— **Second**, the cycle that we're now in is approximately one-fifth of the bigger cycle (the fifth and last world of the Meso-american traditions) that describes the *precession of the equinoxes*—our 25,625-year journey through the 12 constellations of the zodiac, commonly rounded to 26,000 years.

The input into the Time Code program was ready. The seed date was 1941. The cycle length was 5,125 years. With all of the information at my fingertips, I began the calculations. Immediately, two dates emerged. Each indicated a time when America could reasonably expect the same themes of "surprise" and "attack" it experienced on that historic day of infamy.

The Time Code Works

The first date that the program identified was 1984. When I saw it, the year surprised me and didn't make much sense—that is, until I discovered a little-known and frightening fact that was revealed to the world only after the end of the Cold War.

History shows that 1984 marked a time of some of the greatest tension between the United States and the former Soviet Union. The threat of a nuclear exchange was so great during that year that the hand of the famous Doomsday Clock (maintained since 1947 at the University of Chicago by the board of directors of the *Bulletin of the Atomic Scientists* to keep the world informed of the threat of global catastrophe) was moved to three minutes before the worst possible time of midnight.[3] The move represented only the second time since the clock was put into place that the world had been so close to atomic war. It was not until the end of the Cold War, however, that we really knew just *how* close. In the early 1990s, Russian authorities declassified the records describing an event that brought us even closer to that war than we had known.

In September 1983, the Soviet military mistakenly shot down Korean Air Lines Flight 007, a civilian jumbo jet that had strayed into Russian airspace. All of the Boeing 747's 269 passengers and crew were killed, including U.S. Congressman Lawrence McDonald. During that time, the tension between the superpowers was so high that the Russians feared America would view the mistake as an act of war. Recently declassified records show that the Soviet Union, assuming that it was only a matter of time before the United States acted in retaliation, had actually planned a preemptive attack—*a nuclear attack*—to preserve their first-strike advantage.[4]

For reasons that could fill a book, history will show that, fortunately, the attack did not occur. The key here is that the conditions for a surprise attack against America *did* exist and were in place in 1984, just as the Time Code program predicted they would be.

The next date that arose was a time when America wasn't so lucky. The program calculated that the next time we could expect the conditions leading to "surprise" and "attack" would come precisely when it did, in the year 2001 (Figure 1).

Output from the Time Code Program

Seed Date: 1941
Seed Event: The United States is "surprised" and "attacked"

Calculated Dates for Repeat Conditions		Actual Events
Date 1:	August 1984	Preemptive attack planned against the U.S.
Date 2:	June 2001	Terrorist attack planned against the U.S. and later carried out

---

Figure 1. Example of how fractal patterns play out as events in time. The surprise attack upon the United States in 1941 planted the "seed" for a cycle that continues today. The Time Code program uses the principles of fractal patterns and natural cycles to tell us when we can expect the conditions of the 1941 surprise and attack to repeat (see Appendix A).

While the relationship between these dates certainly deserves additional study, there are three facts that we cannot discount:

1. Based upon a documented seed date, when the conditions of "surprise" and "attack" were set into motion, the Time Code formula successfully identified the next two times when America could expect those conditions to repeat themselves.

2. On both of the predicted dates, a plan to surprise and attack America actually existed.

3. On one date, the plan was actually carried out.

The data are clear. While this example is for a single, graphic, and horrible event that is now part of our history, it is just that: an *example* to illustrate how events within a cycle can be related. The Time Code Calculator works for other occurrences as well. From the joys and crises in our personal lives to the wars and peace between nations, it appears that the conditions leading to the pivotal moments of life repeat themselves as cycles. Now we must ask ourselves the following:

- What do such patterns mean for today?

- What can they tell us about our future?

- Can nature's Time Code shed any light on

the frightening predictions for the mysterious Mayan date of 2012?

• Can the program give us a solid basis for the beliefs of many New Age gurus, numerous self-help prophets, and every major religious and spiritual tradition of the last 5,000 years?

In the chapters that follow, we will answer each of these questions in detail and learn to think of time and the things that happen in the world from a powerful new perspective. With our new understandings firmly in hand, we'll apply what we know to everything from our personal lives to our global future. For such a perspective to make sense, however, we've got to think about our world from the vantage point of those who dedicated their lives to understanding vast cycles of time—the timekeepers of the past. What better way to begin than by exploring their view of time and the great world ages of long ago?

※　※　※

CHAPTER TWO

OUR JOURNEY THROUGH TIME: THE DOCTRINE OF WORLD AGES

"The Hindu religion is the only one of the world's great faiths dedicated to the idea that the Cosmos itself undergoes an immense, indeed an infinite, number of deaths and rebirths."

— Carl Sagan (1934–1996), pioneering astronomer

"Our distant ancestors understood the true astronomical meaning behind the doctrine of World Ages."

— John Major Jenkins, contemporary expert on Mesoamerican cosmology

---

There is little doubt in the minds of the world's indigenous elders that present-day events are the fulfillment of their ancestors' prophecies for the end of time. Although many of the details for such prophecies have been shrouded in secrecy to preserve their integrity, those who have held them sacred are now openly sharing them with the world. Sensing that now is "the time," they believe that people of all nations and beliefs can benefit from the wisdom of the past. While the specifics of how we may recognize the significance of the early 21st century vary from tradition to tradition and from telling to telling, common themes weave the different prophecies into a consistent story. Those of the Hopi of America's Desert Southwest offer a beautiful example.

The Four Worlds of the Past

In words that are simple and direct, the Hopi recount a story that many people today prefer to think of as a metaphor for the past rather than a factual history. Maybe it *is* easier to think of the following prophecy in that way. If the story is true, it tells of a past that is just too frightening and too painful for many to accept.

It's the story of Earth, and human history on it, punctuated with times when the unthinkable has happened: the planet changed so quickly and drastically that life as it was known before the change forever disappeared. In his landmark book *Meditations with the Hopi* (1986), scholar Robert Boissiere illustrates the clarity and simplicity of the Hopi worldview. Following are brief excerpts from a longer narrative he gathered while living among the Hopi for years, having been accepted as family.

On the destruction of the first world:

The remnants of the first people moved in with the ant people to be safe when Sotuknang [the sky God] destroyed Tokpela, the first world, with fire.[1]

On the destruction of the second world:

[Then] some became greedy!—though life was plentiful. Greed made them fight one another. . . . So Taiowa [the Creator] said to Sotuknang, "Destroy this second world!" . . . The [second] world froze solid from pole to pole, and in its imbalance, the world stopped spinning for a while.[2]

On the destruction of the third world:

In this [third] world, humankind grew and grew, spreading everywhere. . . . Some became so powerful, they waged war on the others, annihilating them with their machines. . . . Then Sotuknang destroyed the third world. A great flood covered the Earth; it rained for a full moon.[3]

These excerpts describe three vast cycles of time, three previous worlds that existed before the fourth one of today. Each of the preceding worlds concluded with a great cataclysm: the first with earthquakes and the sinking of continents, the second with the earth covered in ice, and the third with a great flood. The prophecy says that the fourth world will end in our lifetime and that we will soon be living in the fifth.

Although the words are nonscientific, the Hopi description of the events that ended each era is eerily similar to the history of the earth that is preserved in the geological record. Recent data from ocean sediment and polar ice cores confirm that the planet has, in fact, undergone a cyclic history of cataclysm from fire, ice, and water, as well as recovery periods. There was a period of earthquakes and volcanic activity around 20,000 years ago. The ice age peaked about 11,000 years ago, and there was a deluge that is believed to have been the biblical Flood, which occurred approximately 4,000 to 5,000 years ago.

According to the Hopi, the same cycles of time and nature that have heralded such changes in the past are now bringing the present world to an end as the next begins. What makes the Hopi worldview so important going forward is its accuracy regarding the past. The key here is that the Hopi knew of these cycles long before modern researchers could confirm them scientifically. If such indigenous knowledge of cycles is so accurate for the past, then what does that mean for their predictions of what's to come in the future?

Our Journey Through the Zodiac

From the oral traditions of the Hopi to the 5,000-year-old records of the ancient Sumerians, among others, a growing body of evidence suggests that humans have long understood our journey through the heavens. In their understanding, they also recognized that the familiar stars and constellations of the night sky seemed to change their positions in space during that journey.

Just the way the sun shining on the Northern Hemisphere appears lower in the sky during the winter than in the summer, the constellations appear to rise and set at different times and locations depending upon where we are in our journey. This change, known as the *precession of the equinoxes,* has been recognized by many civilizations, from ancient India to Egypt. The bottom line to the precession is that the scenery of the night sky changes as we trace our path through the heavens over time.

Historically, our journey across the universe has been described as a circular path that carries us through the 12 familiar zodiac signs. Because there are 12 constellations that we pass through, each is assigned one piece of the circle (12 constellations × 30 degrees each = 360 degrees of the orbit).

Historical records show that our speed through the heavens has varied throughout history. Modern satellites reveal that it takes Earth about 72 years to pass through 1 degree of our zodiac orbit. This means that at the present time it takes us about 2,160 years to pass completely through one zodiac sign. This makes perfect sense, as the present Age of Pisces is believed to have begun about 2,000 years ago, and we are nearing its end as we transition into the new Age of Aquarius.

Based on Earth's current speed through the cosmos, this also means that our entire journey through all 12 constellations takes about 25,625 years. For ease of use, this number is commonly rounded to 26,000 years. This is our voyage through the zodiac, our "precession" through the equinoxes. Our knowledge of this journey gives even greater meaning to the doctrine of World Ages, as well as to our passage through the cosmos.

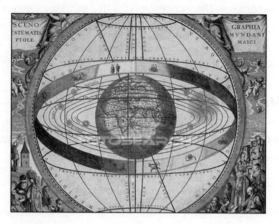

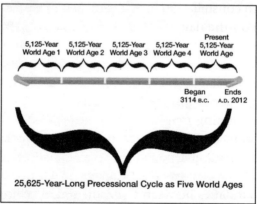

Figure 2. Ancient civilizations, such as the Greeks and Egyptians, used the changing constellations of the night sky to mark the progress of our 25,625-year journey through the zodiac. *Top:* Within that period of time, Earth passes through five world ages lasting 5,125 years each. *Bottom:* When we divide the length of the full zodiac cycle (25,625 years) by the length of the present world age (5,125 years), the number is exactly 5. In other words, there are five world ages in a full cycle of our journey through the zodiac signs.

Time Code 7: Ancient traditions divide Earth's 25,625-year orbit through the 12 constellations of the zodiac—the precession of the equinoxes—into five world ages lasting 5,125 years each.

The Meaning of the Ages

Because the speed of our journey through the constellations has varied in the past, there are different ideas of precisely when one zodiac age ends and the next begins. This is important because the name that we give to our time in history—our zodiac age—is determined by which constellation provides the backdrop for the rising sun on the day of the spring (vernal) equinox each year. At the present time, for example, we're in the Age of Pisces.

The Piscean Age is believed to have begun 2,160 years ago, just before the time of Jesus. As of 2008, we are transitioning *from* the Age of Pisces *toward* the Age of Aquarius. But don't expect the transition to be a fast one. As mentioned previously, the change is a process rather than an event. The problem is that there are no clear boundaries between the zodiac signs telling us an exact time when one ends and the next begins. Instead, there is an overlap as we phase out of one and into the next. So it would be fair to say that although we are technically in the Age of Pisces, we have entered into the zone of the Aquarian Age as well.

I find this particularly interesting, as each zodiac sign

has been associated with traits that are unique to its time in history. It's probably not a coincidence that before the present Piscean Age, the ram's head that signified the constellation Aries played such a powerful role in the ancient world. The Egyptians of the New Kingdom era (16th century B.C. to 11th century B.C.), for example, embodied the symbol of Aries in their representation of the god of the sun, the ram-headed Amen Ra. And it's probably not by accident that the early Christians chose for their religion the same symbol as that of their zodiac age, the two opposing fish of Pisces.

In her beautifully worded interpretation of the significance of the zodiac ages, author and medical intuitive Caroline Myss describes the duality of the Piscean symbol:

> . . . the fundamental blueprint of Pisces (two fish swimming in *opposite* directions) expressed itself in a continual need to divide and conquer, separate and study, split East and West, body and soul, male and female, yin and yang, the left-brained from the right-brained, the intuitive from the intellectual . . .[4]

These are arguably the characteristics of our world for the last 2,000 years.

Because there is no clear boundary between the end of one age and the beginning of the next, today we are experiencing the transition that embodies the qualities of both: the Aquarian Age, and the qualities that it brings, with the attributes of the Piscean Age. Once again, Myss eloquently characterizes this shift:

. . . Aquarian consciousness holds the template of holism (holy)—to draw humanity together. Thus, holism has become the template for medicine, the environment for the beginnings of a global community, and for how we now model ourselves: body/mind/spirit. Holism has become the new soul impulse. We are now living between eras—half in Pisces, an age of separation—and Aquarius, an age of unity and holism.[5]

While the precise timing of the zodiac ages varies, from about 9600 B.C. until the present, the general descriptions for what happened during the last six of them do not. To identify each age, scholars and historians have chosen one defining event that marks each period of time. Following is a brief summary of those characteristics:

Zodiac Age	Defining Historical Event
Leo	Global warming/ melting of the glaciers
Cancer	The biblical Flood
Gemini	The rise of alphabets and writing
Taurus	Egyptian civilization
Aries	The Iron Age
Pisces	The birth of Christianity

Figure 3. The last six zodiacal ages and their defining events. While other things certainly happened during the ages, these events are used as touchstones to give meaning to historical comparisons.

There are places in the world where ancient timekeepers used explicit symbols to describe the cycles of zodiac ages, as well as the longer world ages. The lasting rock of the temple walls where they engraved their time maps has preserved their message in a way that cannot be mistaken. With the clarity of their records, any doubt as to whether or not our ancestors, or at least some of them, understood Earth's movement through the ages quickly disappears.

One of the clearest, as well as one of the most mysterious, of these artifacts is the beautiful zodiac disk embedded into the stone ceiling of the Dendera temple complex on the west bank of the Nile River in Egypt.

The Mystery of the Dendera Zodiac

The sun had already descended into the thick evening mist of the Nile Valley by the time we reached the temple complex. Our day of exploring Egypt's Valley of the Kings near Luxor had started before sunrise that morning. *What a beautiful place to end this day,* I thought, *the 1st-century B.C. Dendera temple dedicated to the goddess Hathor and to ancient principles of healing.*

I had met with the Egyptologist John Anthony West in a hotel lobby in Cairo a few days earlier. As we each had our respective groups touring Egypt during the same time, we agreed to combine them briefly for an evening of dialogue and conversation. It was during that time that West had given me a copy of his newly released book, *The Traveler's Key to Ancient Egypt.* In Chapter 17, I had found the image and description of the place that was one of the primary reasons why I'd invited my group to take this trip. It was a chamber among the rooftop chapels in the temple where we had just arrived: the Temple of Hathor at Dendera.[6]

The eerie afterglow of sunset was settling into the valley, and now every minute counted. I knew that we had less than a half hour of light remaining before the authorities closed the site for the day and we would be forced to leave. While a portion of the group followed our Egyptian guide through the halls filled with immense columns and high-relief hieroglyphs, others followed me to the tall, narrow passages to the roof of the complex. As I turned the corner, I found the steep stairs that led to the elevated sanctuaries above. This was the place I'd been looking for.

I knew that just beyond the top of the stairs was the room I'd discussed with West in Cairo—the one that I'd come halfway around the world to see for myself. Stepping from the stairway into the remaining light illuminating the temple's roof, I followed the walkway directly into a small room with a ceiling so low that we had to stoop as we passed through the entrance. The faint light of sunset that filtered through the doorway had little effect inside the tiny chamber, and I closed my eyes for a few seconds to acclimate to the shadows.

"There it is!" I heard someone whisper in awe under his breath. "It's so beautiful!" Turning my gaze to the place where the people in the room were pointing, I found that I was directly beneath the ancient relic that made seeing this temple so worthwhile to me. Directly above my head was an eight-foot-diameter sandstone disk *embedded into the stone of the ceiling itself:* the mysterious Dendera zodiac.

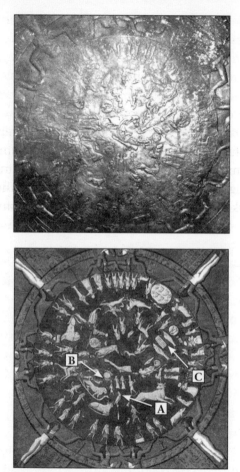

Figure 4. *Top:* Looking up to the zodiac disk on the ceiling of Egypt's Temple of Hathor at Dendera, which is near Luxor, Egypt. *Bottom:* A schematic drawing of the Dendera zodiac showing the constellations as they appeared during the time the disk was constructed.

In high relief and with perfect detail, this ancient celestial map held all of the information needed to calculate Earth's journey from one zodiac sign to the next across an entire 25,625-year precessional cycle. While controversy remains as to whether or not ancient civilizations understood this cycle, *I* had no doubt that I was staring directly into undeniable evidence that the sculptors of the Dendera zodiac did understand—and they understood really well.

As I studied the disk above me, I was mesmerized. It was even more beautiful and detailed than I had imagined. This was more than just a two-dimensional outline of the familiar signs of the zodiac. From the images in the center of the disk representing the polestars, which change over a span of 15,000 years (Thuban, the polestar during the time of the biblical Exodus of the Hebrews from Egypt; Polaris, our current polestar; and Vega, the polestar of the coming world age), to the alignment of the constellations Sagittarius and Scorpio, which show the way to the mysterious center of our galaxy, it was clear that the designers of this amazing artifact could track the movement of our planet through the stars.

If there was any lingering doubt regarding the zodiac's accuracy, it quickly disappeared when I recognized the intentional alignment of the temple with the brightest star in the sky, Sirius. In Egyptian hieroglyphic writing, this celestial body is commonly associated with Horus, a form of the Egyptian god of light. On the Dendera zodiac, we find Horus portrayed in two places: he is simultaneously perched on a papyrus stalk located precisely along the axis of the temple itself (see Figure 4, arrow A) as well as on the true north/south axis touching the sign of Cancer, which is where the sun would have risen and illuminated the sky map of the disk itself during the summer solstice when the temple was built (see Figure 4, arrow B).[7]

It's precisely *because* the Dendera zodiac appears to be so accurate that one of its unsolved mysteries with regard to the way it depicts an aspect of our time in history is significant: the shift between the ages of Pisces and Aquarius. As you can see in Figure 4, the familiar 12 zodiac signs are arranged reasonably close to one another on the disk. Each one follows the previous sign and precedes the next so closely that there is no room for other symbols to be inserted between them, except in the case of the world's zodiac sign for the last 2,000 years, Pisces, and the sign we are transitioning to next, Aquarius.

There's an inordinate amount of space between the Piscean fish and the Aquarian Water Bearer that's sometimes called the "anomaly" or "discontinuity" between the two signs. What makes this spacing on the Dendera zodiac disk particularly interesting is that the area also contains a peculiar symbol known as the *Square of Pegasus* (see Figure 4, arrow C), which appears between the two fish of Pisces and has markings that can't be read on the disk itself. Tradition associates this symbol with an actual artifact—a physical tablet—that holds what are called the *programs of destiny.*

How might the programs of destiny relate to our experience of the shift between the zodiac signs, as well as to the world ages? How does the curious space that only appears between the two zodiac signs matching our time in history relate to the close of our world age?

While the experts continue to speculate on the answers to both questions, we may not have to wait much longer to understand what the disk is telling us. It's obviously about *here* and *now*. Clearly the Dendera zodiac is a message of time. Specifically, the disk I saw above my head in the rooftop chapel is an ancient map of our journey through time, a celestial clock that is still ticking away the changes in our relationship to the heavens.

The Dendera zodiac is the only artifact of its kind known to exist today. While there's controversy surrounding whether the disk originated somewhere else and was transported to the temple or whether the Egyptians who constructed the temple also built the disk, one thing is certain: whoever created the zodiac disk at Dendera understood our journey through the heavens. In that understanding, they also showed us when to expect the great shift from one world age to the next.

I later learned that the disk installed in the Dendera temple roof today is an exact replica of the original, which was sold to the Louvre museum in Paris. In an effort to re-create the most delicate details of the original disk, the replica has even been blackened in the way the original artifact was discovered, the result of centuries of smoke and soot burning on the floor just below it. (I did have the opportunity to see the original Dendera zodiac disk in Paris a short time later and was happy to see that the reproduction appeared to be a precise replica of the one in the Louvre.)

The Doctrine of World Ages

The Dendera zodiac tells us that long before modern scientists began looking seriously at the implications of Earth's location in the heavens, ancient civilizations had already done so. From the oral traditions of the indigenous North and South Americans to the written records of cultures that inhabited ancient India, Tibet, and Central America, we learn that civilizations of our past identified key locations along our planet's path through the heavens, as well as patterns of stars that would tell us when we have reached those locations. They did so using more than guesswork or superstition. They used science.

Specifically, they used their knowledge that Earth's orbit around the sun and its radiant energy is part of a larger orbit that carries us around the energy radiating from the core of our galaxy. Also, they knew that at certain places along our journey, Earth's orientation would create changes that would affect the planet's life and civilizations. While the knowledge of the earth's passage during such huge periods of time may have originated long ago, it's far from a primitive idea. In fact, it is based upon a very sophisticated understanding of planetary and galactic cycles and how they influence our journey through the heavens.

Every 5,125 years, the natural changes in Earth's position in space create an astronomical alignment that signals the end of one cycle around the galaxy and the beginning of the next. The ancients called the periods of time between such alignments *worlds* or *world ages*. The changes in climate, sea level, civilization, and life that have accompanied the shifts in the past have been so great that when they've occurred, the existing world is said to have ended. For clarity here, it's not the planet itself that ends, but our location in an orbit that changes.

Just as the end of the night is a necessary part of our 24-hour day and makes the day that follows possible, the end of one age is a necessary part of our 5,125-year cycle that gives birth to the next. As John Major Jenkins describes beautifully in *Maya Cosmogenesis,* the Maya actually viewed the time within a world age as a gestation period.[8]

Rather than giving birth to an individual life, like at the end of a human gestation, the Maya foresaw something much grander. They viewed the conditions of the galaxy as converging in a perfect way to serve as a cosmic midwife. From this perspective, the great birth that 2012 is facilitating is a spiritual one: humankind's evolutionary leap in response to the cyclic changes of Earth's orbit. The knowledge that such cycles occur, and of what happens when they do, is known today as the *doctrine of World Ages.*

Time Code 8: The position of the earth within our galaxy creates powerful changes that signal the end of one world age and the beginning of the next. The knowledge of these cyclic changes is known as the doctrine of World Ages.

The study of the vast cycles of time required for a

world age is a science that we are only beginning to recognize in the modern world. It's a good thing we are, because the secret preserved by such high knowledge may hold the key to avoiding the suffering that our ancestors experienced during the last time a 5,125-year-long great cycle came to a close.

The World Ages Agree

Among the most ancient and cherished traditions of our past there is a remarkable consistency with respect to the descriptions of previous worlds and how each one ended. Perhaps the most ominous thread they share is that the cataclysmic event that brought each to a close and began the next was seen as a necessary "cleansing" that paved the way for the upcoming cycle.

	Comparison of World-Age References		
Tradition	**Number of World Ages**	**Name of Ages**	**How Each Age Ends**
Hopi	4	Worlds	Cataclysm
Ancient India	4	Yugas	Cataclysm
Aztec	5	Worlds	Cataclysm
Maya	5	Great Cycles	Cataclysm

Figure 5. A brief comparison of diverse ancient traditions shows the common theme of world ages and cycles. While the number of them varies, the way in which each ends does not. Each tradition describes an event that "cleanses" one age and prepares the world for the next.

It's generally accepted that the first written

documentation of world ages is found in the Vedas, the traditional literature of ancient India. While oral transmission of the same stories probably existed for thousands of years prior to the literature, the formal texts were not written until about 1500 B.C. While the Vedas were intended for scholars, another set of texts was created for everyday use by nonscholars. These are the 18 books known as the Puranas, which together contain the essence of the Vedic literature.

The Vedas describe huge expanses of time lasting so long that they challenge our modern notion of the past. These texts include the familiar Rigveda, as well as the Samaveda, Yajurveda, and Atharvaveda. In them we find some of the earliest descriptions of how the universe is periodically created, destroyed, and reborn over vast spans of time called *yuga cycles,* or simply *yugas.*

Interestingly, the actual length of each yuga is determined by the interpretation of the texts themselves. As is the case with many ancient writings, interpretations vary. In his scholarly investigation of Vedic cosmology *Mysteries of the Sacred Universe,* mathematician Richard L. Thompson acknowledges these varying points of view. "There is some controversy regarding the history of the *yuga* system. The traditional view in India is that the *yugas* are real and have therefore been going on for millions of years. The view of modern historians is that the *yugas* are mere ideas that developed historically through a series of stages."[9] Regardless, though, scholars seem to be in general agreement as to the way the yugas work.

Vedic cycles of creation and destruction are based in the repeating series of four yugas, each representing a different length of time. Together, they form a steplike progression of increasingly longer periods determined by multiplying the shortest yuga by the simple formula of 1:2:3:4. In the traditional interpretation, the Kali Yuga is the briefest cycle, lasting for a period of 1,200 years, which is multiplied by the first number of the formula, 1, to arrive at its length. The Dvapara Yuga, the next cycle in the series, is computed by multiplying the length of Kali by the next number in the formula, 2, to arrive at its own length of 2,400 years.

Following the same formula, the Treta Yuga and the Satya (also known as Krita) Yuga last for 3,600 years and 4,800 years, respectively.

Human Time or Divine Time?

So far, so good. But here's the catch: the texts identify the yugas as being *divine years*.[10] This is where the uncertainty comes in. Scholars have different opinions as to precisely what a divine year means to us here on Earth. Thompson summarizes this uncertainty when he asks, "Could it be that divine and human cycles of 12,000 years are both intended by the yuga system—with one representing events on a cosmic scale and the other mirroring the petty pace of human affairs?"[11]

I find this possibility fascinating because of the nature of the universe and time itself. Scientists tell us that both are made of little cycles within bigger cycles within bigger cycles and so on. In other words, they are fractal. The very definition of a fractal is a pattern that repeats itself in similar ways on different scales.

We may well discover that whoever designed the

ancient yugas understood such fractal principles beautifully. If so, then we may use the Vedic system of time to go beyond simply tracking days, centuries, and millennia. It may be, in fact, that the yugas describe a special relationship between us and time: a fractal interplay between planets, galaxies, and our lives, which is described by an ancient axiom: "As above, so below."

While Vedic scholars may not agree on the length of a divine year, they do agree that the four traditional yugas are equal to one *divine yuga*. In other words, 12,000 divine years equal 4,320,000 years of Earth time. When we consider that a single day of Brahma, the Hindu god of creation, is 1,000 of these cycles (4,320,000,000 Earth years), it may be no coincidence that this number is so close to the scientific estimates of the earth's age, now placed at about 4,500,000,000 years old!

In the traditional texts, each of the yugas is multiplied by a sacred number that converts it from divine years into the longer human equivalent. The conversion factor is the single elegant and powerful number that defines one of the most mysterious shapes in the universe—the circle. The number that defines it is 360. When we apply this factor of 360 to the yugas described previously, we see where the controversy and the uncertainty come from.

Multiplying the traditional 1,200 years of the Kali Yuga by 360 increases the figure to 432,000 years. When we do the same multiplication, the Dvapara Yuga jumps from 2,400 years to 864,000 years. The Treta Yuga goes from 3,600 years to 1,296,000 years, and the Satya Yuga from 4,800 years to 1,728,000 years. Suddenly these cycles become such vast periods of time that they stretch our sensibilities and challenge our present ideas of time and human history.

As mentioned before, some scholars have suggested that these values are based on an esoteric interpretation of the original texts, one that doesn't apply to actual human years on Earth. It may be for precisely this reason that alternative interpretations of the original texts are gaining popularity today. While such readings still describe four yuga cycles, they do so with shorter periods of time. The work of Sri Yukteswar Giri[12] and renowned Jyotish astrologer Dr. David Frawley (Vamadeva Shastri),[13] illustrate these updated interpretations.

Frawley describes yuga cycles of approximately 2,400 years long based on his rendering of the traditional Manu Samhita text.[14] Modern scholars are drawn to this interpretation because it makes more sense with what we now know about the precession of the equinoxes. Frawley also suggests that the shorter yugas place the age of important historical Indian figures, like Lord Krishna, into a meaningful context that makes sense with the accepted age of human history.

I mention both the traditional and alternative perspectives of the yugas here to show that even the Vedic experts are divided when it comes to the lengths and the timing of the cycles. *What's important is that while the interpretation of yuga lengths varies, from thousands to hundreds of thousands of years, the number of yugas in a given cycle does not.* The Vedas, like the Mayan calendar, agree that the history of the world exists as four great cycles. Both systems agree that we are in the final one of those cycles.

Signs of the Age

In addition to the consensus among Vedic scholars that there are four yugas contained within each cycle, it's also agreed that each one has a specific quality that it brings to the age when it appears. Each of these qualities describes a form of self-realization that relates to Earth's position in the heavens. The closer we are to our galaxy's core, the greater our degree of enlightenment. At the most distant portions of our orbit, we must make greater efforts to find our personal enlightenment.

Tradition states that within each age there is a 25 percent change in the degree of enlightenment of the collective culture from the previous cycle. So when we are in the ascending portion of the orbit that carries Earth closer to the Milky Way's core, we become more conscious. When we're in the descending orbit that carries Earth away from the core, it's just the opposite. It's through these qualities that we can see the gradual and temporary rise and fall of spiritual awareness that comes with our progression from the lightest to darkest cycles.

— According to traditional interpretations, the **Satya Yuga** is said to have been the last golden age of light. It's characterized as a time of peace, wisdom, and highest enlightenment. The Vedic literature states that during this time, humans had life spans that were essentially limitless. For those living then, this cycle of peace and wisdom would have been the ideal time to enjoy such longevity!

— Although the next period, the **Treta Yuga**, or the

Silver Age, is still characterized as one of great virtue, it is described as a time of 25 percent less enlightenment than the longer Satya Yuga. With the loss of awareness, human life spans decrease to a maximum of 10,000 years.

— The third yuga of the cycle is the **Dvapara Yuga**, or Bronze Age. This is the time of a 50 percent loss of enlightenment from the people, said to be an era when human character is equally divided between "virtue and sin." Once again, with the decline in self-awareness, life spans decrease to a maximum of 1,000 years long.

— Regardless of what length of time the experts assign to each yuga, the fourth is always the shortest of the four cycles. This is fortunate for us because this yuga, the **Kali Yuga**, also known as the Iron Age or Black Age, is the period of the greatest darkness for humankind. It's also the time of the briefest life spans of any cycle, with humans living only between 100 and 120 years. While there are exceptions, for the most part those living in the Kali Yuga are said to have lost 75 percent of their self-awareness. Because most experts agree that we are either near the end or just completing the Kali Yuga, we will explore what it means to be part of this cycle a little more deeply.

The Dark Yuga

The Puranas describe the historical characteristics that we can expect to see throughout the darkness of a Kali cycle. It's the similarities between these qualities identified in ancient times and those that seem to permeate our world today that make this ancient perspective so interesting. The dominant theme of a Kali cycle is one of discord, contention, and quarrel. Examples of these traits[15] include:

- The appearance of rulers who are unreasonable and levy taxes unfairly

- The time when people become addicted to intoxicating drinks

- The period when famine and death are common

- The age when the helpless become targets to be preyed upon

Many of the preceding characteristics look surprisingly similar to those we find in our world today. If we are, in fact, living at the close of the Kali Yuga, then they are surprisingly accurate as well, especially when we consider that they were documented thousands of years ago.

According to the Puranas, the traditional date for the beginning of the Kali Yuga is February 18, 3102 B.C. On this date, mythology states that the Hindu god Lord Krishna left the earth. While it's certainly difficult to confirm the details of Krishna's departure from this world more than 5,000 years ago, there are astronomical events that mark this time as well. Their dates *can* be verified in historical accounts.

The anonymous author of a 9th-century text, *The Book of Thousands,* describes a pattern of galactic cycles that last for 180,000 years each, ending with the conjunction of all the planets of our solar system in the beginning of the zodiac sign of Aries.[16] What makes this account so interesting is that the last occurrence of such a conjunction was the same time that a global "deluge" (which sounds hauntingly like the biblical Great Flood) covered the earth. According to the author's calculations, the date of the conjunction was the day before the Kali Yuga began: February 17, 3102 B.C.

While the traditional (divine) interpretation of the yuga cycles places the end of the Kali Yuga well into our future, it also states that a rare sub-cycle occurs 5,000 years after the yuga begins. If, as tradition suggests, we are five millennia into the dark yuga that began in 3102 B.C., this places us more than 110 years into the unique sub-cycle that began around 1898.

This sub-cycle is akin to an oasis in the middle of a vast desert. It suggests that 5,000 years into the darkest portion of our journey through the stars, an awakening occurs that prepares us for the remainder of the dark cycle and for the transition into the next yuga of light. This cycle-within-a-cycle is described as a time of increased *bhakti* (Sanskrit for "devotion") influence. It is a period of heightened devotion believed to last for about 10,000 years.[17]

While the realistic nature of such vast periods of time is still debated by scholars today, I describe this cycle and its duration here for one reason. The fact that it lasts so long is a powerful indication that the Vedic traditions *do not* see 2012 and the end of our world age as the end of the planet itself. Rather, they seem to agree that the Kali Yuga's "darkness" is a time of necessary turmoil that makes way for our evolution from one way of being to the next.

Time Code 9: The Vedic traditions describe an extended time of devotion, expressed in action (bhakti), that began around 1898 and lasts well beyond the 2012 Mayan end date.

Regardless of whether or not we use the traditional interpretation of the yugas, the message of the cycles is the same. Either we are near, or at, the end or we are now in a special sub-cycle of the Kali Yuga, the briefest and darkest time in the Vedic worldview. Perhaps it's no coincidence that this dark yuga occurs only during the times when the Mayan calendar indicates that we're at the farthest point from the center of the Milky Way.

To get to such a point means that we have traveled a predictable path, marked by predictable milestones, during a predictable length of time. While this is common knowledge to the Vedic scholars of today, just how well our ancestors understood Earth's journey through the stars remains a topic of heated debate in scholarly circles.

The Ancient Ages of an Ancient Sky

To help scientists validate astronomical alignments such as those of the Vedas, advanced computer programs now take the guesswork out of what the night sky may have looked like during the cycles of history in times past. Using simulations produced by software, such as SkyGlobe™, we can now re-create any portion of the night sky from any period in the past, as well as project what the sky will look like at any time in the future.[18] The use of such software has become a powerful tool in exploring the theory that ancient temples, pyramids, and monuments were built the way they were to match precise alignments with stars and constellations as they would have appeared in the past. In the mystery of Egypt's Great Sphinx, for example, this kind of exploration adds to the mounting evidence that the structure was built long before the 2450 B.C. date traditionally found in textbooks.

Because Egypt's mysterious Sphinx is made in the image of half-man and half-lion, a growing number of scholars now suspect that it was built as a lasting marker for the transition from the age of Virgo, the virgin, to that of Leo, the lion, at the time when the world ages shifted in our distant past. But if the transition from age to age is so gradual, then the question becomes: *precisely when did it occur?* Author and researcher Graham Hancock has pioneered a revolutionary perspective of our past and offers concrete evidence that may finally answer this question.

In his book *Heaven's Mirror,* Hancock explains:

Computer simulations show that in 10,500 B.C. the constellation of Leo housed the sun on the spring equinox. Specifically, the simulations show that during the hour before dawn, the lion in the stars would have looked like it was reclining to the east along the horizon, in precisely the place where the sun would rise.

Hancock elaborated on the significance of this correlation, stating:

> This means that the lion-bodied Sphinx, with its due-east orientation, would have gazed directly on that morning at the one constellation in the sky that might reasonably be regarded as its own celestial counterpart.[19]

That constellation is Leo.

What does such a correlation tell us? Is it just a coincidence that the timeless sentinel of half-man and half-lion in Egypt's desert is precisely aligned with the only constellation that bears its namesake? While this correlation may go a long way toward solving the mystery of one of the best-known monuments in the world, it also opens the door to even deeper questions.

If the Sphinx was truly built to commemorate Earth's transition from the constellation of Virgo to Leo, and it was built during the years around 10,500 B.C. (approximately the time when the last ice age ended), who was here to build it? Who in Egypt was tracking cycles of time that are so vast that it would take technology developed over 500 generations later to confirm them? Maybe more important, *why* were they tracking those cycles?

Why did civilizations from Egypt to the Yucatán dedicate entire temples, texts, and monuments in their time to immortalize a single date that would not occur until the end of time, more than 50 centuries into their future?

CHAPTER THREE

THE END OF TIME: OUR DATE WITH 2012

"The ancients knew something which we seem to have forgotten."

— Albert Einstein (1879–1955), physicist

"By examining these core [Mayan] traditions, we can reconstruct and revive the original 2012 revelation."

— John Major Jenkins, contemporary expert on Mesoamerican cosmology

It was a headline seen around the world. On July 6, 2008, the first news item that flashed to users across the Internet was an article titled "Thousands Expect Apocalypse in 2012," excerpted in part from an ABC News investigation of the global rise in "doomsday cults." The first sentence of the article said it all: "Survival groups around the world are gearing up and counting down to a mysterious date that has been anticipated for thousands of years: December 21, 2012."[1]

Only weeks before, approximately two dozen members of a Russian survivalist group—mostly grown women, but including four children—had emerged from a underground bunker where they had sealed themselves from the outside world in November 2007. The group was convinced that the unthinkable would happen well before 2012. They fully believed that the world would end by May 2008, within six months of their entry. When it did not, the group's followers had begun to trickle out a few at a time over the winter. Following the tragic deaths and burials of two members *within* the bunker, the partial collapse of the cave's ceiling due to spring snowmelt, and a shortage of food, the remnants of the group emerged in May 2008.

According to the article, while they seemed mystified as to why the world was still here, they were convinced that it was only their calculations that were off. They still believed that a great apocalypse and the end of the known world were just around the corner.

As extreme as such beliefs and reactions may sound, they're not all that unusual these days. The same article states, "From across the United States, Canada and throughout Europe, apocalyptic sects and individuals say that is the day [December 21, 2012] that the world as we know it will end."[2]

While it's obvious that the year 2012 is on the minds of a lot of people today, when we step back for a bigger historical perspective, we discover that these beliefs are actually part of a tradition that began a very long time ago. While there seem to be as many different ideas of what we can expect as there are people *with* such ideas, there also seems to be a general agreement as to the reason for the 2012 focus. It's all about our location in the heavens and the cycles of time that bring about the changes.

History Points to Now

As we saw in Chapter 2, there is a universal consensus among the indigenous peoples of the earth that our time—spanning the last years of the 20th century and the early years of the 21st century—is no ordinary period in the history of humankind or of the earth. With their prophecies, traditions, and systems of time-keeping, they remind us that during our lifetime we'll experience a repeat of the cycle that sparked the dawn of recorded history.

Over the centuries that followed the last shift of world ages, the themes of what happened then, and humankind's response to it, have been incorporated into myriad religious and spiritual practices. As diverse as they appear, the common thread that joins them together offers a clear message for us today. It's only in recent times, with the aid of 20th-century science, that their message has started to make sense.

What a message it is! Using everything from prophetic visions to the dates of precise astronomical alignments, our ancestors devised every method imaginable to alert us to a single fact: now is the time of the most extraordinary conditions and opportunities that accompany the rarest of events, the shift from one world age to the next.

❋

The ancient Aztec traditions of central Mexico share the Mayan belief that the universe exists as great waves of energy that repeat as cycles of time. A key aspect of their understanding is that each cycle has a unique characteristic based upon the wave that carries it. As the wave ripples through creation, its movement synchronizes nature, life, and time with its passing. It's from their understanding of such waves that the ancient Aztec timekeepers knew that our moment in history would bring the beginning of a new cycle that they simply called a "sun."

The Aztec cosmology describes the history of the Earth as a series of such suns. The first, named *Nahui-Ocelotl,* was characterized as a time when giant creatures lived within the earth. As strange as it may sound, this account actually sounds similar to biblical ones that describe a time in our past when humans encountered larger-than-life creatures. According to the Aztecs, this period ended when the animal kingdom overcame the human kingdom.

The second sun, named *Nahui Ehécatl,* was noted as a time when humans learned to cultivate and crossbreed plants. This cycle ended with what is described as a great wind that swept across the earth, clearing everything in its path.

During the third sun, *Nahui Quiahuitl,* the people of the earth formed huge cities and great temples. The

Aztecs describe a phenomenon that occurred during this time: the Earth opened and the sky was filled with a "rain of fire." The geological record does, in fact, show a time in our past when portions of the earth were covered with fire. The ash that is found in the rock record is generally believed to have come from the impact of a huge object from space, possibly an asteroid, about 65 million years ago. The fourth sun ended with a global cooling that is also confirmed in the geological record.

According to the Aztec traditions, today we are living in the last days of the fifth sun. The timing for the next Aztec sun is based on the same cycles that the Maya used in their calendar. With these relationships in mind, the fifth sun of the Aztecs is believed to occur within the same zone of time as the Mayan 2012 alignment. As with the other Mesoamerican traditions, modern Aztecs and Maya believe that the chaos triggered by the end-of-cycle changes is a necessary passage of purification to pave the way for a better world to follow.

Modern Prophets of the New World Age

The visions of a world-age transition, and what follows it, extend far beyond the ancient and indigenous worldviews into the era of recorded history. For more than 400 years such visions of the future have fallen into the realm of *prophecy,* and the word itself has been nearly synonymous with the names of great seers such as Edgar Cayce and Nostradamus.

Born in 1503, Nostradamus was fascinated by the profound visions of ancient oracles and studied them to work on his own techniques of prophecy. Using what he learned, Nostradamus developed a gift of second sight that allowed him to peer—*to remote-view*—well into his future and even beyond ours, to witness events that had yet to occur with extraordinary detail and accuracy. In what is arguably his best-known work, *Centuries,* he recorded what he saw from his vantage point in the 16th century, through the next ten centuries, and then even beyond our time, ending in the year A.D. 3797. Some scholars believe his future sight may have extended even further.

Because of the stigma surrounding the use of prophecy in his time, Nostradamus couldn't write about his visions directly. Instead he recorded them in a coded format called *quatrains*—mysterious verses of four lines each. By the time of his death, Nostradamus had set down his visions for each century as 100 verses of such quatrains. While many of the things that Nostradamus recorded do appear to be surprisingly accurate, just as we find for other prophecies, without specific dates they are open to interpretation.

Among the dates that are noted, however, are the specifics for the two world wars that cannot be mistaken. Nostradamus also recorded Hitler's name and a description of the swastika; the discoveries of penicillin, nuclear energy, and the AIDS virus; the failure of Communism; and the assassination of U.S. President John F. Kennedy. Even though the interpretations are subjective, scholars generally agree that he did foresee a great change on a global scale around the transition from the 20th to the 21st century. Similar to the Native American and biblical traditions, the changes that Nostradamus witnessed in his visions were accompanied by tremendous cataclysm.

Only when he felt that the event in his vision was critical or urgent did Nostradamus include an actual date. On the rare occasions that he did so, those dates have become the touchstones to orient us in history for the things that happen before and after. For this reason, I find it fascinating that one of those rare dates occurs in the late 20th century. In his book *Centuries X,* quatrain number 72 reads: "In the year 1999 and seven months, / A great King of Terror will come from the sky. / He will bring back the great King Genghis Khan [of the Mongols] / Before and after Mars [war] rules happily."[3]

In the *Epistle to Henry II,* verse 87, Nostradamus further clarifies this time in history, stating, ". . . this will be preceded by a solar eclipse more obscure and more dark . . . than any since the creation of the world except that after the death and passion of Jesus Christ."[4]

A solar eclipse that was visible throughout much of Europe did occur on August 11, 1999. In verse 88, Nostradamus continues describing the cataclysmic nature of his millennial vision, identifying a specific month of Earth changes: ". . . and there shall be in the month of October a great movement of the globe, and it will be such that one will think the Earth has lost its natural [gravitational] movement . . . there will be initial omens in the spring, and extraordinary changes in rapid succession thereafter, reversals of kingdoms and mighty earthquakes . . ."[5]

While there have, in fact, been record-setting earthquakes (the 2004 Indian Ocean quake registered between 9.1 and 9.3 on the Richter scale) and nations, such as

Iraq and Afghanistan, have certainly changed their affili-
ations and forms of government, it's difficult to say that
these are precisely the things that Nostradamus saw in his
visions. What's important here is that although the specifics of Nostradamus's future sight may vary from those
of other prophets and prophecies, the general theme of
a great change at century's end does not. Although they
were born 374 years apart, there is a surprising consistency between Nostradamus and the man known as the
"Sleeping Prophet" in the 20th century, Edgar Cayce.

In what have become some of his best-known prophecies, Cayce stated that the late 20th and early 21st centuries would herald a time of unprecedented shifts upon
the earth. Just as many ancient prophecies described
two paths that could carry humankind through such
an upheaval, Cayce foresaw the possibility of a future
brought about by gradual change as well as a time of
tumultuous shifts that are obviously catastrophic in
nature. What makes his prophecies especially significant, however, is that he saw *both possibilities* happening
during the *same period of time.*

During his lifetime, Cayce gave approximately
14,000 readings that cover topics ranging from the diag-
nosis of ailments for specific individuals to the future
and fate of humankind and the world. In reading number 826–8, which is dated August 1936, Cayce was asked
specifically about the kind of changes he foresaw for the
millennium that would not happen for another 64 years
into his future. His response was a tangible statement
regarding a measurable change for the Earth: ". . . there
is the shifting of the pole. Or a new cycle begins."[6]

The rapid decline in the magnetic fields of the

Earth—the kind that precedes a magnetic reversal of the poles—has led some scientists to speculate that we may be in the early stages of just such a shift. In the absence of extenuating circumstances, however, and with the insights from our Time Code Calculator (see Chapter 6), it appears unlikely that such a shift will occur in the years immediately before or following 2012.

Although a number of Cayce's early predictions for the new millennium sound catastrophic, later readings take on an interesting, although subtle, change. Reading number 1152–11 in 1939 describes the close of the century as a series of gradual changes rather than the sudden shifts he previously foresaw. Once again, Cayce shares his future visions with the specifics of an actual date. He states, "In 1998 we will find a great deal of activity that has been created by the gradual changes that are coming about."[7]

He continues: "As to the changes, the change between the Piscean and the Aquarian Age is gradual, not a cataclysmic one."[8]

In Chapter 7, we will explore the concept of *choice points,* a physics term that describes moments in time where our choices seem to have a greater impact on the way something turns out. While Princeton University's Hugh Everett III coined the term itself in 1957, Cayce seems to be describing just such a point in his reading numbered 311 10. Here, he suggests that our response to the challenges of our lives may determine, at least in part, how much of the changes he foresaw for the millennium shift we would actually experience: "[It] may depend upon much that deals with the metaphysical. . . . There are those conditions that in the activity of individuals, in line of thought and endeavor, keep oft many a city and many land intact through their application of spiritual laws."[9]

The prophecies of Nostradamus, Edgar Cayce, the Aztecs, the Hopi, the Maya, and others have sent the reverberations of an unmistakable message throughout time. Separated by hundreds of years of history and thousands of miles of distance, all point to *now*. They all see something powerful, possibly wonderful and possibly destructive, happening on a global scale during a time that spans the last years of the 20th century and the first years of the 21st century.

The odds against such similar stories developing "out of nowhere" for such vastly different people and places suggest that this is more than simply a coincidence. What did *they* know that *we've* forgotten? Why did the Mayan timekeepers choose 2012 rather than the 2000 millennium date as the end of their calendar? What difference could those 12 years possibly make in the ending of a 5,125-year-long cycle?

Perhaps the best way to answer that question is through a better understanding of the Maya themselves. To appreciate just what the Mayan calendar and the end of time means, we must look *beyond* the calendar itself. Its symbols and codes are the lasting legacy of an obsession with vast cycles of time and our relationship to that time. It's the Maya's advanced knowledge of the cosmos and their ability to preserve it for generations to come that modern archaeologists have called the "Mayan mystery."

The Mayan Mystery

The Mayan civilization itself is an anomaly in the traditional view of history and culture. Archaeological studies in Mexico, Guatemala, and parts of Honduras and Belize show that the advanced architecture, cosmic observatories, and precise calendars that come to mind when we think of the Maya appeared "suddenly" in the historical sense.

In his exploration of this ancient mystery, archaeologist Charles Gallenkamp, the author of *Maya: The Riddle and Rediscovery of a Lost Civilization,* graphically summarizes the irony of the Mayan presence. "No one has satisfactorily explained where [or when] Maya civilization originated," he states, "or how it evolved in an environment so hostile to human habitation."[10]

It's the advanced technology used by the Classic Maya that sets them apart from the village cultures that came before. Michael D. Coe, emeritus professor of anthropology and emeritus curator in the Peabody Museum of Natural History at Yale University, describes this technology beautifully in his book *The Maya:*

> The Classic Maya of the lowlands had a very elaborate calendar; writing; temple-pyramids and palaces of limestone masonry with vaulted rooms; architectural layouts emphasizing buildings arranged around plazas with rows of stellae lined up before some; polychrome pottery; and a very sophisticated art style expressed in bas-reliefs and in wall paintings.[11]

It is this high level of sophistication and the widespread influence of their civilization that makes the collapse of the Classic Maya so mysterious. Although there are many theories, no one has definitively solved what is called the "Mayan riddle." Charles Gallenkamp elaborates on how little we may actually know about our ancient ancestors, observing that whatever it was that led to "the sudden abandonment of their greatest cities during the ninth century A.D.—one of the most baffling archaeological mysteries ever uncovered—is still deeply shrouded in conjecture."[12]

While the experts may not agree on precisely *why* such a powerful civilization seems to have disappeared, they can't argue over the marvel of what was left behind: temples, observatories, and sophisticated calculations of time.

To put the Mayan phenomenon into perspective, their science and their message could only make sense to the modern world with the emergence of computers and satellite probes in recent years. How could a group of people living in the jungles of Mexico a millennia and a half ago have known so much? To answer this question we must begin with another one: that is simply . . . *why?*

Why did an advanced civilization suddenly appear more than 2,000 years ago, build massive temples and observatories focused on huge galactic cycles, and then vanish? Why does their calendar, identifying cycles that coincide with the 5,000 years of recorded human history, abruptly end on such a precise date—one that occurs within our lifetime?

Figure 6. *Top:* The astronomical observatory of Palenque, Mexico, one of the most beautiful examples of advanced Mayan architecture. This extensive site is believed to have been constructed and used between the 7th and 10th centuries A.D. and then quickly and mysteriously abandoned. (Martin Gray, **www.sacredsites.com**) *Bottom:* A portion of the La Mojarra Stela 1, discovered in 1986 near La Mojarra, Veracruz, Mexico, showing a Long Count calendar date in the left column. From top to bottom, it reads 8.5.16.9.7, translating to A.D. 156 in the Gregorian calendar. (Stela Copyright © 2000, 2001, 2002 used with permission under the terms of the GNU Free Documentation License, Free Software Foundation, Inc.)

It's impossible to answer these questions by simply looking at the Mayan calendar itself. It's also impossible to unlock the secret of Mayan timekeeping by looking at traditional history itself. To do either is to miss the power and elegance of the message that our Mayan ancestors left to us. There is only one way to answer these questions, and that is to think differently about our relationship to the universe than we have since the birth of science 300 years ago.

We must cross the traditional boundaries that have separated science, religion, spirituality, and history—both past and present—and marry these many sources of knowledge into a single new wisdom. When we do, something remarkable happens!

Mayan Time

Any discussion of Mayan accomplishments must acknowledge what is arguably the single most sophisticated achievement of all: their unsurpassed calculation of time. Even today, modern Maya keep track of great cycles, as well as local time, using this system that experts such as archaeologist and anthropologist Michael D. Coe tell us has "not slipped one day in over twenty-five centuries."[13]

Their calculations were based upon their calendar. But it represents much more than simply counting the number of days between the full moon and the new moon. The Maya were tracking cosmic cycles of time, along with the celestial events that occur during that time. Using the most advanced system of calendars the world has seen until modern times, they did something that is almost unthinkable to us today. In the absence of high-speed computers and complex software, they calculated the movement of the earth and our entire solar system as it relates to the core of our own Milky Way galaxy.

The key to the Mayan "galactic timer" was a 260-day count called the *Tzolkin,* or Sacred Calendar. Intermeshed with another 365-day calendar, called the Vague Year, the Maya viewed these two cycles of time as progressing like the cogs of two wheels—progress that would continue until the rare moment when one day on the Sacred Calendar matched the same on the Vague Year. That rare and powerful day marked the end of a 52-year cycle and was part of the even larger expanse of time known by the Maya as the great cycle.

At present, there is no one artifact known to represent the Mayan calendar in its entirety. While modern scholars are able to interpret the Mayan system of timekeeping from their inscriptions, there is another ancient artifact from another culture that has preserved the Mayan view of time as a single calendar and is still in use today. It's the Aztec Stone of the Sun *(Piedra del Sol),* the ancient calendar disk pictured in Figure 7. This monolithic artifact was discovered during excavations in Mexico City's main plaza in 1790.

The huge basalt disk measures about 12 feet in diameter, is almost 4 feet thick, and weighs nearly 53,000 pounds.[14] While the interpretations of the disk sometimes differ in specifics, with new understandings of the Aztec symbols, there seems to be a general agreement as to what it represents. What follows is a high-level description of the key glyphs on the Stone of the Sun. I offer it here to show that the architects of the disk had a deep understanding of cosmic cycles and their relationship to the days of the month.[15]

Figure 7. There is no single artifact that represents the entire system of Mayan calendars. The ancient Aztec calendar (top) is believed to be derived from the Mayan calculations of time. The themes of the present world age and the four previous world ages can be seen clearly in the magnified illustration of the calendar (bottom).

When we look at the Aztec calendar in Figure 7, the most striking image is the face in the center of the disk. The Aztecs accepted the doctrine of World Ages and, like the Maya, believed that we are living in the fifth and final world of a cycle that included four previous ones. The center image is Tonatiuh, meaning "movement of the sun" or "sun of movement," the god of our fifth world. Some scholars interpret the movement implied by the Tonatiuh's role in the cycle as a possible clue to the mystery of what happens at the end of the age.

Surrounding Tonatiuh, four boxes represent where we've been in this cycle: the four suns of ages past. The glyph for each is the deity associated with that particular age. Moving clockwise from the upper left, we find the symbols for wind, jaguar, water, and fire. There is still uncertainty as to whether or not these glyphs represent the dominant theme of the age or the cause of its end.

Moving outward from the circle of world ages, the next ring we see contains 20 squares that depict the 20 days of the Aztec month. The eight arrows (angles) that point away from this circle are the eight cardinal points of the sun's rays (north, northeast, east, southeast, and so on).

At the bottom of the disk (not pictured) are the symbols of two serpents. Each is divided into sections believed to represent the limbs of jaguars and flames. While scholars have yet to arrive at a consensus as to precisely what these symbols mean, it is generally believed that they represent the 52-year cycles of the Aztec century, which is also 52 years long.

The images on the Aztec disk are intact, readable, and still used today by the indigenous peoples of Central America. On replicas found throughout Mexico and the Yucatán, this ancient map of time is the standard for everything from setting daily watches to planting annual crops. To those knowing the language of the disk, it's a beautiful map of our relationship to time, covering everything from thousands of years to the present moment.

Reading the Mayan Map of Time

The Aztec calendar is just one artifact, representing only a partial understanding of the Mayan system of timekeeping. While many of the subtleties are missing, the Stone of the Sun still conveys the big message of the great cycle.

The date that both the Mayan and Aztec calendars indicate as the end of the present cycle is the same: December 21, 2012. On this day, the winter solstice signals the close of the present world age, the calendar resets itself, and we begin a new world age. Similar to the way the odometers on some cars return to all zeros after reaching the 100,000-mile mark, the Mayan calendar "resets" to a new start date of zero and the cycle begins anew. The Mayan timekeepers encoded the end date and the system that keeps track of it into the massive tablets and temples they built throughout territory that is now Mexico and Guatemala.

While Mayan priests marked the key dates for these cycles on their monuments more than 2,000 years ago, it was not until early in the 20th century that their message made sense within the framework of our familiar Gregorian calendar. It was during this time that the original calculation of Mayan scholar Joseph T. Goodman (1905) was confirmed by Yucatán scholar Juan Martínez Hernández (1926) and English archaeologist J. Eric S. Thompson (1935) and has become the generally accepted date for the beginning of the Mayan great cycle.

In recognition of each man's contribution to it, the result of the mutual effort uses one letter from each scholar's name and is called the *GMT correlation*. Based on this understanding and the traditions of the Mayan priests themselves, the calendars indicate that the last great cycle began on the Mayan date 0.0.0.0.0, which translates to August 11, 3114 B.C.[16]

When I read about such an ancient date, if I can think of it in terms of something else that was happening at the same time, it helps me to grasp its meaning. So as a reference point for the start of the current great cycle, the beginning identified by the ancient calendar is about the same time that the first hieroglyphs appeared in ancient Egypt. From that point to today, the balance of the cycle encompasses the entire span of time that we typically think of as recorded human history.

What Does It Mean?

The Mayan timekeepers were obviously tracking more than the minutes of the day with their calendars. They were using their sophisticated timepieces to count down the years that would culminate with a rare celestial event. Through his scholarly diligence, John Major Jenkins recognized that event in the 1980s, and with that recognition, we now know why the end of our particular cycle was so important and so anticipated by the Maya.

At the end of the cycle, our solar system, our sun, and our planet move into an alignment with the core of the Milky Way galaxy, or more precisely, with the equator of the galaxy—an alignment that will not happen again for another 26,000 years.[17] While it does mark the end of this particular great cycle, the Mayan tradition says that the end is the *beginning* that we've been waiting for.

From the Mayan perspective of cosmology and myth, consciousness and human awareness progress through stages of growth that cover the vast periods of time encompassed by the cycles. With each new cycle, we have the opportunity to move beyond the thinking that has limited or destroyed us in the past. This growth is achieved as cycles within cycles that create the gestation period mentioned in the last chapter.

Jenkins eloquently describes this idea of human life cycles within cosmic, spiritual cycles: "The 260-day tzolkin calendar is based upon the 260-day period of human embryogenesis, and, on a higher level, the 260-day tzolkin symbolizes, or structures, the 26,000-year period of precession, what we might call human spiritual embryogenesis."[18]

Time Code 10: The present world age began on August 11, 3114 B.C. Its end is signaled by the rare alignment of our solar system with the core of the Milky Way galaxy on December 21, 2012— an event that last occurred approximately 26,000 years ago.

Modern scientists acknowledge that this galactic alignment is happening. They also acknowledge that the Mayan calendar marks the event. "There's no question that one of the great cycles of the traditional ancient Mayan calendar comes to a completion of its count at that time in 2012," says E. C. Krupp, Ph.D., director of the Griffith Observatory in Los Angeles, California.[19] The question most often asked is simply, "What does it mean?" On the one hand, there are those who discount the phenomenon as little more than an interesting oddity that we are lucky to see in our lifetime. Others suggest that the close of the great cycle marks the convergence of rare cosmic processes, with implications that range from the joyous to the frightening.

José Argüelles, Ph.D., author of *The Mayan Factor*, which sparked a modern interest in Mayan time during the 1980s, suggests, for example, that the first years of the new millennium are part of a sub-cycle that began in 1992 and mark the emergence of what he calls "non-materialistic, ecologically harmonic technologies . . . to complement the new decentralized mediarchy information society . . ."[20]

Using the same information, however, other scientists and researchers have a very different idea of just what the Mayan calendar is showing. They warn that the end of the Mayan great cycle coincides with celestial events that may hold profound and even dangerous consequences for life on Earth as we know it. *India Daily*, an online magazine based in India, for example, carried an editorial article in the March 1, 2005, edition describing the results of the Hyderabad Computer Model for a polar shift to coincide with calendar's end date. Its frightening headline reads: "Computer Models Predict Magnetic Pole Reversal in Earth and Sun Can Bring End to Human Civilization in 2012," and the editorial describes a worst-case scenario of what a world without a magnetic field could mean.[21]

These are obviously two very different ideas of what we can expect the end of the great cycle to bring our way. That is precisely why I'm sharing them here. While in later chapters we will explore possibilities ranging from peace to a polar shift, the point is that Mayan timekeepers were trying to tell us about a date that none of them would even live to see.

While there are many ideas of what we may expect as the end date of the Mayan calendar draws near, most people feel that *something* is going to happen. Because 2012 is only a few short years away and it happens to coincide with unprecedented changes that are already happening in our solar system as we speak, a growing number of scientists suggest that it is in our best interest to understand what the Mayan timekeepers were trying to tell us.

The best place to begin is with the Mayan calendar itself. Perhaps retired California State University professor Ricardo Duran says it best. In an interview discussing the significance of the 2012 end date, Duran explains, "It [the last day of the cycle] is called a four movement day. That's the name of the date, and this means a very profound change by movement."[22]

Two Cycles, Same End Date

In addition to the 2012 winter solstice marking the end of the Mayan great cycle, December 21 also signals the completion of an even larger cycle: the great or *precessional* year that began approximately 26,000 years ago. It was then that we began the journey that carries us through the celestial path of all 12 signs of the zodiac. As we cross the threshold of the Milky Way's equator in the 2012 time frame, we not only begin a new 5,125-year-long world age, but we also complete one precessional year of all 12 zodiac constellations and begin the next.

The rarity of these two cycles completing simultaneously, and the fact that we are living at a time when they converge, tells us beyond any doubt that these are truly extraordinary days. This also adds credibility to the wisdom of the ancient timekeepers who have held the knowledge of this convergence of cycles for thousands of years until modern science could accept its meaning.

Although the details of the Mayan cycles sometimes differ from those of the world's oldest cosmologies, in general the similarities are striking. The following chart summarizes parallels to the Vedic system of yugas.

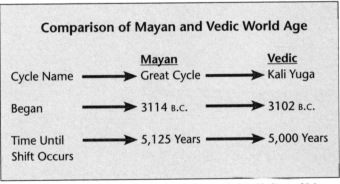

Comparison of Mayan and Vedic World Age

	Mayan	**Vedic**
Cycle Name	Great Cycle	Kali Yuga
Began	3114 B.C.	3102 B.C.
Time Until Shift Occurs	5,125 Years	5,000 Years

Figure 8. The accounts of world ages recorded in Vedic and Mayan writings are strikingly similar. Both describe the beginning of our present age approximately 5,000 years ago as a portion of a greater cycle. Both describe a momentous change expected approximately 5,000 years into the cycle that coincides with a rare astronomical alignment that will not recur for another approximately 26,000 years.

Both traditions state that we are presently in the last cycle of a great world age. Both cycles are believed to have started approximately 5,000 years ago, and there is a difference of only 12 years between their dates of origin. With such close agreement between two very different civilizations existing on two different parts of Earth, and in light of the accuracy of additional cosmic timelines (such as the agreement between the scientific and Hindu versions of Earth's age), we owe it to ourselves to ask, "What are these cycles of time telling us?"

To answer such a question, we must take a deeper look into an experience so common that we seldom give it a second thought. At the same time, it's one that is so puzzling to scientists that modern physicists even have a special way of referring to it when they consider solutions to the mysteries of the universe. As we'll see in the next chapter, it's called the "problem of time." The answer to what 2012 means in our lives comes down to our understanding of the mysterious essence of time itself.

※　※　※

CHAPTER FOUR

THE KEY TO THE UNIVERSE: TIME AND NATURE'S MOST BEAUTIFUL NUMBERS

"Mathematics is the language with which God has written the universe."

— Galileo Galilei (1564–1642), astronomer

"God used beautiful mathematics in creating the world."

— Paul Dirac (1902–1984), physicist, 1933 Nobel Prize laureate

Any discussion of time and the 2012 Mayan calendar end date would be incomplete without mention of ethnobotanist and visionary author Terence McKenna. Before his death in April 2000, McKenna was exploring time in a way that sounds more like the wisdom of an ancient shaman than that of a 20th-century researcher. That may be precisely where the inspiration for his powerful ideas came from. Co-authored with his brother, Dennis, McKenna's books *True Hallucinations* and *The Invisible Landscape* describe how their experiences with indigenous people in the jungles of Colombia led them to think of time and the way things change within it as waves that have structure and lead somewhere.[1]

TimeWave Zero

In 1998, McKenna sent me a copy of his TimeWave Zero software, a computer program he had developed to open a window of insight into the past, as well as our present time in history. Due to compatibility issues between his program and my computer, I never had the opportunity to actually use TimeWave Zero. It was the letter that McKenna included in his correspondence, his innovative thinking, and his marriage of science and indigenous tradition that intrigued me. Just as I had found in my pilgrimages from Egypt to Peru, he agreed with the ancient idea of time as a moving essence that travels in cycles across the universe. It was the way he thought of those cycles that made me want to read more.

Using the King Wen sequence of the *I Ching* (the ancient Chinese "Book of Changes") as a key, McKenna believed that he had found a way to plot the newness and growing complexity of change throughout the course of time. He called these unique conditions "novelty." According to McKenna, when novelty is plotted on a chart, a special waveform known as *timewave zero,* or simply the *timewave,* results.[2]

The reason why I mention McKenna's TimeWave Zero program here is because of its results. There is a single year that it identifies as the point when we can expect what he called *maximum complexity* and novelty in our world. It probably comes as no surprise that it's also the one that's already deeply ingrained into our collective psyche: the 2012 end of the Mayan great cycle.

In McKenna's own words, he described the significance of his program and what he believed it revealed. "We are on the brink of possibilities that will make us literally unrecognizable to ourselves," he stated, "and those possibilities will be realized, not in the next thousand years but in the next 20 years because the acceleration of invention and novelty and information transfer is at this point so rapid."[3] In other words, McKenna's program identified 2012 as the time when all combinations of everything that we may conceive of in our minds become possible at once.

Without a doubt, McKenna's idea of novelty has opened the door to new possibilities in our understanding of time. The mathematics supporting his work is complex. To some, it's also controversial. Before his death, he and mathematician Matthew Watkins worked together to identify the strengths and weaknesses in his program.[4] Using Watkins's discoveries, nuclear physicist John Sheliak then revised McKenna's original software to correct for the errors that were identified.[5]

As we approach 2012, McKenna's ideas and his

TimeWave Zero program continue to offer the framework for insights into the meaning of this date. Even after it passes, however, I have no doubt that his work will continue to pave the way for new understandings of nature's cycles.

While McKenna's ideas offer powerful insights into life's complexity, to answer my questions about 2012 I needed more than the information his program could provide. If the events of the past do, in fact, become the seeds of future conditions, I had to understand the patterns themselves. I needed to find the rhythms that repeat from cycle to cycle, rather than the novelty of events and when they converge.

The Simple Universe

Edward Teller, the man known as the "father" of the hydrogen bomb, once said, "The main purpose of science is simplicity." Clarifying what he meant, Teller concluded, "As we understand more things, everything is becoming simpler."[6] From my experience as a scientist and a student of ancient cultures, I have found that this principle seems to be universal. The more we understand about life and nature, the simpler things appear to become. This includes the secrets of the universe itself.

We can describe the forces of nature in technical terms that give scientists the vocabulary to explore our world. But my sense is that we don't need to. When we get right down to the essence of what makes the universe tick, those understandings are, in fact, based in simple ideas. While the laws of nature and time certainly exist in the universe on a huge scale, they are still grounded in very simple concepts. They unfold in simple ways in our lives. And they can be shared simply through words and examples that make them meaningful. So it appears that nature and time are only as complex as we choose to make them.

The key to making sense of the big things in the universe is to understand what makes those things work on a small scale. Then we can apply what we've learned to the larger world. That's precisely how one of the greatest minds of the 20th century reached one of the most profound conclusions about reality itself. He took a principle that he was developing on a small scale at his desk and wondered if it could apply to the whole universe. The implications of what he found now form the basis for an entire branch of science, one that is just coming into its own during the early years of the 21st century.

Nature's Programs

In the 1940s, Konrad Zuse, the man credited with developing the first modern computers, had a flash of insight into the way the universe may work. While he was developing the simple programs to run those early computers, he asked a question that sounds more like the plot of a novel than something meant to be taken as a serious scientific possibility.

What Zuse wondered was simply this: *is it possible that the entire universe operates like the computers I am building?* This is clearly a huge question, with implications that rattle everything from the ideas of life and evolution to the basis of religion itself. These are the same implications that spawned the hugely popular 1999 film *The Matrix*.

In the 1940s, Zuse was obviously a man ahead of his time. In recent years, new discoveries have directed scientists right back to his original ideas. In 2006, Seth Lloyd, the designer of the first feasible quantum computer, took Zuse's thought of a computerlike universe one step further. In light of new technology and new discoveries, he elevated it from a question of "What if" to the statement of "It is." Based upon his research in the new field of digital physics, Lloyd describes the implications of an emerging view of reality: "The history of the universe is, in effect, a huge and ongoing quantum computation."[7]

Just in case there is any doubt in our minds about precisely what Lloyd is saying here, he clarifies his ideas. Rather than suggesting that the universe may be *like* a quantum computer, he blasts us into the most radical description of reality to emerge in the last 2,000 years, stating: "The universe *is* a quantum computer."[8] From Lloyd's perspective, everything that exists is the output of the universe's computer. "As the computation proceeds, reality unfolds," he explains.[9]

The reason comparing the universe to a computer is important is that regardless of its size or how sophisticated it may appear, each computer follows the same basic principle: it uses programs to get things done. With this in mind, the similarities between nature and a computer become obvious. In both, there are codes that make things happen. If we can understand the codes, then we can understand how things work and how to make changes when we need to.

While some people may find the thought of life's beauty stemming from a "program" somewhat unsettling, except for the language it may not be so different from what our own science has already discovered. The definition of a *program* is that it's a code that "sets a series of events into motion." We know that from atoms to cells, from orbits to seasons, the universe keeps itself going by following patterns. We also know that those patterns repeat as cycles. These are the programs of nature.

Nature's programs exist because something, or someone, has put them there. While the descriptions of that something or someone range from "colliding particles releasing energy" to "God," the principle is the same: there is a great cosmic engine that drives things forward. So it's really not such a stretch to say that the universe, and everything in it, is what and where it is because a code—nature's program—has put it there.

The key to understanding such a cosmic program is to recognize what it does—the patterns that it creates. And to work with those patterns, we must understand the numbers that make them possible. Because nature operates on simple principles, it should come as no surprise to discover that the numbers describing nature's cycles are simple as well.

Nobel Prize–winning physicist Paul Dirac captured the essence of this simplicity: "God used beautiful mathematics in creating the world."[10] The beauty is found in the elegant simplicity. In a very real sense, when we understand the numbers that make natural cycles possible, we are also learning the language of God. When we learn to apply those numbers to bridge the past and the future, we are speaking the divine language of the great programmer of the universe.

While there are textbooks full of complex mathematics that describe nature's codes, our ancestors left us the same ideas as the two simple keys that are explained in the following section. Through the powerful number that seems to govern so many of nature's patterns and their precise repetition, the scientist-shamans of our past created a beautiful bridge between the worlds of sensual beauty and time's cycles. Through that bridge, the secret of time becomes obvious: it's all about recognizing the way cycles of patterns play out in our lives.

Patterns: Nature's Keys to the Universe

My first winter in northern New Mexico's high desert happened to be one of the coldest ever entered in the record books. Even the elders of the nearby native pueblos said that no one remembered it having been so cold, for so long, as during the dry winters of the early 1990s. While my scientific mind knew that cold air is heavier than warm air and tends to settle in the valleys at night, until that first winter I never really realized just how cold those nights could be. The first December evening that I walked outside my house to look at the stars and check the thermometer near the woodpile, I found out.

I quickly learned that high-desert valleys could

create dangerous conditions where bare skin can freeze in minutes. After I tapped the mercury a couple of times to make sure the reading wasn't stuck, I dashed back inside for a warmer coat. *The temperature was 50 degrees below zero!*

When the sun came up the next morning and temperatures rose into the mid-40s above zero, I drove into town. Everywhere I went the conversation was the same. People were talking about the record cold and what it had done to their livestock, water pipes, and crops the night before. One man at the local hardware store, who'd had to be on the job before the sun warmed the world, found that morning as he rolled out of his driveway that the rubber on his tires had become so brittle from the cold that they had actually cracked and broken. Later that night, the temperatures dropped again, and once more thermometers read nearly 50 degrees below zero.

While I was walking in the fields surrounding my home the next day, I noticed that the occasional anthills dotting the property seemed to be larger than normal—and not just a *little* larger: these were anthills that measured a foot and a half or more above the ground and could be seen for acres before I got to them! There were some that even towered above the sage plants and desert shrubs that grow wild in the valley. I knew that for the mounds to be so large, the ants had to go really deep into the ground. I also knew that the deeper ant colonies built their tunnels into the earth, the warmer the temperatures of the ground surrounding them became. What I *didn't* know was if there was a link between these facts and the record temperatures. In other words, had the ants somehow "known" that an extremely cold winter was on the way and built their homes accordingly?

The next winter, the weather patterns changed. While the December temperatures were still cold and well below the zero mark, they were not *50 degrees* below. Throughout the autumn I had watched the ant-hills across the fields and noticed that they didn't seem to be as big as the year before. *Hmm,* I thought, *maybe the ants are telling us that this won't be such a cold winter.*

I soon discovered that what I'd seen in my fields is part of well-known lore among the native people and historical residents of the high deserts. It's a pattern. And that pattern is part of a cycle. It's as predictable and reliable as any high-tech forecasts from the computer models, but it comes even earlier than they do.

The pattern is clear: the higher the mounds, the deeper the ants have tunneled into the ground, and the colder the winter will be. By the time the trees begin to turn in the fall, if the ants go really deep, it means that I can either schedule my seminars in a part of the world where the temperatures are at least a little above zero at night . . . or stock up on some extra firewood. The point is that the anthills and the weather are patterns that can be recognized. Together, their cyclic patterns are part of even larger patterns of seasons. The patterns are consistent, and they appear like clockwork.

The more we learn about our relationship to nature and time, the clearer it is that patterns and the cycles of time are more than simply an interesting phenomenon of life. *The cycles of time are life.* In fact, it's fair to say that for everything from the biology of DNA and the laws of physics to the history of our planet and the evolution of the universe, our world of matter follows very precise rules that allow things to "be" as they are.

While it may sound like the only time we escape the effect of cycles is at the end of life, even in death we appear to be part of a larger cycle. Almost universally, our most cherished spiritual traditions remind us that death is merely the end of one cycle and part of a greater one that mirrors the creation/destruction/birth/death theme of the universe itself.

With these ideas in mind, nature offers us two powerful keys that make it possible to predict repeating patterns in the cycles of time. Regardless of the scale, whether the cycles last for a nanosecond or for tens of thousands of years, the keys work the same way.

- The first key is the principle of *fractals.* These are the patterns that nature uses to fill the space of the universe.

- The second key is the *golden ratio.* This is the number that determines how frequently nature repeats the fractals that fill space.

Separately, each key stands on its own as a powerful tool to understanding everything from the secrets of atoms and the inner workings of solar systems to the cycles of personal success and betrayal. Combined, they offer an unprecedented insight into the language of time itself.

As we'll see in the following chapters, when we apply these two simple keys to time—past, present, and future—we open the door to powerful insights into when and how often we can anticipate the greatest threats to our careers, our way of life, our civilization, and even our future. If we know when to expect the conditions, we also know how to change the circumstances.

Before we can do any of this, however, we must understand our two keys: the nature of fractal patterns and the ancient secret of the golden ratio.

Fractals: The Code Within the Code Within the Code . . .

In the late 1990s, I had the opportunity to put all of the organizational and planning skills I'd developed in the corporate world to good use for my own family. It was time to move my mother from her home in one city to a different home in a different city. I quickly found, as anyone who has ever embarked upon such a mission has already discovered, that the move itself was the easy part. It was the preparation that had to happen *before* that became the project of a lifetime.

Mom had made the decision that this move was a special one and she was going to do it differently than any she had ever done in the past. Celebrating good health, new beginnings, and new surroundings, in an effort to streamline her life she had chosen this move as the one to *downsize*. This meant that everything she had accumulated for decades would be examined and evaluated, and the things that she no longer needed would find a new home. So before we could even begin to pack, we had to choose what would make the journey.

As we sifted through the boxes and bags that held the accumulated history of our entire family, we found ourselves engrossed in the memories and the meaning that the contents brought to mind. Every few minutes I would hear Mom's excited voice coming from somewhere behind a stack of boxes taller than she was, asking me to look at the treasures she had rediscovered. "Oh, look at this," she would say, holding up something that my brother or I had made for her more than 30 years before.

There was the Valentine's Day card that still had two Tootsie Roll chocolates (now nearly fossilized) taped inside. My brother had made the card and given it to her when he was in the second grade. There were the black-and-white metal-plated photographs of our stern-faced ancestors taken in the late 19th century. Apparently, having a personal photo taken a century ago was serious business. Not one of them was smiling! Then there was my artwork. Mom had all of it, showing the evolution from the simple drawings of nature I'd made in kindergarten to the Asian water-colors of martial artists I'd painted in high school. It was those early drawings that bring this story to mind in this chapter.

As I unfolded the brittle construction paper and darkened crayon images, I was amazed by what I was seeing. As I child, I had done my best to reproduce the beauty of northern Missouri's trees and the changing of the seasons. The thing was that the drawings on the paper looked nothing like the trees that made up the forested bluffs overlooking the Missouri River. My trees resembled triangles on skinny poles! The puffy clouds that dotted the sky were empty circles hanging above the horizon, and the rocks on the ground looked like a pile of tiny squares.

What I had recorded on paper was a primitive rendition of what I had actually seen with my eyes. What's important here is that I expressed what I'd seen using the tools that I'd been taught represent our world: the geometry of shapes. Because the geometry that we've typically learned in the past is based on forms that we don't find in nature, the drawings were approximations. I'd expressed what I'd seen as a child through the shapes with the closest resemblance. Now we know that this type of geometry—Euclidean geometry—simply can't do the job. The reason is that nature isn't made of circles, triangles, and squares. Clearly, we need a different kind of geometry to describe the world that we experience through our senses.

Now we have one. A new mathematics has burst onto the scene, forever changing the way we think of everything from nature and our bodies to wars and the stock market. It's called *fractal mathematics,* or simply, *fractals.*

In the 1970s, a mathematics professor at Yale University, Benoit Mandelbrot, developed a way for us to see the underlying structure that makes the world as it is. That structure is made of patterns—specifically, patterns within patterns within patterns . . . and so on. He called his new way of seeing things *fractal geometry.* His work *The Fractal Geometry of Nature* is now recognized as one of the most influential books of the 20th century.[11]

Before Mandelbrot's discovery, mathematicians

employed the Euclidean geometry that I'd used as a child to describe our world. The belief has been that nature is too complex and too fragmented to have a single mathematical form, or formula, that represents it accurately. It's for precisely this reason that children's first drawings of trees usually look like lollipops on sticks. It was from an epiphany that Mandelbrot experienced as an adult studying the world's architecture and the inadequate tools he had to re-create what he saw, that he began a search for a new way to express his experiences.

Describing this realization, he said, "I don't feel that Euclid is the way to start learning mathematics. Learning mathematics should begin by learning the geometry of mountains, of humans. In a certain sense, the geometry of . . . well, of Mother Nature, and also of buildings, of great architecture."[12]

With these words, Mandelbrot stated what we all know intuitively. Nature does not use perfect lines and curves to build mountains, clouds, and trees. Rather, it uses irregular fragments that, when taken as a whole, *become* the mountains, clouds, and trees. The key in a fractal is that each fragment, no matter how small, looks like the larger pattern that it's a part of. This will be important when we begin to think of time as fractal patterns in the next chapter.

When Mandelbrot programmed his simple formula into a computer, the output was stunning. By depicting everything in the natural world as small fragments that look a lot like other small fragments, and by combining these similar fragments into larger patterns, the images that were produced did more than simply approximate nature. *They looked exactly like nature.*

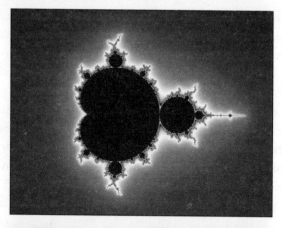

Figure 9. In the 1970s, Benoit Mandelbrot programmed a computer to produce the first fractal images, such as the one seen here on the top, called the Mandelbrot set. When we zoom in on each piece of the pattern, we find that no matter what the scale is, the overall pattern repeats itself and looks remarkably self-similar. Scientists have found that self-similar principles describe nature and can mimic even the most complex patterns, such as the fern leaf on the bottom.

This is precisely what Mandelbrot's new geometry was showing us about our world. Nature builds itself in fragments, and each one is made of patterns that are similar yet not identical. The term to describe this kind of similarity is *self-similarity.*

Time Code 11: Nature uses a few simple, self-similar, and repeating patterns—fractals—to build energy and atoms into the familiar forms of everything from roots, rivers, and trees to rocks, mountains, and us.

Seemingly overnight, it became possible to use fractals to replicate everything from the coastline of a continent to an alpine forest—and even the universe itself. The key was to find the right formula—the right program. This is the idea that brings us back to thinking of nature as a program that drives the universe.

If the entire universe is really the output of an unimaginably huge, ancient, and continuously running program, such as Zuse and Lloyd have suggested, then that program must be producing the fractal patterns that we see as the world around us. This fractal view of the universe implies that everything from a single atom to the entire cosmos is made of just a few natural patterns. While they may combine, repeat, and build themselves on larger scales, in their complexity they can still be reduced to a few simple forms.

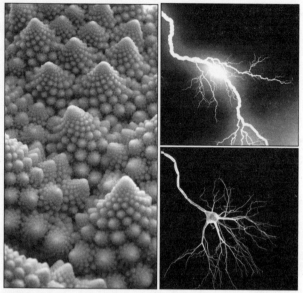

Figure 10. Examples of fractals in nature. The image on the left is of Romanesco broccoli. From the individual flowers to the entire stalk, the same patterns repeat on varying scales to create the head of broccoli. The image on the top right is of a bolt of electricity discharging as lightning from the atmosphere to the ground. The image below the lightning is of a magnified neuron—a specialized cell of the nervous system that carries electrical information within the body. Both sets of images illustrate how self-similar, repeating patterns can be used to describe the universe from the very small to the very large, while differing only in scale.

The idea is certainly attractive. In fact, it's beautiful. Thinking of the universe as a fractal reality crosses the artificial separation that we have placed on our knowledge in the past, weaving very different disciplines of science and philosophy together into one great, elegant story of how the universe is constructed. The fractal view of the cosmos is so complete that it even accounts for the aesthetic qualities of balance and symmetry that artists, mathematicians, philosophers, and physicists aspire to in the highest forms of their crafts.

The universal appeal of this way of thinking certainly fulfills pioneering physicist John Wheeler's prophetic statement of simplicity's time-tested truth. Before his death in 2008, Wheeler predicted that everything must be based on a simple idea. Once we discover that idea, he said, it would be "so simple, so beautiful, so compelling that we will all say to each other, 'Oh, how could it have been otherwise?'" A universe of fractal patterns certainly fits Wheeler's prediction.

In addition to accommodating the requirements of so many different ways of thinking, the fractal model of our universe has another important advantage as well. It holds the key to unlocking nothing less than the inner workings of nature's patterns. If we can understand the pattern of an atom on the small scale, for example, then the fractal pattern of a solar system will begin to make sense. From our understanding of a solar system, the patterns of a galaxy should begin to fall into place. While each of these systems is very different in size, they are expressions of a common pattern; they are fractals of one another.

Time Code 12: Everything we need to understand the universe lives in the simplicity of each piece of it.

Through his unique gift of finding just the right words to create just the right mental images, poet

William Blake captured the essence of a fractal universe in the simplicity of only four short verses. Preserved in what may be his most popular poem, "Auguries of Innocence," Blake reminds us:

> To see a world in a grain of sand,
> And a heaven in a wild flower,
> Hold infinity in the palm of your hand,
> And eternity in an hour.

Through the beauty of these words, we're reminded that everything we need in order to understand the vastness of the universe lives in the simplicity of each fragment.

Nature's Most Beautiful Number

In January 1986, I walked onto Egypt's Giza plateau for the first time. Towering into the sky above me was the marvel that represents one of the greatest unsolved mysteries in the history of our species and the monument that had fascinated me since the first time I saw an image of it as a child. I was standing at the base of the Great Pyramid.

It looked different up close, even more weathered and ancient than in the classic photographs that fill the pages of the travel guides. Although I should have been jet-lagged from the long flights and unexpected delays that it took for me to be in the shadow of the pyramid, I felt none of that in the moment. Immediately, I wanted to know more. How could such a mystery remain in the technological world of the 20th century? Who put it there? And how?

The Great Pyramid is one of those enigmas that seem to be a bottomless pit for questions. Rather than the traditional process of solving the puzzle by discovering facts, the more we know about this ancient mystery, the more we discover that we *don't* know. But even in the light of all of the mystery, one fact about Egypt's Great Pyramid has become abundantly clear: Whoever built it understood the power of the single number that seems to permeate life and form throughout the universe. It's the same number that became the focus for one of the most successful mystery novels in history.

In Dan Brown's best-selling novel *The Da Vinci Code,* the main character, Robert Langdon, leads his students through the exploration of a powerful number—a code—that the ancients recognized as a constant that exists throughout nature and the universe. Using words that sound more like a reference to a magnificent work of art than a code to history's greatest secret, Langdon states that the number, named *phi* (usually pronounced with a long *i,* like the word *eye*), is "generally considered the most beautiful number in the universe."[13]

While phi may be secretly encoded into the work of great masters such as Michelangelo and Leonardo da Vinci, it was certainly no secret to the architects of the Great Pyramid. The consistent accuracy of the pyramid's construction leaves little doubt that the numbers and relationships used to build it were applied with great care.

The Great Pyramid is made of an estimated 2.3 million individually formed stones, some weighing up to 70 tons each. It covers 13 acres of native rock and is nearly perfectly level across the entire area (it's believed that the structure was once exactly level and that the small variance seen today is due to shifting earth over the centuries). The pyramid's height is 5,449 inches, the same number as the average height of the Earth's landmass above sea level, and its location in Egypt is also the geographic center of the landmass for the planet.

With these facts in mind, we can be sure that the use of nature's most beautiful number in the pyramid's construction is intentional. It should come as no surprise, then, that the very dimensions that make this mysterious monument possible are due to the use of phi. A line drawn from the projected top (apex) of the capstone to the edge at the base of each face produces a measurement that is phi units.

The ongoing controversy over the age of the Great Pyramid gives such measurements an even greater significance. If the revised date for the building of the structure turns out to be older than the conventional theory of 2560 B.C., then it means that its builders not only had the advanced knowledge to create such a structure, but they also encoded it with the essence of the number that seems to govern much of the universe: the mysterious phi.

The Mystery of Phi

Phi is the number that we get when we compare one part of a "something" to another part of itself, after that something is divided in a very precise way. The result of the comparison is the ratio.

While there are an infinite number of ways that something may be divided into two parts of different sizes, the one that the universe seems to favor has been recognized for hundreds of years. During that time, it's been given names that vary, from the *golden proportion* and the *divine ratio* to the *golden ratio*. Although the names vary, the number they represent is always the same: *Phi* with an uppercase *P* is 1.618; and its close relative, *phi* with a lowercase *p,* is .618. Both are a form of the golden ratio. For the following chapters, we will use phi as .618 for the Time Code calculations.[14] The illustration that follows offers an example of precisely what these ratios are and how they work.

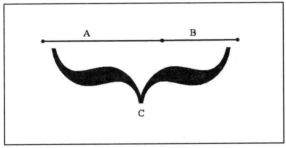

Figure 11. The golden ratio describes a special relationship between two parts of a whole. In this illustration, we can demonstrate this for ourselves by taking the large section length (A) and dividing it by the smaller section (B). No matter what number we assign to the overall length of the line (C), when we divide it with the proportions shown above, the relationship of the smaller section to the larger one will always approximate 1.618, while the larger to the smaller will approximate .618.

During the early 14th century, Leonardo Fibonacci, an Italian mathematician, discovered what is believed to be the never-ending series of numbers that creates the golden ratio. The best way to see how this works is to look at an example. Following are the first 20 members of Fibonacci's numbers, which are known as the *Fibonacci sequence:* 1; 1; 2; 3; 5; 8; 13; 21; 34; 55; 89; 144; 233; 377; 610; 987; 1,597; 2,584; 4,181; 6,765 . . .

A closer look at each number will show that it is the result of adding the two numbers before it. For example, 1 + 1 = 2; 1 + 2 = 3; 3 + 2 = 5; 5 + 3 = 8; and so on.

The next thing we see is that if we divide any number in the sequence by the one that immediately precedes it, the result is close to the golden ratio—very close, *but never it exactly.* The division always gives us a value that is either slightly higher or lower, but never equal to, the golden ratio.

The reason is that such a division creates a number that falls into a class of numbers that simply cannot exist in our way of thinking of numbers. (It's an *irrational number,* which simply means that it can't be described as an exact fraction.)[15] So each number in the sequence dances just above or just below the golden ratio. The larger the numbers we divide, the tighter the dance and the closer we get to the precise number of 1.618.

Once again, the best way to illustrate how nature approximates the golden ratio is by example. Following are a few showing that the ratio of each pair of Fibonacci's numbers is either slightly higher or slightly lower than the golden ratio itself:

1 ÷ 1 = 1.00—less than 1.618
2 ÷ 1 = 2.00—greater than 1.618
3 ÷ 2 = 1.50—less than 1.618, but closer than the last ratio
5 ÷ 3 = 1.66—greater than 1.618, but closer than last ratio

8 ÷ 5 = 1.60—less than 1.618, but closer than the last ratio
13 ÷ 8 = 1.625—greater than 1.618, but closer than last ratio
21 ÷ 13 = 1.615—less than 1.618, but closer than last ratio
34 ÷ 21 = 1.619—greater than 1.618, but closer than last ratio

Whether we're talking about the proportions of the human body or those of the elegant temples in ancient Greece, this universal ratio seems to be the template for what we accept as beautiful in the world.

Fact: The proportions of the human body are governed by the golden ratio:

- Ratio of navel height to total body height is .618.

- Ratio of length of hand to that of forearm is .618.

- Ratio of human face from the brow to the chin is .618 of that from the chin to the crown.

- The body's ratios continue with additional proportions and even the location of organs determined by .618.

Fact: The orbits of planets, such as Mercury and Venus, are approximated by the golden ratio.

Fact: The spirals that form everything from the arms of the Milky Way galaxy and the vortices of a hurricane to the way hair grows on the human head and the pattern of seeds in a sunflower are governed by the golden ratio.

Fact: The spiral paths traveled by quantum particles in a laboratory bubble chamber are governed by the golden ratio.

The golden ratio is everywhere. Because it surrounds us, it's probably no accident that it embodies the proportions of things that we are most comfortable with. While the precise reason why things based upon these proportions are so pleasing to us remains a mystery, the fact is that they *are*. It's almost as if we're hardwired to be drawn to such a powerful standard of beauty—and maybe we are.

In addition to being the number that governs much of the world around us and the parts of our body that we can see, it's also key for the things we *can't* see. The golden ratio applies to everything from the brain states of consciousness to the proportions of DNA itself. For example, one complete turn of a DNA strand is 34 (angstrom units) in length and 21 wide. Each of these lengths is a member of Fibonacci's sequence shown previously, and as with the other such numbers, 21 to 34 approximates the golden ratio of .618.

While we all may know this intuitively, it's important to understand that our idea of beauty may not be the universal one. If we suddenly find ourselves on an alien world someday, with beings that are based upon a different proportion, because we are so powerfully compelled to hold the golden ratio as our standard of beauty they may seem strange and unpleasing to us.

At the same time, however, if our alien friends do

happen to have bodies based on a different proportion—say, one that represents half of the golden ratio, of 1:309—then we may find that we look just as strange to them as they do to us. Knowing where our ideas of beauty come from may help us be more tolerant of other possibilities. This simple understanding of our local world could actually go a long way in developing good relations in our galactic neighborhood.

For reasons so numerous that they've filled entire books in the past, the golden ratio seems to be the guiding principle in nature's cycles of growth and proportion, as well as in the timing that separates the things that happen in life.

It's precisely *because* the golden ratio applies to the natural world in a way that is so universal that we shouldn't be surprised to find that it applies to the mysterious essence separating one moment of life from the next. The golden ratio applies to time itself.

The Mystery of Time

When physicist John Wheeler was once asked to define "time," he did so with a simplicity that we might expect from an ancient mystic isolated in a remote monastery at the summit of a snow-packed mountain in the Himalayas. "Time," he said, "is what prevents everything from happening at once." While we may laugh when we first hear such a simple answer from such a brilliant man, if we really think about it, it is clear that Wheeler had a deep understanding of what may be the most common yet mysterious relationship that each of us will experience in life—our relationship with the time that defines our existence.

Our bizarre relationship with time, as well as our attempts to describe it, is nothing new. In words that are as meaningful today as they were in his time, Saint Augustine identified the irony of our relationship with time. "What is time?" he began. "If no one asks me, I know what it is. If I wish to explain it to him who asks, I do not know." Sixteen hundred years ago, Saint Augustine seems to have zeroed in on the crux of time's mystery.

Without a doubt, time is the most elusive experience to define and the most difficult to explain. The reason is that no one has ever seen it, measured it directly, or experienced it by itself. We can't capture it or photograph it. Contrary to what "daylight saving time" seems to suggest, it's impossible to collect it in one place and use it later somewhere else. When we do try to describe what time means in our lives, we find that the only way to do so is to describe our experiences *within* time, rather than the time itself. We say that something happened *then* in the past, that it's happening *now* in the present, or that it *will* happen at some point in the future.

In other words, it's as if time cannot be separated from the events themselves. This is precisely the key to what may well be one of humankind's greatest leaps in understanding the way the universe works: the fact that time and the things that happen within it are intimately connected as two parts of the same essence—they cannot be separated.

Two revolutionary discoveries of the 20th century forever changed the way we think of time. With those discoveries, it became possible to link time with the things that happen within it. In other words, it became scientifically "legal" for us to think of time as *stuff*. If it behaves like stuff, then we can measure it as stuff.

Because time is a natural process and so much of nature is governed by the golden ratio, it would make sense that time would follow the same patterns of fractals and the golden ratio as well. And it does. To understand how this paradigm-shattering way of thinking connects the things that happen in the future with those of the past, we must first take a closer look at the mystery of time itself.

Space and Time Redux

Until the 20th century, the Western world typically thought of time in a poetic sense, as something that exists only because we need it to exist in our experience. Philosopher Jean-Paul Sartre described time as "a special kind of separation" between the events of life. It's this separation that creates what he called a "division that reunites."

The Greek philosophers were among the first who tried to give a definition to time. In his work *Timaeus,* for example, Plato describes how time was created along with the heavens for a specific reason. "[The Creator] sought to make the universe eternal, so far as might be," he begins. But recognizing that the life *within the universe* would not share the eternal attribute *of the universe*, Plato reasoned that the Creator "resolved to have a moving image of eternity, and when he set in order the heavens, he made this image eternal but moving according to number, while eternity itself rests in unity; and this image we call time."[16] From this description, we see that Plato believed time originated with the birth of the universe and was God's way of assuring a lasting creation.

With the birth of science in the 17th century, time began to take on a new meaning. When Isaac Newton formalized the laws of motion in 1687, he recognized that his theories, as well as his equations, were based upon time. So to identify the nature of the stuff that his work depended on, he defined pure time as something that "flows equably without relation to anything external."[17]

In other words, Newton thought of time as an absolute quantity. It "is" what it "is" and *isn't* influenced by the universe or events of the world. This view of time works as if there were an independent clock ticking away somewhere *outside* of the universe tirelessly tracking the constant flow of time. Newton's ideas were accepted quickly because they seemed to work well—so well, in fact, that he developed calculus, an entire mathematical system based upon his notions of time.

The implications of Newton's view of time as an absolute quantity are still with us today. If his ideas are correct, then it means that we should be able to calculate the location of every particle in the universe. And if we could know where each particle is and how fast it's moving, then we should be able to calculate its precise location at another moment in time.

With the acceptance of Newton's ideas, the whole universe began to look like a big machine made of particles that could be tracked from one place to another.

It's this mechanical view of reality and our bodies that has led to the present-day split between thinking of our world as individual particles that can be known and measured absolutely (classical physics) and conceptualizing it as zones of energy described by probabilities (quantum physics).

With Einstein's theory of relativity in 1905, these poetic views changed forever. Rather than thinking of time as its own experience and separate from everything else, Einstein suggested something so radical that even scientists had to rethink the foundation of physics to grasp what he was saying. The bottom line of Einstein's theory was simply this: *time is part of the universe and cannot be separated from the space it travels in.*

Figure 12. What does space-time look like? Scientists often illustrate it through images that look like the one above, where the waves of space are bent and shaped by things like black holes and the gravity of planets. Because time and the events of life cannot be separated, however, in reality we see space-time all around us as our everyday world. From the waves of the ocean to the person sitting next to you, all that we know as our world *is* the space-time of the universe frozen into the "now" of the present moment.

In other words, time and space are two parts of the same stuff. And just the way two threads become intimately enmeshed in the same strand of yarn, time cannot be separated from the space it moves through. It is space and time, married together as *space-time,* Einstein said, that forms a realm beyond our familiar world of three dimensions of length, width, and height. He called this realm the *fourth dimension.* With the acceptance of Einstein's ideas, time became more than a casual philosophical concept. Suddenly, it was a force of nature that scientists had to seriously deal with.

While Einstein is credited with the publication of the theory of relativity, the idea of time and space woven together actually arose from one of his colleagues and friends, Hermann Minkowski. It was Minkowski's elaboration upon Einstein's ideas that he described at the 80th Assembly of German Natural Scientists and Physicians in 1908. Minkowski began the program with the following now-famous words:

> The views of space and time which I wish to lay before you have sprung from the soil of experimental physics, and therein lies their strength. They are radical. Henceforth space by itself, and time by itself, are doomed to fade away into mere shadows, and only a kind of union of the two will preserve an independent reality.[18]

Acknowledging that both Einstein's relativity and Minkowski's revisions led to one of the most revolutionary ideas in science, the complete term for the realm that Minkowski was describing is now known as *Einstein-Minkowski space-time.*

Einstein knew that what he had proposed in his original papers of relativity was complex. In a letter to Heinrich Zangger in 1915, he stated: "The theory is beautiful beyond comparison. However, only *one* colleague has really been able to understand it and [use it]."[19] (That colleague was mathematician David Hilbert.) Once the idea of relativity caught on, however, there was no turning back. Suddenly everyone seemed to be talking about it, and more than 30 years later Einstein was still baffled by why his ideas of space and time were received so well by the public at large.

In a letter to Philipp Frank, for example, in 1942, Einstein wrote: "I never understood why the theory of relativity . . . should have met with such a lively, indeed passionate, reception among a broad segment of the public." In another letter to his friend and colleague Marcel Grossmann, Einstein described just how much his ideas of relativity had permeated the public at large: "At present every coachman and every waiter argues about whether or not relativity theory is correct."[20]

In words that gave an entirely new meaning to our idea of time, Einstein described its mysterious nature, explaining, "Time cannot be absolutely defined, and there is an inseparable relation between time and signal velocity [speed of a wave]."[21] With this single sentence, 300 years of the way we think of time and the things that happen within time changed forever. We continue to talk about the implications today, and many of the questions that were sparked by Einstein's ideas still have not been answered.

The "Problem" of Time

Perhaps the two questions of time that baffle scientists the most are the following:

1. Is time real?

2. Why does time seem to flow only in one direction—forward?

While these two questions may sound like something we'd expect to hear on the first day of a college philosophy course, the answers are the key to the meaning of the Mayan calendar and the mystery of 2012. Mainstream scientists are seriously asking both. The reason is that they must be answered before scientists can move on and solve some of the greatest mysteries of physics and the universe.

The effort is paying off. Recent studies are producing new evidence that has catapulted physicists into a new way of thinking of the universe. This new way of thinking is leading to precisely what we need to solve the mystery of 2012. So let's take a deeper look at each question and see where the evidence leads.

1. Is Time Real?

If we ask anyone who is stuck in traffic on one of America's gridlocked freeways if time is real, the answer will be the same. Most will find a direct correlation between the level of their blood pressure and the time of their commute. Their answer would be: "Yes! You bet, time is real." And, from the quantum perspective of creating our reality in terms of the way we perceive our world, they are absolutely right.

Time is as real as we agree it is. But while "watch time" ticks away the minutes it takes us to get from one stoplight to the next, maybe there's another kind we're also dealing with: the time that is the container for the things happening in the world. While he did not have the rush-hour traffic to contend with while he was asking this question, this is precisely the kind of time that Einstein chose to see differently a century ago. When he did, everything changed.

While Einstein's 1905 and 1915 theories of relativity definitely propelled us into a new way of thinking of time, they also created a problem that physicists are still struggling with today. Here's the bottom line to the quandary: the rules that describe the world on the large scale of universes and apples falling from trees (classical physics) do not seem to work with the rules that describe the tiny realm of subatomic particles that the apples and universes are made of (quantum physics). It's all about what time means to us in our reality. Its role has been in question for so long that physicists even have their own lingo to describe the mystery . . . it's simply called "the problem of time."

In 1967, two of the 20th century's most brilliant minds proposed a way to unify the quantum and classical worlds. Physicists John Wheeler (a Princeton University colleague and peer of Einstein) and Bryce DeWitt (of the University of North Carolina) published a paper with an equation that seemed to successfully merge both ways of thinking of the world into a single unified view known as the *Wheeler-DeWitt equation*.[22] For those trying to reconcile the two great theories of physics, this appeared to be great news.

While the specifics of the Wheeler-DeWitt equation are complex, the idea is simple. It's a way to think of the universe from a perspective that weaves the quantum world and classical physics into a single story. There is one small "catch," however: *to solve the Wheeler-DeWitt equation, we have to forget about time*. That's right—it seems that in arriving at the solution, time simply disappears from the equation.

In other words, just when it seems that a couple of the best minds of the 20th century have solved one of the greatest mysteries in the history of science, we find that the only way for them to do so is to discount the very essence of the stuff that keeps everything from happening all at once. So just what is such a discovery really telling us? Could it be that at the deepest levels of reality, time doesn't truly exist?

This is precisely the conclusion that studies at Germany's Max Planck Institute of Quantum Optics seem to be leading to. It's there that physicist Ferenc Krausz has been using laser light to explore the tiniest intervals of time imaginable: quantum time. His work has taken him to a place that sounds more like a fairy-tale world of imagination than the reality of a laboratory experiment. In Krausz's lab, the things that happen during the study occur so quickly, and on such a small scale, that scientists have had to create a whole new vocabulary just to describe them.

An *attosecond*, for example, is a measure of time

that's equal to one-quintillionth of a second. That is the number 1 followed by 18 zeros. It's in these mind-bogglingly tiny instants of time that scientists have discovered a place where there *is* no time, a realm where the space between one thing happening and the next has no meaning and makes no sense. It's called *Planck time*. Planck time is measured as anything that happens in an interval of 10^{-43} seconds or less. Just for scale, one unit of Planck time is less than a trillionth of a trillionth of the attosecond described above! At least for now, it is the smallest unit of time that has any meaning in the physical world.

This brings us back to the reality of time itself and what happens at intervals that are *less than* Planck time. The bottom line is this—for things that happen below the Planck scale, time disappears. In other words, the things that happen at such small scales appear to have no meaning in our physical world. This has led to the controversial idea that time may not be as important as we once thought it was, or it may be that it doesn't exist in the way we've thought of it in the past. Carlo Rovelli, a physicist at the University of the Mediterranean in Marseille, France, sums up this possibility: "It may be that the best way to think about quantum reality is to give up the notion of time—that the fundamental description of the universe must be timeless."[23]

With these words Rovelli describes just how far we have come in our thinking of what time means to us. While we used to think of it as the basis of life and the universe, we may be discovering that time, at least in some places, doesn't even matter. We now have everything we need to address the question that began this section: *does time really exist, or is it our experience that gives it meaning?* Interestingly, the answer to both parts of the question appears to be the same. It's yes. It all depends upon what level of reality we're talking about and our place in that reality.

When "Then" Is "Now": The Language That Mirrors Reality

While modern science is still coming to terms with the reality of time and what it means for the concepts of past and future, our indigenous ancestors were already well aware of these relationships. When linguist Benjamin Lee Whorf explored the language of the Hopi during the mid-20th century, for example, he discovered that their words directly reflected their view of the timeless nature of the universe. Their idea of time and our place in it was very different from the way we typically think of ourselves. They saw the world as a single entity, with everything connected and happening in the present of "now."

In his pioneering book *Language, Thought, and Reality,* Whorf summarized the Hopi worldview: "In [the] Hopi view, time disappears and space is altered, so that it is no longer the homogeneous and instantaneous timeless space of our supposed intuition or of classical Newtonian mechanics."[24] In other words, the Hopi simply don't think of time, space, distance, and reality in the way we do. In their eyes, we live in a universe where everything is alive and connected. Perhaps most important, they see everything as happening "now." Their language mirrors their view.

When we look at an ocean, for example, and see a wave, we would typically say, "Look at that wave." But we know that in reality, the wave we're looking at doesn't exist alone. It's there only because of other waves. "Without the projection of language," said Whorf, "no one ever saw a single wave."[25] What we see is a "surface in everchanging undulating motions," he explained. In the language of the Hopi, however, they would say that the ocean is "waving" to describe the action of the water in the moment they see it. More precisely, clarified Whorf, "Hopi say *walalata*, 'plural waving occurs,' and can call attention to one place in the waving just as we can."[26] In this way, although it may sound odd to us, they are actually more accurate in how they describe the world.

In this expanded view of the universe, time as we tend to think of it takes on a brand-new meaning within the traditional beliefs of the Hopi. Whorf's studies led him to discover that the "manifested comprises all that is or has been accessible to the senses, the historical physical universe . . . with no attempt to distinguish between present and past, but excluding everything that we call future."[27]

In other words, the Hopi language uses the same words whether describing what "is" or what has already happened. Knowing that the quantum world holds the blueprint of all possibilities, this view of time and language makes perfect sense. When the Hopi say that something "is," they are describing the quantum possibility that has become manifest, while also leaving the future open to other possibilities.

From the implications of the Hopi language to the now-common laboratory examples proving that observation affects reality, it's obvious that there is more to our relationship with time than using it to gauge when we are at the right place at the right moment of the day. While it may not exist in the unseen quantum world, time definitely exists in the world of big things like universes, patterns, and cycles. Where there's time, it seems to always flow in the same direction. This leads us to our second mystery.

While the mathematics describing time appear to allow for it to move either forward or backward, our everyday world seems to be locked into a place where we experience only the future motion physicists refer to as the forward "arrow of time."

2. Why Does Time Seem to Flow Only in One Direction?

When physicists talk about time, their ideas generally follow one of two ways of thinking. One way says that time is a subjective experience and that the way we experience it is determined by whoever is doing the experiencing. From this perspective, the past, present, and future all exist, all of the time. In every moment, they each exist as a flow of energy and events that we experience as "now."

Perhaps this way of thinking of time is best described by Einstein himself in a letter sometime around 1931. "For those of us who believe in physics," he said, "this separation between past, present, and future is only an illusion, although a persistent one."[28] While many physicists believe that our "illusion" of time may be the way the universe really works, when it comes to the mathematics that describe time, there's a mystery that seems to be as persistent as the illusion itself. It's called the arrow of time or, more commonly, the "problem of time."

Simply stated, the problem is this: Time seems to flow only in one direction. It moves from the present to the future. While there is nothing in physics that says time must go in one direction, we all know that it does. Or at least that's the way it seems to *us*. Any doubt of this fact quickly disappears when we think of the way things work in our everyday world.

If an egg slips from our fingers and shatters onto the kitchen floor, for example, while we're rushing around to make breakfast in the morning, that egg is pretty much irreversibly broken. And we can safely assume that it will remain that way forever. The possibility that the fragmented, shattered shell will reassemble itself into the familiar shape of the original egg, coupled with the possibility that the yolk spread across the floor will suddenly gather itself back into a round mass that was neatly packed inside of the shell, is slim.

What makes this so interesting, however, is that there is nothing in our understanding that prevents these things from happening. Just to be clear, there's absolutely nothing in the laws of physics, at least as we know them today, that states that the egg must remain broken forever. In fact, the physics suggest just the opposite: the principles that determine the flow of time in the universe are said to be symmetrical—that is, they can go in either direction.

But we know that they don't. All we have to do is to think about that shattered egg on the kitchen floor, the flow of money from our checkbook, or the way we change as we age to be a firsthand witness to the arrow of time. The question is *why?* What is it that seems to force time to flow in one direction, and why is that direction always toward the future?

The answer to this question is the second key to understanding the mystery of 2012. It all comes back to Einstein's brilliant realization that time and space are inseparable.

For the most part, the prevailing view of the way things began in the universe is encapsulated as part of what is called the *big bang theory.* Simply stated, the big bang proposes that a primal release of energy set the universe into motion. While there is controversy as to precisely when this event happened and what, if anything, existed before it, the data strongly suggest that it did take place. Recent information from satellites, such as NASA's Chandra Observatory and the Cosmic Background Explorer (COBE), shows what are believed to be the remains of the massive release of energy that birthed our universe about 14 billion years ago.[29] What's important here is that the energy appears to be *moving away* from one place in the center of the universe. As it does, the data show that it is expanding and cooling.

It's in the outward expansion of the universe from a central point that we may find the clue to time's mysterious flow in one direction. Just as our egg on the kitchen floor does not reverse the sequence of events that led to its shattering, the universe does not reverse the flow of the outward expansion that began with the big bang— or at least not in the current cycle of the universe as we know it. *Because time is the space it travels in, it expands with the flow of space: outward and away from its source.*

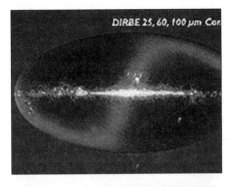

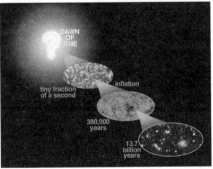

Figure 13. *Top:* NASA image from the COBE satellite showing the concentration of energy left over from the original release of the big bang. *Bottom:* Artist's illustration showing the energy of the universe expanding outward and moving away from a central point. Because time and the space it travels in cannot be separated, the outward and ongoing expansion of the universe may explain the mystery of why time appears to move only in one direction and always toward the future.

So while the laws of physics may allow time to move either forward or backward—to the future or the past— it's the outward flow of the universe itself that makes its arrow march in one direction. With this idea in mind, what would happen to time if the universe stopped expanding and began to shrink? Would it start to move in the opposite direction and become "smaller"? This is precisely what the traditional Hindu texts suggest is our ultimate fate.

In the creation story of the Puranas, the existence of the universe is attributed to the inhalation and exhalation of Brahma's breath. Similar to the way scientists describe the big bang as the release of energy that began the universe, the ancient myth traces the beginning of the universe to the release of energy from the god's exhaling breath. As long as Brahma continues to breathe outward, the universe continues to grow and expand.

Furthermore, just as scientific theories identify a time when the forces of gravity and electromagnetism will reach a balance, stop expanding, and begin to contract, the Hindu texts describe a moment when Brahma completes his exhale, pauses, and begins the next part of his breath as an inhale. If space-time truly exists in the way that relativity describes it today, then during this period we would experience time in a very different way than we do now. This is where things get even more interesting.

According to the current theories, the contraction of the universe would cause space to flow in the opposite direction from what we see today. In other words, all of the particles that have moved *away* from the place where the big bang originated would begin a journey backward *toward* their point of origin. Because space is time, time would reverse its flow as well.

So we may well discover that the reason time seems to

move only toward the future is simply that it's following the movement of space. If we ever find ourselves in a place where space is contracting, such as a wormhole or hidden dimensions, the mathematics that we know today would still apply, only in the opposite direction.

The Shape of Time

Because space and time are different parts of the same stuff, and "stuff" has form, the question that comes to mind when we think of time as a wave is: *What does it look like?* What is the shape of time? While it may take a second or two to really wrap our minds around the possibility that time can take on a form, it's certainly not a new idea. In fact, it's precisely the conclusion that some open-minded and far-thinking scientists arrived at early in the last century.

In 1913, the mathematician Élie-Joseph Cartan (1869–1951) proposed a new kind of mathematics that would explain some of the mysteries of space-time that Einstein's relativity theories couldn't account for. The result was the *Einstein-Cartan theory* describing space-time as something that moves in a special way and follows a special path, which creates a special effect. The path is that of a spiral, and the effect is called a *torsion field*.[30]

Thinking of the stuff that the universe is made of in terms of a torsion field carries a number of profound implications. Perhaps the most obvious is that the shape of space-time is the template for the way matter forms in nature. We don't need to look far to find evidence that this is precisely the case. We see nature's spirals everywhere. In fact, they seem to be the pattern for much of the universe as we know it. If we begin with big things, like galaxies, and work our way down to the tiniest that cannot be seen with the naked eye, it becomes clear that spirals of space-time are key to nature's code.

Here is a brief listing of just how universal this form is and how frequently it appears in our world and beyond:

- The spiral that governs the shape of the Milky Way and other "spiral" galaxies

- The spiral orbits of the planets as they revolve around the sun

- The spiral patterns of the weather systems that move across the face of the earth

- The spiral vortex that drains the water in our sink one direction in the Northern Hemisphere and the opposite way in the Southern Hemisphere

- The spiral winds that form the familiar funnel shape of hurricanes, tornados, and dust devils

- The spiral configuration of the seeds that grow in the head of flowers such as the sunflower

- The spiral patterns that form the protective

coverings we see as the beautiful shells we
find on a beach

- The spiral pattern that defines much of the
  human body

And the list goes on and on.

While we may not put a lot of time into thinking
about the role of spirals in nature, visionary natural-
ists, such as Theodor Schwenk (1910–1986) and Viktor
Schauberger (1885–1958), have dedicated their lives to
doing just that. Through the legacy of their unifying
studies, we have clear documentation of the role that
spiral energy plays in everything from the motion of
water in Earth's streams and rivers to the motion of the
blood that courses through our veins to give us life. It's
precisely *because* the spiral pattern and torsion effect
appear to be so universal that it makes perfect sense to
find this powerful shape in the stuff that the universe is
made of, as well.

It's this very idea that brings us back to nature's most
beautiful number. The spiral that we see so commonly
in the world is actually a special kind that is made from
the numbers we explored previously as the Fibonacci
sequence. It's called a *Fibonacci spiral*. So the beautiful
number phi that determines how often things in nature
repeat also appears to govern the very shape of the stuff
(space-time) that those patterns are filling.

So now we can answer the question that began this
section: *what is the shape of time?* The evidence of spirals
in energy and nature suggests that the waves of time follow the paths of those spirals. As they do, they create the

torsion fields that move in cycles throughout the universe. With these ideas in mind, it now makes even more sense to think of the things that happen in life and the world as places appearing along time's ever-expanding spirals. Whether we're talking about that time in terms of seconds, years, or eons, those places can be measured, calculated, and even predicted.

Armed with our understanding of time's shape (spiral) and motion (outward), let's apply what we know to the everyday world. We've all heard that history repeats itself, but what does that really *mean?* How much of history repeats, and can we know when a bad experience from our past (or a good one, for that matter) is likely to show up again in our lives?

In the next chapter we'll use the simplicity of nature's programs to answer these questions. If we know where we are in the spiral of time, then we can discover the seed event that begins a cycle and determine when the personal and global conditions of the past will show up again in our future.

⚡ ⚡ ⚡

CHAPTER FIVE

HISTORY REPEATS IN LOVE AND WAR: FRACTAL WARNINGS FOR THE FUTURE

"There are cycles in everything. There are cycles in the weather, the economy, the sun, wars, geological formations, atomic vibrations, climate, human moods, the motions of the planets, populations of animals, the occurrence of diseases, the prices of commodities and shares and the large scale structure of the universe."

— Ray Tomes, contemporary philosopher

"The eternal flow of time goes through cyclical periods of manifestation of the universe . . ."

— Alexander Friedman (1888–1925), cosmologist

The look on my teacher's face that day is something I'll always remember. She was obviously shaken as she walked into our classroom and asked us to remain calm, collect our coats and supplies, and walk quickly to the buses that were waiting for us outside. It was the middle of the day and much too early for classes to end. I remember thinking that our teacher knew something she wasn't telling us. Why else would she be wiping tears from *her* eyes while asking *us* to stay calm?

It was a different world in 1963. The Cold War between the Soviet Union and the U.S. was at its peak. The frightening image broadcast around the world of Soviet leader Nikita Khrushchev shouting to America, "We will bury you!" was still fresh in my memory. I remember thinking of it each week as our class practiced dropping to our knees and ducking under our desks to protect ourselves in the event of a surprise atomic attack. I also remember thinking that if we *were* ever actually bombed, my desk probably wouldn't be much protection from the force of an atomic blast!

Only a year earlier, in October 1962, everyone had breathed a sigh of relief as the two superpowers backed away from one of the Cold War's most visible confrontations and the brink of nuclear war—the Cuban missile crisis. The girl in the seat next to me remembered it, too, and whispered that maybe the missiles were "back." We all knew that *something* had happened. We just didn't know what. It's with the backdrop of such a world that I joined hundreds of thousands of other children across the country who left school early that day. It was November 22, 1963.

As we filed toward the only door leading out of the

classroom, the last thing I heard was my teacher's voice attempting to provide some kind of explanation. "Your parents will have to tell you what has happened," she said. "We're not allowed to do so in school." And just like that, I walked with my classmates to our buses with absolutely no indication of when, or even if, we would return.

When I arrived home, our family living room was like a replay of what I had experienced at school. My mother's eyes were red from crying, and she was obviously frightened. "Here, take a look at the television," she said. Together we watched our family's tiny black-and-white TV as the unthinkable unfolded. Each station was showing the same images, with the same story: the President of the United States had been assassinated. The nation was in shock. There were so many unanswered questions. Who did it? Why? How could such a thing have happened?

Déjà Vu, 100 Years Later

Just a couple of days after John F. Kennedy's assassination, our local newspaper printed a story that rekindled my fascination with patterns. While I was moved by the life, ambition, and vision of Kennedy himself, the story was about the curious circumstances that surrounded his death. I read it and reread it. The title of the article was "History Repeats Itself." Its focus was on the eerie set of "coincidences" that connect the 1963 assassination of President Kennedy to another that had occurred nearly 100 years before—that of Abraham Lincoln. While I had always been interested in patterns and cycles, I had never really thought of them in terms of things like the deaths of Presidents.

At first I simply skimmed the statistics out of curiosity. While they were interesting, they seemed so generalized that I was unconvinced that there was any great mystery. My thought was that any similarities were just that: parallels that the staff writers were drawing to create a flashy story. Both Presidents, for example, had been deeply involved with racial equality and civil rights. Both had wives who had lost children while living in the White House. Both had been shot on a Friday. Both had died from a gunshot wound to the head.

All were certainly uncanny coincidences, but not enough to convince me that anything out of the ordinary was being revealed. The more I read, however, the more specific and bizarre the parallels became.

Lincoln, for example, was sitting in box number 7 of Ford's Theatre when he was killed. Kennedy was riding in car number 7—the make was a Lincoln offered by the Ford Motor Company—when he died. Both were with their wives at the time. Before his presidency, Lincoln had been elected to Congress in 1846. One hundred years later, in 1946, Kennedy was elected to Congress. Lincoln became President in 1860, Kennedy 100 years later in 1960. The last name of the men who replaced them in office was the same—Johnson—and both Johnsons were born 100 years apart. Andrew Johnson was born in 1808, while Lyndon Johnson was born in 1908.

As the comparisons continued, the similarities certainly seemed to be more than coincidence. They even went beyond the assassinations themselves, weaving their way throughout the personal lives of the men, their families, and their friends. Both Presidents had four children, and both had lost two of them before they reached their teens. Both had lost a son while they were serving in the White House. The doctors for Lincoln and Kennedy had the same name: Charles Taft. The name of Lincoln's private secretary was John (Kennedy's first name), and that of Kennedy's secretary was Lincoln (Abraham's last name).

The patterns even extended into the lives of the men who killed them—into their personal histories, their motivations, and their captures. A law-enforcement agent named Baker, for example, detained Lincoln's assassin, John Wilkes Booth. An officer who was also named Baker held Kennedy's shooter, Lee Harvey Oswald, in custody.

It seemed that the patterns were endless. But perhaps more important, they are undeniable. Regardless of why or how these two events separated by 100 years could be so similar, the fact is that they are. While this example could be chalked up to some sort of bizarre karma between these two men, the reality is that it exists. Whether we like to admit the similarities or not, the answer to our question of whether or not history repeats itself appears obvious. For at least these two events, it appears to be *yes*.

Along with our answer comes an even deeper question: Are the similarities that we see between the assassinations of two American Presidents separated by 100 years part of a greater pattern? If so, what is the pattern, and what does it tell us about the cyclic nature of time?

The 20-Year "Curse"

In the same way we search for patterns to find meaning in the mysterious events of our day, scholars do the same thing with historic moments of the past. Following the tragic death of President Lincoln in the 1860s, for example, historians began to suspect that his assassination might be part of a pattern that was emerging. Little more than 20 years earlier, another President had tragically died in office. In 1841, William Henry Harrison had become ill and died of pneumonia.

With President Harrison's death, it seemed that the seed had been planted for a pattern of such tragedies. In the years that have followed, the suspicions of those early scholars have been confirmed. For reasons that are as eerie as they are mysterious, in the nearly 160 years that followed Harrison's death approximately every 20 years the U.S. President has either died in office or has survived an attempt on his life (see Figure 14).

With the unsuccessful attempts to assassinate Ronald Reagan and George W. Bush, the conditions of the pattern seem to have held true. The question that historians are now asking is whether or not their survival after these assassination attempts has put an end to the "20-year curse" of American Presidents. The presidential cycle of 2020 will tell the story. When we look at the statistics, however, they seem to speak for themselves.

Whether we're talking about the 100-year coincidences between Kennedy and Lincoln or the 20-year presidential "curse," three facts are obvious:

Year Elected	President	Event
1840	William Henry Harrison	Died in office
1860	Abraham Lincoln	Assassinated
1880	James Garfield	Assassinated
1900	William McKinley	Assassinated
1920	Warren Harding	Died in office
1940	Franklin Roosevelt	Died in office
1960	John F. Kennedy	Assassinated
1980	Ronald Reagan	(Survived assassination attempt)*
2000	George W. Bush	(Survived assassination attempt)**

*The wounds from the gun used by John Hinckley, Jr., were serious but not fatal.

**Bush avoided injury from a grenade that was tossed in his direction during a 2005 visit to Georgia, the former Soviet satellite state.

Figure 14. Since the election of the United States President in 1840, the country has lost a sitting President to illness or violence every 20 years. (The election years given for McKinley and Roosevelt are for reelections.)

Fact 1: There are cycles underlying both events.

Fact 2: Both cycles are "triggered" by a seed event.

Fact 3: The conditions of the seed event repeat at regular intervals.

The facts are undeniable. The question for us is, what do they mean? What are such obvious cycles telling us about the nature of our lives, our world, and even time itself?

We may find that the message encoded into a 3,000-year-old manuscript holds the answer. But, as is so often the case, with it we open the door to an even greater mystery.

The 3,000-Year-Old Map of Time

In November 1995, Yitzhak Rabin, the prime minister of Israel, was assassinated in the city of Tel Aviv. While the event itself shocked the world, there was an aspect of Rabin's assassination that rumbled like an earthquake through the scientific community, with aftershocks that continue to this day. Before the day of his death, Rabin had been warned that he was the target of an assassin. What made the warning so unusual, however, was that it didn't come from a secret informer or as a result of a detective's work—at least not one working in law enforcement. Instead, the information regarding Rabin's death was based upon a prophetic code discovered in a document created more than 3,000 years ago: the Bible.[1]

Specifically, the researchers who had warned Rabin had discovered the details of his death in a particular portion of the Bible. The first five books of the Christian Old Testament are the same mysterious five books that form the Hebrew Torah, one of the stablest documents in human history. A comparison of today's Torah with the oldest known versions shows that it has not undergone the edits and revisions of other sections of the Bible. In fact, only about 23 letters have changed in 1,000 years.

So when we study the Torah, we can trust that we

are reading the original text, just as it was intended more than 30 centuries ago. It's for this very reason that Rabin followed the schedule on the day he was killed. He was a deeply spiritual man and believed in the Torah so much that he felt that if his last day on Earth was truly encoded into such an ancient and holy text, then the events of that day must be destined to occur. On November 4, they did.

It is within the Torah, and only the Torah, that Israeli mathematician Eliyahu Rips, Ph.D., discovered "the Bible Code," which has been reviewed and validated by scientists in leading universities worldwide, as well as technical agencies that specialize in encryption decoding, such as the U.S. Department of Defense. Rips and Michael Drosnin, the journalist who wrote the first book describing the code, uncovered details that they shared with Rabin. The Bible Code described the specifics of the event and did so with such accuracy that there could be no doubt as to what was being revealed.

The prime minister's name, Rabin, had been spelled out, along with the date of the assassination, the name of the city it would occur within, and even the assassin's name: Amir.[2] In some ancient and mysterious way, the details of the event that changed the course of history for Israel had been encoded into the fabric of the most beloved book in the world, a text that appeared upon the earth more than 1,000 years before the time of Jesus.

The Code Within the Code

For more than 200 years, scholars have suspected

that the Torah holds more than the words that are read sequentially on each page. An 18th-century scholar known as the Genius of Vilna once stated: "The rule is that all that was, is, and will be unto the end of time is included in the Torah, from the first word to the last word. And not merely in a general sense, but as to the details of . . . everything that happened to him from the day of his birth until his end."[3]

Mathematicians study the Torah's encrypted messages of time, past and future, by creating a matrix from the letters of the Bible's first five books: Genesis, Exodus, Leviticus, Numbers, and Deuteronomy. Beginning with the first letter of the first word, all spaces and punctuation are removed until the last letter of the last word is reached, leaving a single sentence thousands of characters in length.

Using sophisticated search programs, the matrix of letters is examined for patterns and intersecting words. In the book of Genesis, for example, the word *Torah* is actually spelled out with sequences of 50 characters between each letter of the word. The same sequence is found in the books of Exodus, Numbers, and Deuteronomy. Only in Leviticus is the code absent, for mysterious reasons that may unlock an even greater secret within it. As early as the 1940s, Rabbi M. D. Weissmandel found these sequences, and the word *Torah* became the key to unraveling the code within the code of the text.

With the development of high-speed computers, the extent of the Bible Code was finally recognized. The new computers replaced the tedious manual decoding that had driven Bible scholars to madness for centuries. Running against control groups of other texts, such as *War and Peace, Moby-Dick,* and even the Yellow Pages telephone directories, only the Bible was found to have the encoded messages. According to Harold Gans, a former code breaker with the U.S. National Security Agency (NSA), there is about a 1-in-200,000 chance that the information revealed in the Bible Code is a coincidence. Vertically, horizontally, and diagonally, the names of countries, events, dates, times, and people intersect with one another in a way that sets the Bible apart from any other text, giving us a snapshot into the events of our past and a window into our future.

While the reasons why such an ancient prediction tool could see into 3,000 years of time so accurately remain a mystery, the big question is, *how does it relate to our future?* In light of its accuracy for events ranging from World War II, the Shoemaker-Levy comet impact with Jupiter, the Scud missiles discovered during the first Gulf War in Iraq, and the Kennedy assassination, how reliable can this ancient matrix be when peering into the years to come?

In answer to this question, Dr. Rips suggests that the entire Bible Code had to be written all at once, as a single act, rather than developing over time. The implication of such a statement is mind-boggling. It means that when the Torah was transcribed, all possibilities and all possible futures already existed and were already in place. "We experience it like we experience a hologram," he suggests. "It looks different when we look at it from a new angle—but the image, of course, is pre-recorded."[4] The key to applying this ancient Time Code to future events may lie in thinking of it through the eyes of what we now know about cycles of time.

Planting the Seeds of Time

Whether we're talking about world ages that last for 5,125 years at a time or the link between the events of 1941, 1984, and 2001, it's clear that cycles are involved and that each has a beginning. In every instance, that beginning—*the seed event*—sets the conditions that will repeat at various future dates. From our understanding of natural rhythms and cycles, we can calculate when similar conditions and events will repeat throughout the cycles of time.

So here's the question: Is it possible that everything from the war and peace between nations to the love and heartbreaks of life began with a seed event somewhere in our distant past? In other words, are we living out a pattern that was initiated with the beginning of time—the beginning of our cycle in 3114 B.C.—and will complete with the end of the cycle in A.D. 2012? If so, is the Bible Code the "map" that describes the cycles, as well as the seed events that set into motion all the human dramas playing out across our world today?

Admittedly, these are huge questions and deserve more attention than we can do justice to in this book alone. But the ideas are worth considering and may go a long way to help explain the mystery of the Bible Code and what the Torah is really telling us about our future. Whether or not we actually believe in the literal accuracy of this sacred book is less important than our understanding of the themes it describes.

In the fourth chapter of Genesis, for example, the Torah "time map" describes the first betrayal of one human by another, the violence of brother against brother when Cain took the life of Abel. From the perspective of repeating patterns and cycles, we can think of this primal act of betrayal as the seed event that anchors the repeating pattern of betrayal throughout the history of all remaining cycles.

Not long after this original betrayal, in the same chapter we also find the first acts of forgiveness. Among them is the story of Joseph, who was one of 11 brothers. As Joseph was his father Jacob's favored son, his brothers became jealous and sold Joseph into slavery. In the second confrontation between brothers in Genesis, this story has a different outcome from the first, that of Cain and Abel. The powerful act of forgiveness Joseph shows his brothers many years later becomes a seed event for the conditions of forgiveness that permeate the rest of the biblical traditions and our lives today.

Just as the seeds of "surprise" and "attack" began in 1941 and repeat at intervals that can be known and predicted, the Torah may actually be the map of all possibilities that the Genius of Vilna was describing in the 18th century. Since it's a map based upon cycles that begin with a seed event, and as the seeds are described within it, we should not be surprised to discover that the Torah also contains the patterns showing when and how those patterns repeat. It's all about the cycles.

If the cycles are still repeating and we're part of them, what can they tell us about our personal lives and our global future?

Hot Spots and Flash Points for the Future

"In a time of drastic change, it is the *learners* who inherit the future. The *learned* usually find themselves equipped to live in a world that no longer exists [my emphasis]." With these words, social philosopher Eric Hoffer beautifully described the difference between meaningful knowledge and information without meaning. In a world of constant change, to simply know the facts as the "learned" is not enough. To know that a village pump brings the water of a well to the surface, for example, is great as long as the pump is working. If it fails, however, and the mechanism that makes it work is a mysterious "black box" that no one understands, then it may be a long time until the village has its own water again.

I've witnessed such a crisis personally in a Tibetan village. The entire population relied upon a single well with an antiquated pump for all of their water. During one of our visits in the late 1990s, the village elders informed us that the pump had not worked for nearly a month. A closer inspection of the machinery quickly revealed the problem.

The pump had been built in 1910, and no one in the village knew how it worked or how to fix it. When the villagers understood that they could bypass the pump and bring their water up by hand using a "dip" system, they no longer had to travel to a nearby town for the tedious task of importing their water. They could get their own from the same well that they had always used in the past; it's just that to do so was a manual effort. It's all about bringing what we know to bear upon the conditions of the moment.

Hoffer's simple yet profound statement brings the idea of time's cycles directly to our lives today. As noted in the Introduction, both the scientific experts and the ancient traditions tell us that we're living a time like no other in the recorded history of humankind. While there seems to be agreement that the early 21st century is a period of great change, the reasons behind the change could not appear more different.

Scientists describe our time of change as a series of separate crises that just happen to be occurring at the same time. From the shift in climate; rising sea levels; and depletion of food, water, and oil to the tilt of the earth's axis and one of the strongest solar cycles in history, modern experts see our time as a convergence of multiple—yet separate—challenges that face our planet simultaneously.

While many indigenous traditions acknowledge the same problems, from their ancient worldview they are anything *but* separate. Following the wisdom of their ancestors' instructions, those who live a little more aligned with the principles of nature see modern crises as a by-product of something greater, as the changes that always seem to come with the end of time and the beginning of a new world age.

If we bear this idea in mind, what can *we* learn from studying the cycles of time? Now that we know that they exist and how they work, are there pitfalls from the past that we may recognize, prepare for, and even prevent in the future? Once again, our Time Code Calculator helps us answer this question.

History will show that the 20th century witnessed the greatest suffering, with the greatest number of lives lost at the hands of other humans, in the entire history of the species. Any doubt as to the truth of this statement disappears with historian Eric Hobsbawm's direct assessment of the 20th century as the "most murderous century in recorded history."[5]

Zbigniew Brzezinski, the former U.S. national security advisor under the Carter administration, estimated that by the 1990s, before the century was even complete, violence stemming from what has been called "man's inhumanity to man" cost between 167 and 175 million lives—roughly the equivalent of the populations of Great Britain, France, and Italy combined![6] The cause of the deaths was largely due to two world wars; the violent competition for land, oil, minerals, and other resources; and the seemingly relentless efforts to "cleanse" entire societies based on principles of race, religion, and ethnic background.

While the same century that witnessed so much suffering saw many good things happen as well, it's the great tragedies that leave us reeling and asking the question "Can the same thing happen again?" From the perspective of cycles, the answer is *yes*. It seems that once the patterns that spawn such tragedies are created, they continue to repeat at rhythmic intervals until something changes them.

While I've stated this before, it's important to note that it's the conditions that repeat, not the events themselves. If we know that the time is ripe for the conditions to appear, we can take extra steps—such as global prayer, sensitive dialogue, and measured tolerance during tense situations—to be certain that we don't fall into the ancient trap of where the cycles may have led in the past.

Time Code 13: Our knowledge of repeating cycles allows us to pinpoint times in the future when we can expect to see the repeating conditions of the past.

Is it possible to look ahead and anticipate the flash points of the future so that we can prepare for them in the present? Absolutely! The Time Code Calculator can help us identify precisely where they are. Let's begin by looking at the events in the last century that led to some of the greatest tragedies in history. If we recognize these cycles of possibility and when they will reappear, then they also represent the greatest window of opportunity to avoid the suffering and replace it with healing and peace.

In the following section, we will identify key events of the last century to determine when the conditions that they created will repeat again. The cycles that stem from each event will be summarized in the familiar format that we used in Chapter 1. As before, the actual calculations have been placed in the appendices (see Appendix B) for continuity and ease of reading.

So let's begin where we left off in Chapter 1, with the relationship between 1941, the year of the seed event, and the conditions for September 2001 that it spawned. The dates for the return of the 1941 cycle after 2001 were intentionally omitted. To list them would have made little sense until we had the opportunity to explore the nature of cycles—how they work and why they repeat.

Now that we've done so, we can answer the lingering question as to when, or even if, any dates between 2001 and the 2012 end of our present world age hold the potential for repeating the conditions of "surprise" and "attack" for America. The following chart summarizes the output from the Time Code perspective.

Summary 1

Cyclic Conditions for Surprise Attack on the United States Created in 1941

Seed Year: 1941
Seed Event: Surprise attack upon the United States

Calculated Dates
for Repeat Conditions   Actual Events

Date 1:   1984   Planned nuclear strike against U.S. during Cold War averted

Date 2:   2001   Attacks of September 11 carried out

Date 3:   2007   Planned attacks against U.S. and interests foiled in Germany and Saudi Arabia

Date 4:   2010   ?

While historians analyze and dissect the wars of the last century, in many respects, a strong argument can be made that they essentially originate with the first great conflict of the century: World War I. Although technically the war ended and peace treaties were signed, the root causes of the political unrest remained; and the rise of dictatorships throughout Europe, including those of the Soviet Union, Yugoslavia, and Spain, can be directly linked to the way the First World War ended.

It's for this reason that some historians suggest that, in effect, there was only a single great war in the 20th century, one that never really ended and has continued through subsequent conflicts since that time. Whether we subscribe to such a perspective or not, the fact remains that World War I, and the loss of more than 40 million human lives, began with the seed events of 1914. The conditions of 1914 are the primer for the effects that are still seen to this day. So it makes tremendous sense to begin with this date to calculate when the patterns that it set into motion will return as the ripples of its repeating cycle.

As with any pattern, the conditions that it creates continue until they are broken by the introduction of a new pattern. Knowing when and how the cycles of the 1914 seed date will appear in our lives gives us the edge to do just that: recognize the symptoms of war-producing conflict when it appears and prepare for what it may bring, while working at the same time to break the cycle by introducing a new pattern of peace.

The following summary tracks the Time Code calculations from 1914 to the end of the 2012 great cycle to show us when the choice points of peace (see Chapter 7) reappear. Similar to the way McKenna's TimeWave Zero program exhibited more complexity compressed into briefer periods of time toward the end of the cycle, the

Time Code calculations after 2011 are so frequent that I have shown only the first as an indicator of when the window of opportunity appears.

Summary 2

The Cyclic Conditions of World War Created in 1914
Seed Year: 1914
Seed Event: The start of World War I

Calculated Dates
for Repeat Conditions   Actual Events
Date 1:   1973   Middle East Yom Kippur War (aka the Ramadan War)

Date 2:   1997   U.S./Iraq crisis begins in November

Date 3:   2006   U.S. presence in Iraq sparks tension in the Arab world

Date 4:   2009   ?

Date 5:   2011   ?

The years shown in Summary 2 are the times when the cyclic conditions for global war have been, are, or will be present. Just as we discovered with the 1984 expression of the 1941 seed date in Chapter 1, the presence of the conditions does not always mean that what happened on the seed date will occur again. It tells us that the conditions are in place and that the event *may* repeat. The Arab-Israeli war of 1973 is a perfect example of what I mean here.

Known by names that range from the Yom Kippur

War and the Ramadan War to the October War of 1973, the conflict began when a coalition of Arab states led by Egypt and Syria attacked Israel on October 6, 1973, in a dispute over borders. While the entire war lasted only 20 days, it occurred within the context of the global tension created by the Cold War. As is so often the case in regional wars, the two sides directly involved had ties with the larger nations and superpowers. It is those ties that carry the potential to escalate the conflict into a larger war, one even on a global scale. This is precisely what happened during in 1973.

A request from Egypt's president, Anwar el-Sadat, asking the Soviet Union for military aid; the Russian response to mobilize troops in preparation for bestowing that aid; and the U.S. decision to move American military forces to a Defense Condition (DEFCON) 3, a rare heightened state of alert used in preparation for possible war, were the catalyst for yet another crisis that brought the world to the brink of a confrontation between the two Cold War superpowers. Fortunately, through a series of sensitive negotiations, which *excluded* the United States President at the time, cooler heads prevailed. The Egyptians retracted their request for help from the Soviet Union, and the United Nations Security Council passed Resolution 339 on October 23 asking the warring states to honor an earlier cease-fire.

The point here is that the conditions were in place and the stage was set for a regional conflict to escalate to a global war during the year when the cycle carrying those conditions was repeating. The Time Code Calculator demonstrates this beautifully, showing that 1973 is precisely the year when the 1914 conditions of world war would appear as a repeating cycle (see Appendix B, example 5). Now that we know how the cycles appear, the additional dates in Summary 2 will be the opportunity to put into place what we've learned to head off such close calls.

Only two atomic weapons have ever been used in wartime against civilian populations. Both were detonated by the United States. Both events happened in the same year, 1945, at the end of World War II.

Summary 3

The Cyclic Conditions Created in 1945 (Use of Nuclear Weapons and the End of WWII)

Seed Year: 1945
Seed Event: The end of World War II

Calculated Dates
for Repeat Conditions   Actual Events
Date 1:   1985   Nuclear weapons spread
                                              beyond the superpowers

Date 2:   2001   Intelligence reveals terrorists have
                                              nuclear capabilities

Date 3:   2008   North Korea and Iran actively
                                              seeking nuclear capabilities

Date 4:   2010   ?

Summary 3 clearly shows how the conditions created by this single event planted the seeds for a cycle that has repeated these conditions throughout time. In each year indicated, the stage was set for the conditions of atomic capabilities to threaten the world once again. Fortunately, while the conditions have been present and there has been a focus upon nuclear capabilities, the events themselves haven't lived up to the fullest expression of the cycle's potential. The year 2010 will be the next opportunity for the return of the conditions of 1945, as well as the opportunity to break the cycle and set a new pattern for the new world age.

While our ability to recognize such cycles doesn't necessarily change them or prevent their parallel conditions from recurring, it does give us a powerful insight into when to be on the alert for a repeated cycle. It offers us the opportunity to respond to the parallel conditions in a responsible manner when they show up. If we know, for example, that a nation's acts of aggression, such as the 1990 invasion of Kuwait's oil fields by Iraq, is happening during a cycle that carries the 1914 conditions of World War I, then we also know that clear communication and sensitive diplomacy will be especially important during this vulnerable period of time in order to keep the conflict from blowing out of control and fulfilling the cycle's seed potential.

It's at precisely such times that a response meant to send a clear signal that "enough is enough" can be misread and escalate before we know it. As declassified NSA documents revealed in 2005, Vietnam's Gulf of Tonkin incident is a perfect example of just how easily unnecessary results can be triggered by wartime fears.[7]

In the midst of the Cold War tensions in 1964, the actions of two reported naval engagements between the United States and North Vietnam sparked America's first large-scale troop deployments into Southeast Asia. The incidents occurred within two days of one another in the waters of the Tonkin Gulf. The declassified documents show, however, that only one of the reported events actually occurred.

The first incident, between the U.S. destroyer *Maddox* and three North Vietnamese torpedo boats on August 2 of that year, is verified and well documented. The second incident is where the uncertainty, and mystery, lies. What the declassified documents show is that the "attack" that the U.S. destroyers reported, and returned fire to, never happened. While the American destroyers *did* fire at what they *believed* was a threat at the time, the reports show that, in fact, there was none. The exact words of the declassified report state: "In truth, Hanoi's navy was engaged in nothing that night but the salvage of two of the boats damaged on 2 August."[8]

Under the suspicious atmosphere that became the hallmark of the Cold War, and with the crew's anxious state of mind following the artillery exchange only two nights before, some historians suggest that the U.S. sailors may have mistakenly read unusual radar blips on the night of August 4. Believing that they were under a second attack from the North Vietnamese, they fired in response to what they thought was a follow-up attack. While the mystery of that night may remain unsolved, the fact is that the American response meant to signal strength and resolve to ease the rising tensions actually had the opposite effect and was a direct factor leading to the escalation of the war that would last into the next decade and cost approximately 58,000 American lives.

America's Economic Collapse: No Secret to the Cycles!

"It's official: the crash of the U.S. economy has begun." With these words, writer and consultant Richard C. Cook began an article published by the Centre for Research on Globalization.[9] While such captions were common during the autumn 2008 meltdown of the world's financial markets, at the time when this headline appeared nothing could have sounded more ominous— or more unlikely. *Ominous* because of what such a crash would mean. *Unlikely* because, at least on the surface, America's economy appeared to be nowhere near any kind of collapse. The date was June 13, 2007: full 14 months before the actual crisis of 2008 occurred.

Cook's article describes the work of two leading economists who were looking beyond the outward signs of America's seemingly booming economy at something much deeper. Steven Pearlstein, a Pulitzer Prize–winning columnist for business and economy who writes for *The Washington Post,* and Robert Samuelson, a contributing editor for *Newsweek* and *The Washington Post* since 1977, both saw the same fracture in the economy at the same time. And what they saw was frightening.

They were concerned about the growing number of companies that had huge amounts of debt compared to their profits and the vulnerability of those companies to buyouts that were financed through borrowing even more money (leveraged buyouts). In words that clearly reflected his concern, Pearlstein stated: "Across the board, stock prices and company valuations will fall. Banks will announce painful write-offs, some hedge funds will close their doors, and private equity funds will report disappointing returns. Some companies will be forced into bankruptcy or restructuring."[10] Even for those not familiar with the technical-sounding lingo of stock-market analysts and economists, the message was clear. This was a warning, and those with interests in the American economy were being warned.

What these economists and others like them were telling the rest of us was that 2007 marked the year when the conditions fell into place for the perfect global economic storm to unleash its fury. Whenever it happened, the U.S. economy would be directly in its path. While they accurately predicted the scenario, it's unclear if even Pearlstein and Samuelson could have known how the storm they described would trigger the collapse of an entire world's economy.

We've all heard it said that vision is always 20/20 in hindsight. In other words, it's easy to look back at everything, from a military crisis to the loss of an NFL championship—or even to the end of a marriage—*after it is over* and be able to see all of the things that could have averted the crisis. Hindsight is easy. And it's accurate for one obvious reason: everything we're looking at has already happened!

All the same, as I watched the earnings of the New York Stock Exchange plunge further and further into negative territory on September 29, 2008, I had the same feeling and asked the same questions that had occurred to me on September 11, 2001: *Is this crisis part of a larger pattern? If so, could we have known in advance and acted differently to avert it?*

Unlike the seven years that separated the crisis of September 11 and the development of the Time Code Calculator, I didn't have to wait long for my answer. I had watched America's financial meltdown from a series of cities and hotel rooms where I was doing business at the end of September 2008—without access to the Time Code Calculator. As soon as I returned home, I immediately went to the appendices for this book to discover what role, if any, economic cycles were playing in the world's financial chaos.

Using the same process described earlier in this chapter, I went through the steps of Mode 1 of the calculator in order to find out when the conditions of a past event were most likely to reappear. I began by identifying the date when the seeds of the 2008 economic collapse could have been planted. From the experts along Wall Street to the commentators in the nation's media, the comparison was obvious and nearly unanimous.

Before the stock market lost 777 points in the largest single-day drop in the history of the New York Stock Exchange (NYSE), the previous record had been held by another loss that occurred in the same market 79 years earlier. Over the course of two autumn days in 1929, the "Black Thursday" of October 24 followed by the "Black Tuesday" of October 29, America's young stock market lost 23 percent of its previous value. The panic and sell-off that followed led to a decline in the American financial system that would continue until it bottomed out nearly three years later. It was then that the Dow Jones

Industrial Average closed at a reading that sounds impossible by today's standards. Incredibly, by July 8, 1932, the New York Stock Exchange had lost 89 percent of its previous value and closed with a reading of only 41.22 points. Clearly, the conditions of 1929 are the logical comparison for the crash of 2008. Except for the magnitude of the loss, at first glance the outward conditions seem eerily similar.

Summary 4

The Cyclic Conditions Created in 1929 (Crash of the U.S. Economy)

Seed Year: 1929

Seed Event: The "crash" of the stock market in October of 1929

Calculated Dates
for Repeat Conditions   Actual Events

Date 1:   1979   Surge in oil prices and economic contraction

Date 2:   1999   Surge in oil prices and 6 percent drop in NYSE in October

Date 3:   2007   Unsustainable debt / profit ratios poise markets for 2008 collapse

Date 4:   2010   ?

Using 1929 as the seed year for the Time Code calculations, the process quickly revealed the next date when we could expect the conditions of an economic collapse to reappear. That date was 1979. Just as we did in the previous examples, 1979 then became the new seed date for the next round of calculations, yielding the second opportunity for economic chaos to repeat: 1999. These calculations were performed two more times to find the remaining years before 2012 when the cycles for economic collapse in the U.S. and the world were likely to repeat. Summary 4 shows the results for the calculations located in Appendix B (beginning with Example 10).

Because the stock-market crash that I was seeing in real time was taking place in 2008, at first the dates made little sense. Why did the calculator indicate 2007, for example? Why not 2008? I searched the literature and returned to Pearlstein and Samuelson's findings for a deeper understanding of what the cycles were actually showing. In two sentences I found the bridge between the calculator's results and the reality of the September stock-market collapse. *"It is impossible to predict when the magic moment will be reached* and everyone finally realizes that the prices being paid for these companies, and the debt taken on to support the acquisitions, are unsustainable [my emphasis],"* Pearlstein stated. Leaving little doubt about the consequences of such a realization, his next sentence said everything: "When that happens, it won't be pretty." From an economist's perspective, the "magic moment" arrived on September 29, 2008.

With this observation, my questions had been answered.

The calculator was showing that the *conditions* for the economic chaos predicted by the article had arrived precisely on schedule in 2007. As Pearlstein stated, however, the unknown factor was *when* investors would recognize the conditions and react to what they had discovered. What's important here is that experts "in the know" saw what was happening beforehand, such as the sharp rise in oil prices that seems to precede such chaos, and realized that the crash was inevitable. They announced what they knew when the conditions were in place in 2007.

But what about the other two dates: 1979 and 1999? Obviously there was no financial meltdown anywhere near the size of those during 1929 and 2008. What was the calculator telling us?

As I researched both dates, I realized that we were very lucky on both occasions. In the same way that a sharp rise in oil prices had triggered a domino effect that highlighted the weakness of the economy in 2008, something very similar had happened in 1979 and 1999. During both years another perfect economic storm was looming when unexpected conditions converged. And during both a global economic crisis had been a very real possibility. Fortunately, it was only the *conditions* that were present. For reasons that will follow, the storm that the conditions could have spawned never materialized. The year 1979 is a perfect example of a crisis averted.

At the beginning of the year, the indicators used by experts to gauge the health of the economy (things like customer demand, strong sales, and lean inventories) looked promising. There was every reason to believe that it would be a good year for the nation's finances. But there was one factor that even the experts hadn't taken into account, the same one that began the decline in the 2008 economy: the price of oil. Through increases that occurred during two critical times of the year, at the beginning and again at the end, the price of crude oil rose nearly 100 percent. When it did, shock waves of reduced spending rippled throughout the American economy. Similar conditions led to a loss of 630 points on the NYSE in October 1999 and set into motion the conditions for the economic slowdown that followed in 2000.

While there are probably a number of reasons why the economy didn't completely collapse during the 1979 time frame, an analysis by the Economic Research Department of the Federal Reserve Bank of Minneapolis may explain one of the most significant. According to the report, the 1979 rise in oil prices automatically caused the federal budget to tighten in response.[11] In doing so, individual incomes were placed into higher tax brackets, which forced a decrease in the spending habits of some citizens. In other words, the higher taxes reduced the amount of money available, and spending was curbed, which ultimately slowed the growth of the economy.

Unfortunately, for reasons that are beyond the scope of this section, that system didn't operate as it was designed to when the oil prices skyrocketed to their highest in history during summer 2008. The key here is that such market extremes appear to be linked to a cycle, one that may be known and predicted.

The Time Code Calculator indicates that we may be faced with similar economic conditions and the possibility of yet one more financial crisis before the present cycle ends in 2012. Interestingly, the year that it indicates is the same one when the conditions of a number of other seed dates may reappear as well: the year 2010. As different and disparate as the seed dates appear, from the cycle of "surprise" and "attack" that began in 1941 and reappeared in 2001, to the use of atomic weapons in 1945, and the crash of the United States' economy in 1929, the opportunity for the next appearance of each of these conditions occurs within the same year.

While it's probably not insignificant that so many cycles are converging during such a small window of time, it's important to remember that the end of any cycle also marks the beginning of the next. As we'll discuss in Chapter 7, this is the good news that the convergence of so many cycles may be calling to our attention. At the end of one and the beginning of the next, nature offers us the greatest chance for change. So it's precisely because so many different cycles—of such great magnitude, representing so many different kinds of experiences—are ending within the same period of time that the 2010 time frame may well represent one of our best junctures to make new choices. As the old cycles end and the new ones begin, we share the rare opportunity to reset the course of our personal and global paths for the future. We may also find that it's the perfect time to do so, well *before* the 2012 window arrives.

As with any window of change, the power of the opportunity begins with acknowledgment that a choice is possible.

The Seeds of Love and Betrayal

The cycles of nature apply to our personal lives as well as to global events. While we probably know this relationship intuitively, it often shows up in our lives in ways, and at times, that are the least opportune or that we least expect. For example, we've all heard of people who leave their relationships, jobs, and friends and move to a new city for a "fresh start." You can probably guess what often happens to those of us who do.

While a change of scenery can sometimes be just what the doctor ordered, it's not uncommon to find that while the people, weather, and skylines changed, the circumstances that we thought we were leaving behind us may not. Why would they? The cycles of our world and our lives are made of time and space, the stuff of the universe that cannot be bound by a building or a city. When we think about our lives from this perspective, it should come as no surprise that the cycles that play such a powerful role in the world play an equally powerful role in our personal lives. Once again, the key to uncovering such patterns is to recognize where they begin.

The house felt different that morning. Although it was a Saturday, a day that my father normally used to catch up on the sleep he'd lost from working long hours earlier in the week, he and my mom were up early. It just didn't feel like a typical weekend. There was no singing from my mom as she went about her endless routines of homemaking. The TV screen that would normally echo the news of the week was black and cold; and there was no radio blaring Peter, Paul and Mary songs from my parents' bedroom. Even though my mom and dad were up, except for the shuffling of footsteps moving from one room to another across the hardwood floors, the house was absolutely silent.

Cautiously, I tiptoed from my room down the hallway and peeked into Mom and Dad's bedroom. My father was there with a small suitcase open on the bed, packing his crisp corporate shirts. "Good morning, son," he said as he caught sight of me from out of the corner of his eye. "Come in here for a minute. I want to talk to you." Things had been tense in our house for a while. I knew that my parents were having a tough time, and my first thought was that I was going to get an explanation at last. I was right, but it wasn't the one that I'd expected.

"I'm going away for a while," my father said, "and I'm not sure when I'm coming back." That was it. I watched as he closed his suitcase and followed him as he walked down the hallway and passed my mom in the kitchen. Her eyes were still red from crying after the conversation they'd had the night before. Together, she and I watched as my dad left our house that day. I didn't know it at the time, but I had just witnessed the ending of my parents' marriage. I was 11 at the time.

It wasn't until years later that I began to understand how much that moment affected me. As I came to terms with what that day had meant to me, I realized that I had lost not only my father, but also my family—at least the way I had known them for the first 11 years of my life.

At first I believed that, except for not having my dad around, everything in my life would continue as normal—everything, that is, except those things where other boys my age had their fathers present and I didn't.

From parent/teacher nights at school and father/son weekends with the Boy Scouts, to my first public speech to our church congregation and awards presentations at my swim meets, I began to realize that something was missing in my life and that I'd lost something else on that Saturday morning as well.

The reason why I'm sharing this story here is because it offers an example of how an experience carrying a strong emotional imprint at one time in life can become the primer for the conditions of that experience to repeat throughout other times. Just as the seed event that established the pattern for "surprise" and "attack" on American soil was set in 1941, the meaning that we give to a traumatic experience can set into motion a cyclic pattern that can follow us throughout our lives.

If the experience is a positive one of love and life-affirming emotions, then it's probably not a problem. There's certainly no need to recognize it and heal anything. My sense is, however, that we seldom complain of finding ourselves "stuck" in mysterious patterns of joy, healing, and peace in our lives. When we do, it's probably not something that we want to change.

It's the negative patterns that will inevitably arise from the situations of everyday life—moments of loss, hurt, and betrayal, for example—that can become the unconscious seeds for a pattern that shows up again and again. Fortunately, just as repeating cycles are also opportunities to change the patterns for war and aggression on a worldwide scale, if we know our individual cycles and how they work, they can become powerful allies in healing some of the greatest hurts of our personal lives.

Calculating Personal Cycles

The Time Code Calculator can help us find such cycles in our lives. To the calculator, a cycle is a cycle, whether it is personal or global. The key is to recognize that life follows nature's rhythms, and our emotional patterns are part of life.

Time Code 14: The Time Code Calculator can pinpoint personal cycles of love and hurt, as well as global cycles of war and peace.

Using Mode 3 of the Time Code Calculator, we can calculate the times in our lives for the repeating conditions of any emotional experience that has left its imprint on our hearts. It's amazing to see how deeply the experiences from one time in life—from our greatest loves to our deepest hurts—can impact other relationships after the seed is planted.

If we can identify one of two keys, then we can also bring to light those patterns and be aware of when they may repeat in our business, casual, and intimate relationships. So let's begin with the example that we started this section with: my feeling of losing my family.

Although my mom, my younger brother, and I were still together and outwardly we still worked as a family unit, the key is that *I felt* I'd lost my family. In that feeling, I also experienced a sense of loss and betrayal. So just as "surprise" and "attack" are the clear descriptors for what happened on September 11, 2001, *loss* and *betrayal* are those for my personal experience. They became the seed for a pattern that would continue until I recognized its presence.

In the example that follows, I use my experience of loss and betrayal to illustrate this point. Because the calculations are brief, I have included them here in the text rather than creating a separate appendix.

Mode 3: Find the time we can expect the conditions of a personal experience from the past to happen again. To answer this question, we need a single piece of information.

- **Input:** Our age when an obvious momentous event (the seed) occurred

---

The Time Code Calculation

Step 1: Identify your age at the time of the seed event, *Seed Event Age* (SEA$_1$).

Step 2: Calculate the phi ratio interval of your age during the seed event (I$_{phi}$).

Step 3: Add the phi ratio interval back to your age during the seed event to determine your age when the conditions will repeat (SEA$_1$ + I$_{phi}$).

In my case, this would look as follows:

Step 1: My age at the time of seed event (SEA_1):
11

Step 2: Calculate the I_{phi} of the SEA_1:
.618 × 11 = 6.798 (I_{phi})

Step 3: Add the I_{phi} to the SEA_1 to find the next
repetition:
6.798 + 11 = <u>17.798</u>

From this simple calculation, it's evident that the age of 17.798 is when the conditions of betrayal and loss that I experienced at 11 years old could be expected to repeat. As the examples of global war and peace in the preceding section illustrate, although the conditions *may* lead to a repeat of the seed experience, the presence of the conditions isn't a promise that it *will* repeat. However, in my case, it did.

It was during this time that I lost two relationships in my life, both for the same reason. One was a friendship and the other was a romance; and both involved what I perceived as betrayal of trust, confidences, and promises. (If I had known then what I now understand about cycles, I might have saved myself years of asking why.)

When we use these calculations in our lives, there are seldom absolutes and rarely exact repeats of earlier situations. What we are looking for are general patterns that can give us a "heads-up" in business or romance. Following is a partial list of how the cycles of betrayal and loss continued for a number of years in personal and business relationships, until they were recognized and replaced with a new pattern of clear communication and discernment.

Summary 5

Personal Cycles—the Cyclic Conditions Created from the Loss of Family
Seed Age: 11
Seed Event: Loss and Betrayal

Calculated Ages for Repeat Conditions		Actual Events
Age 1:	17.798	Personal betrayal and loss of significant relationship
Age 2:	24.596	Academic betrayal and loss of significant relationship
Age 3:	38.192	Business and financial betrayal and loss of friendship
Age 4:	44.99	Business betrayal followed by healing of friendship (seed pattern was replaced with a new pattern)

The cycles identified by the Time Code Calculator work for positive experiences of success and accomplishment as well as for the lessons of hurt. Just as the first experience of emotional trauma creates the pattern of repeating cycles, the gratifying feelings of accomplishment and success are the conditions created as the seed events following their first appearance in life.

In all likelihood, *our very first examples* of such grati-fying experiences may have faded from memory by the time we reach adulthood, so our earliest recollection of accomplishment that follows the original experience will serve as the seed event for these calculations. To find patterns related to an experience of success and accom-plishment, we again turn to Mode 3 of the Time Code Calculator.

Mode 3: Find the times we can expect the condi-tions of a success and accomplishment from the past to happen again. To answer this question, we need a single piece of information.

- **Input:** Our age when an obvious pattern (the seed) occurred

---

While I was still in high school, I knew that I wanted to study earth and space sciences at the college level. I also knew that I would be the first person in my family to obtain a university degree, and that the tuition to do so would be my responsibility. Looking for a way to earn and save as much money as I could as quickly as pos-sible, I found a copper mill in a nearby town that paid union wages, had a full-time night shift, and could help me turn my college dream into a reality. Each Wednes-day I would walk directly onto the factory floor and talk to the supervisor about a job. Each week for four months he said there were no openings.

Just after my 16th birthday, all of that changed. I was hired as a full-time employee on the 4 P.M. to midnight shift. Two years later I had saved enough money to pay the out-of-state tuition at the Florida Institute of Technology in Melbourne, Florida. The elation and sense of accomplishment I felt the day I was hired was the seed for a pattern that has repeated like clockwork throughout my entire adult life since then.

Here is how a calculation based on the seed of my successful life experience looks:

Step 1:   My age at the time of seed event (SEA_1): **16**

Step 2:   Calculate the I_{phi} of the SEA_1:
$.618 \times 16 = 9.88$ (I_{1phi})

Step 3:   Add the I_{phi} to the SEA_1 to find the next repetition:
$9.88 + 16 = \underline{25.88}$

The age of 25.88 is when the conditions of accomplishment that I experienced at the age of 16 could be expected to repeat. Following is a partial list of how the cycles of accomplishment and success continued for a number years in my personal and business relationships. Interestingly, some of them actually overlap with the earlier cycles of loss and betrayal that I described. That's precisely what cycles do: they play out again and again as nested experiences within nested experiences.

Summary 6

Personal Cycles—the Cyclic Conditions Created From Success and Accomplishment
Seed Age: 16
Seed Event: Job success/accomplishment

Calculated Ages
for Repeat Conditions | Actual Events
Age 1:   25.88   First corporate position based upon college expertise

Age 2:   35.768   Received award for lead role in Cold War software project

Age 3:   45.648   First corporate publishing contract

When we look to the cycles of our lives, it's important to remember that there are no absolutes. Because we are dealing with natural processes that follow the rhythms of natural cycles, the choices that we make at any time in our lives can forever change the course of a given cycle. When they do, we begin the new patterns of a new one.

The key in exploring personal cycles is to recognize, first, that it's happening; and, second, the frequency with which it repeats. In doing so, we can prepare for the conditions the cycle offers while making the choices that become the new patterns of the future.

Herein we find the value of using the Time Code Calculator for the 2012 end date. Just as we can explore our personal histories to find the seeds of what we can expect in the future, we can use our knowledge of fractal patterns and nature's cycles to discover the key dates that tell us where to look in the past for the conditions that we can expect for 2012 . . . and beyond.

❋ ❋ ❋

CHAPTER SIX

THE END OF TIME REVISITED: WHAT CAN WE EXPECT?

---

*"The future has already happened,
it just isn't very well distributed."*

— William Gibson, contemporary science-fiction writer

"Will you change it?"

— Coded message regarding prophecies of destruction,
discovered in the ancient Torah

"7.8 Earthquake Rocks China."
"Baton Rouge Takes Brunt of Hurricane Gustav."
"Southern California Declared Disaster Area."
What were once rare captions that commanded our attention have become all too frequent. While we're still in awe of the power of Mother Nature to destroy

centuries of history and lifetimes of human effort in a single day, we're probably less surprised because we've seen it happen so many times. In the first years of the 21st century, tornados, hurricanes, severe thunderstorms, massive flooding, earthquakes, and droughts have taken an unprecedented toll upon human life, property, and a major portion of the world's infrastructure.

One earthquake alone in China's Sichuan Province, for example, killed more than 69,000 people and caused an estimated $20 billion in damages. Cyclone Nargis in Myanmar killed at least 84,000 people and left in excess of $10 billion in damages. In North America, Hurricane Katrina devastated the city of New Orleans, leaving over 1,000 people dead and more than $81 billion in damages.

There can be little doubt in the minds of anyone in the world today that life on planet Earth simply isn't business as usual. It's clear that something is happening—and it's big. But just what, and how big, is "it"? Maybe Peggy Noonan, a journalist for *The Wall Street Journal,* best summarizes the uniqueness of our time: "We are living Days of Lore. Days of big history." Clarifying what she means by "big history," she continues, "We are living through an epoch scholars 50 years hence will ask about and study. . . . They will see us, you and me, as grizzled veterans of something big."

From the 8,000-year-old Hindu Vedas and the ancient Mayan calendar to the indigenous prophecies of Asia and the Americas, the timekeepers of the world seem to agree with Noonan. They have predicted, anticipated, welcomed, and feared the events of our time. As frightening as some of the stories and prophecies are, however, it's important to note that *there is nothing in any of them that tells us unconditionally that the world itself ends, or leaves any doubt that we will survive what lies before us.* What they do say is that the cycle that has spawned the world as we know it is over and the next begins. As we've seen in the preceding chapters, it all happens in our lifetime.

"There it is!" I heard someone exclaim as we rounded the curve that marked the top of the mountain pass. Holding on to the overhead rail where I was standing, I ducked my head to see out the dusty window on the right side of the bus. As my eyes scanned the barren rock that filled my entire view, the landscape suddenly changed. The dark cliffs gave way to the blue-white ice of a glacier that seemed to hang suspended from the jagged cliffs above.

"How beautiful," I whispered to myself. "How absolutely beautiful." The steam from my breath hung in the early-morning chill inside our vintage bus. It had been driven from the Chinese mainland and into Tibet at our request, just for this journey across the high plateau. While it was definitely old, we also knew that this ancient-looking bus was more rugged and reliable than the newer vehicles—shiny low-riding tour vans that could never have made it over the trails and washed-out roads that led to this glacier. "Rest stop," I heard our translator blurt out as our bus slowed to a halt on the side of the road.

Revelation at 16,000 Feet

We had just crossed a pass that was 16,000 feet above sea level, the highest point of the day on our journey out of Tibet toward the Nepalese border. The air under the mountain clouds was cold, thin, and magnificent. As I hopped from the last step of the bus onto the smooth rocks that marked the edge of the valley, I was greeted in a way that I would never have expected in a million years.

The flap of a primitive-looking tent made of thick, dark yak fur flew open and a beautiful young Tibetan woman emerged, looking more than a little surprised to see us. Dressed in brightly colored skirts and robes, she was a powerful contrast to the dark hues of the mountain as she walked directly toward me.

Without taking her eyes from my face, she directed a question to our translator where he stood nearby. Following suit, he turned his face toward her, even as he addressed me with his translation of her words. "She has asked who we are and why we are here," he said.

"Please tell her that we've come halfway around the world for a visit," I said, hoping that a little humor would translate well and put her at ease. As the Tibetan version of my answer reached the woman, her concerned expression gave way to a widening grin. The translator continued. "She says that she doesn't get many visitors here," he said, "and she says that we are welcome."

With that, everyone was smiling. Our group of 22 (too many to fit into one tent) was immediately divided into smaller groups and escorted out of the wind and into the shelter of various tents for hot yak-butter tea.

Our guide and I followed the woman who had greeted us. Suddenly she stopped in her tracks and turned to me. Right there in the middle of the field, she began firing sentences at me so fast that I could only wait for the translations to catch up. When they did, I couldn't believe what I was hearing.

"Do you know how special this time is in the history of the world?" she began. "Do you know that everything is about to change?" For the next ten minutes or so, I listened as the woman shared the tradition that her people have held sacred for centuries: preparing for global change and doing so *now*. Except for the specifics, such as the local names for constellations, the ages of the world, and so forth, she was describing in her language the same change that is so familiar throughout other indigenous traditions of the world.

She described the recent extremes in her valley's weather, pointing to the glacier that had hovered for generations over her family's camp, providing water from its melting ice. Due to the warmer summers, it was shrinking. It had already retreated nearly a third of the way up the mountainside. At the present rate, it would disappear altogether in a few more years.

Suddenly tears filled her eyes as she described how many people in neighboring tribes, and even some closest to her in her own family, had died recently. It seemed that a new disease had swept through the local villages and camps, claiming those whose immune systems were the weakest, mostly the elders and the children. I was never clear on precisely *what* the disease was or where it came from. But from the way she described what had happened, it had obviously passed from person to person and was apparently something so new that their bodies hadn't been able to fend it off.

Then she began describing how all of humankind is making the choice now that will determine the outcome for our time in history. While I had heard similar themes discussed by people from the deserts of the American Southwest to the Andes of Peru and Bolivia, after 18 days of travel it was the last thing that I expected in one of the most remote and pristine places remaining in the world, at a mountain pass over three miles above sea level. Except for the specifics, the words I was hearing could have easily come from a New Age program regarding the prophecies of a planetary cleansing.

How powerful, I thought. *The uniqueness of our time in history is such common knowledge that even this nomadic woman, living isolated from the rest of the world in one of the highest inhabited lands remaining on Earth today, knows about it! Her culture has preserved it, and her traditions allow for it. It's like the big secret that everyone on the planet knows except those of us in the "modern" world.*

The Signs of the Time

In some traditions, like that of the Tibetan woman, people just seem to sense that now is the time of change that their ancestors described. In their rural and often isolated existence, with little or no contact from people in the technological world, the things that they know best are their surroundings: the land, the elements, and nature. These are precisely the things that they see changing.

For centuries, their ancestors told them that when they can no longer grow their crops at the right time, when the rivers flood, and when their land and the ice of the mountains begin to disappear, these will be indicators that they are living the time of the great change. From their ancestors' instructions and the signs of nature, they will know when to prepare for the end of one great cycle and the beginning of the next.

Using nature's signs to mark world changes extends beyond the knowledge of today's indigenous people. The "lost" biblical book of Enoch the Prophet offers a perfect example. Enoch is one of the most honored and mysterious of the Old Testament prophets for a number of reasons—not the least of which is the account that states he never died! Instead, at 365 years of age, Enoch left the earth and, as one passage relates, "walked with God."

The wisdom and message of Enoch were greatly revered by the early Christians—that is, before the book of his powerful visions was removed from the official biblical texts. We see evidence from some of the world's great scholars that his wisdom was considered divine, and the Book of Enoch was regarded as a holy scripture. The Roman historian Tertullian, for example, stated that the words of Enoch were "spoken in the same scripture of the Lord, and every scripture suitable for edification is divinely inspired."[1]

Before he walked with God, Enoch revealed his visions of a great change in Earth's future, which the angels had shown him at his request. During the cataclysmic change that he describes as occurring in "those days" when the earth shifts on its axis, Enoch states:

"The rain shall be restrained, and heaven shall stand still . . . the fruits of the Earth shall be late, and not flourish in their season; and in their season the fruits of the trees shall be withholden. The moon shall change its laws, and not be seen at its proper period."[2]

Using the astronomical tables in the Book of Enoch, historians have determined that his prophecies extend from about 5,000 years ago to the present and then continue about a thousand years beyond the 20th century. There is an obvious consistency between Enoch's description of a changing world and the Hopi recital of changes at the end of the fourth world. In no uncertain terms, the Hopi prophecy states: "When earthquakes, floods, hailstorms, drought, and famine will be the life of every day, the time will have then come for the return to the true path . . ."[3]

As much as such descriptions seem to apply to our world today, the problem with Enoch's is that without specific dates or events, it remains open to interpretation. His phrase *in those days* could apply to many times in the five millennia between his era and ours. Without something concrete to relate to, we find ourselves back to the question that began this book: *what can we realistically expect to see in our world as we approach the time that has been calculated, predicted, feared, and welcomed for more than 5,000 years?*

Until now, the answers have been as varied as those who were surveyed. Because we've had few facts to base our ideas of 2012 on, much of the popular opinion has been precisely that: opinion and theory with little concrete information to rest upon. Now, all of that has changed.

With our understanding of nature's cycles, fractal time, and the Time Code Calculator, we can look to the past to see what the future may bring. Specifically, we can examine the years for cycles that have already happened to see what *conditions* they will carry when they return. As we discovered in Chapter 5, the key is that if we know where to look in the past, then we can predict what patterns to expect in the future.

The Time Code Template

Following the success of the Time Code Calculator in correlating the dates leading to September 11, 2001, I began to apply the same principles to explore historic events of the past. While I wasn't surprised by the accuracy of the calculator, I *was* in awe of the patterns. The undeniable relationship between cycles of time and the events of our past clearly deserves more study. From the results revealed to date, however, three principles have become apparent:

1. The *conditions* of nature, including human events, do repeat themselves in cycles.

2. The *conditions* of one cycle often repeat with a greater magnitude of expression in a later cycle.

3. It's the return of the *conditions,* rather than the events themselves, that can be predicted.

It's clear beyond any reasonable doubt: from experiences of marriage, divorce, success, and loss to the cycles of war and peace, the same pattern can show up in life time and again. When it does, it's not uncommon for the repeating pattern to make itself known as an even stronger pattern than before, and often one that really catches our attention. We saw an example of this in Chapter 1 of this book with the patterns of "surprise" and "attack" on the United States that began in 1941. The crisis that drew America into the Second World War became the seed event for the next two times the conditions were repeated, the fractal expressions of that event: the plans in 1984 for a surprise nuclear attack during the Cold War and the reality of the surprise terrorist attacks in 2001.

If the 1984 strike against the United States had actually come to fruition, although it was the same pattern, it would be fair to say that the magnitude of its expression—a nuclear attack against America—would have been greater than the original seed event. The facts of the September 11 attacks followed this pattern as well with respect to the manner and the location in which they were carried out. The key is that patterns identified for an earlier time in history tend to repeat themselves with greater intensity at later dates.

Time Code 15: Patterns identified for an earlier time in history tend to repeat themselves with greater intensity at later dates.

To know what conditions the 2012 calendar end date may hold in store, it's important to bear in mind that 2012 marks the completion of not only one, but *two* nested cycles of time. The 5,125-year great cycle or world age that ends then is part of the larger 26,000-year precessional cycle that's also coming to a close at the same time. If we know how to "read" the key patterns for both, they will each tell us something different about our respective time in history.

The great cycle of 5,125 years, for example, covers about the same period of time as most of what is regarded as recorded history. So we can look to this cycle to see how civilization has been influenced by the changes of the past. This includes things like patterns of war and peace and the rise and collapse of nations and superpowers.

Since the 2012 end date is marked by an alignment of planets and stars *that happened before recorded human history,* we must go back—way back—to the last time such a pattern occurred to get the big picture. This was long before the current world age. It's during this time of an even older cycle that the larger patterns we are living today become clear. These patterns are seen in such things as changes in temperature, the melting of the polar ice caps, solar cycles, and shifts in the magnetic fields of the earth.

So, to answer our question of what 2012 means for us, we must take both of these nested cycles into account. Only then can we give ourselves a realistic picture of the ancient seeds for what we can expect today.

A Window into the Past

As we saw in previous chapters, the Time Code Calculator points us to precise dates in history. But without a way to explore what they mean, they are just insignificant numbers. To give meaning to our historic dates, we need a way to look at different points in time through the same kind of window.

Based upon the conversations I've had throughout the world since my seminars began in 1986, as well as the questions that have followed, I have chosen three categories with which to do just that. The window that will help us make sense of the past is a template made of *human events, Earth events,* and *celestial events.*

Time Code 16: Using a template of human events, Earth events, and celestial events gives us a consistent way to view the past as a realistic window to 2012.

As we use the Time Code Calculator to search the cycles of time, these simple categories will give us a consistent way to keep track of what we've found. Once we do so, the patterns for what we can expect for 2012 will become clear. So let's begin with a brief explanation of each class of events, depicting what it is and why it's important.

Human Events

Human events are those things that happen with regard to civilization and the way we respond to the challenges we face as a collective population. These include the rise and fall of super-powers, cycles of war and peace, and the expansion and collapse of empires.

This is an important category for us today. Historical records suggest a strong link between the physical changes of the climate that come with a shift in world ages (temperature, rainfall or drought, sea levels, and the depletion of resources); the cycles of war; failing economies; and the decline of civilizations.

Earth Events

The category of Earth events includes the systems of nature that tend to be most affected by world-age transitions. History has shown that these are the conditions that drive rapid change in populations and entire civilizations. They also tend to be the events that force us to choose between competition and cooperation as we respond to the changes.

Following is a brief discussion of Earth's magnetic fields, perhaps the most significant factor for changes in global temperature, how much energy we receive from the sun, the melting of polar ice, and the rise and fall of sea levels.

— **Earth's mysterious magnetic fields:** Since the discovery of Earth's *magnetosphere* in 1958, scientists have recognized that one of the most significant roles it plays is serving as the shield that protects us from the harsh effects of solar wind. Every moment of each day, there is a constant emission of radiation and high-energy particles that stream toward us from the sun. It is only because of our magnetic "shroud" that we are saved from the dangerous effects such radiation would certainly have on the delicate tissues of our bodies. It's also due to the strength of the magnetic fields that Earth's temperatures remain within a constant range over long periods of time. And this is where the change associated with world-age cycles comes in.

— **Magnetic fields and climate:** The relationship between the strength of Earth's magnetic fields and the abrupt climate change that seems to accompany their shifts is a controversial area of ongoing study. While scientists have yet to arrive at a consensus—at least at one that is published in the peer-reviewed journals—the documented effects of magnetism on major climate indicators are clear.

Recently two teams of scientists completed a monumental task that gives us an unprecedented snapshot of this relationship for a period of time greater than anything we've seen in the past. In June 1999, a press release announced the successful completion of a drilling project that went deeper into the ice of Antarctica than anyone had ever drilled before.[4] For hundreds of thousands of years a natural process has created and preserved a record of the earth's climate as a layer of air bubbles captured in the Antarctic ice. Each year the topmost layer "freezes" the airborne elements and compounds (oxygen, carbon dioxide, and so on); rain; snow; microscopic life; and the microdust present in that moment of time into a permanent record of that year that adds to the thickness of the ice.

As long as the ice remains, we have a virtual library of our planet's history captured in the thousands of layers that have accumulated over thousands of years. This history includes indicators of global temperatures, available sunlight, sea levels, and thickness of the ice caps.

A new method of using these elements to tell us how strong the magnetic fields were in the past now makes the ice cores even more valuable.[5] While scientists have sampled Antarctic ice before, the 1999 completion of the core samples to the bottom of the ice sheet now gives us an uninterrupted record of Earth's climate for the last 420,000 years—the longest continuous period of time that scientists have ever been able to evaluate. The data revealed from the Antarctic cores give us a powerful key to understanding the many roles that our planet's fields of magnetism play in our climate and in our lives.

In general, it appears that the relationship is as follows: When the field lessens, even a little, the weaker shield allows more of the sun's energy to reach Earth's surface. It's this increased solar energy that begins a period of global warming. As the land, oceans, and atmosphere heat up, their warming sets into motion the events that lead to the climate change seen in the geological record. We don't have to be climate experts to understand what happens next.

The warmer temperatures begin to melt the polar ice, where huge amounts of water have been stored for thousands of years. This melting, in turn, releases the water into the oceans and changes the delicate balance that drives our weather patterns. As the melted water mingles with the ocean currents, it changes the salinity and temperature—two powerful factors that have a direct effect on weather patterns across the planet.

This cycle helps give perspective to what scientists are calling the "abrupt" climate change of today. While the periods of warming are certainly associated with greater levels of "greenhouse" gases, such as carbon dioxide, these processes can clearly be seen on a cyclic basis during times when there was no human industry. In other words, while civilization has certainly contributed to the levels of carbon dioxide that normally exist in the atmosphere, the amount of that contribution appears to have accelerated the effects of a natural cycle that was already under way.[6]

— **Magnetic flip-flops:** When we think of things that are certain in life, we tend to count the magnetic fields of our planet among those certainties. For as long as anyone living today can remember, every time we have looked at the needle of a compass, the northern tip has pointed in the same direction: "up there" toward the North Magnetic Pole of the earth. While we tend to think of Earth's North and South poles as a sure thing, the reality is that our planet's magnetism is anything but certain. In fact, it's a moving mystery.

We know, for example, that every once in a while something almost unthinkable and truly mind-boggling happens. For reasons still not fully understood, and at times that appear to be unpredictable, our familiar North and South poles trade places. The magnetic field of the Earth does a complete a flip-flop.

Although polar reversals haven't happened in the 5,000-year history of civilization, the evidence shows that they *have* taken place routinely in terms of Earth's history. The geological record shows that such magnetic reversals have already happened 171 times in the last 76 million years, with at least 14 of those occurring in the last 4.5 million years alone. And although the geological record indicates that we have come close to a reversal a number of times, scientists believe that the last complete one happened 780,000 years ago during a time called the *Matuyama-Brunhes transition,* suggesting that we may be "overdue" for the next.[7]

— **Magnetic fields and life:** There are countless studies in the scientific literature that describe how many species of animals, from whales and dolphins to hummingbirds and wildebeests, rely on Earth's magnetic "superhighways" to navigate their way to feeding and mating grounds. While we may not use them in quite the same way, it appears that humans are no exception.

In 1993, an international team studying *magnetoreception,* the ability of our brains to detect magnetic changes in the earth, announced a discovery that makes 2012, the Mayan cycles, and Earth's magnetic fields even more important to us today. The team published the remarkable finding that the human brain contains "millions of tiny magnetic particles."[8] These particles connect us, just as they do other animals, to the magnetic field of the earth in a powerful, direct, and intimate way. This connection carries powerful implications. If Earth's magnetic fields are changing in the 2012 time frame, then *we* are affected!

We know, for example, that magnetic fields have a profound influence on our nervous systems; our immune systems; and our perceptions of space, time, dreams, and even reality itself. While the strength of our planet's magnetic field may be measured as a general reading, it varies locally from place to place. Early in the 20th century these ribbonlike patterns were charted and published by scientists as a contour map of the world.[9] The maps display the strength of the magnetic lines overlaying the continents, showing the places on Earth where the people of the world experience the strongest, and the weakest, effects of the planet's magnetic fields. To understand why this is important for the 2012 cycle, we need look no further than consciousness itself.

— **Magnetic fields and consciousness:** If we think of Earth's magnetic fields as a form of energetic "glue," then we can use this metaphor as a possible explanation for why change seems to come faster in some places and slower in others. Such a "magnetic glue" model suggests that the locations with the stronger magnetic fields (more glue) are more deeply entrenched in tradition and existing beliefs and ideas. In places where the field is weaker, the opposite is true. In these places people seem to be compelled to create change. The key is that although areas of low magnetism may be ripe for something new, how that change is expressed is up to those living in the fields.

Even without such evidence, however, all know intuitively that we are affected by planetary magnetic forces.

Any law-enforcement worker or health-care practitioner will attest to the intense and sometimes bizarre behavior that is seen during the full moon each month. When the magnetic strength changes suddenly, it affects the way we feel, and that change can be disorienting if we don't understand why it happens.

To those who do understand, however, such moments can be a powerful gift: an opportunity to release the patterns of belief that have caused pain in their lives, hurt in their families, and disease in their bodies and a chance to embrace new and life-affirming beliefs in their place. Artists and musicians know this and often anticipate the full-moon cycles as periods of great creativity. These existing examples of consciousness and magnetism offer important insights into how future changes in magnetic strength may affect us during the 2012 cycle.

Celestial Events

Although the mystery of Earth's magnetic fields remains, one factor appears certain. Regardless of the *reason* why Earth's magnetic fields to shift over time, the changes begin with a trigger. And that trigger appears to be linked to things that happen beyond the earth: celestial events throughout the solar system, and possibly even the galaxy.

For the purposes of our 2012 exploration, the category of celestial events focuses upon the natural cycles of our sun. Through the geological record and the correlations described previously, we have a reliable record of how much radiant energy—*solar luminosity*—has reached the earth in the past. This factor has been shown to play a key role in driving changes of climate and civilization's response to those changes.

— **Cycles of the sun:** From the time Galileo's first telescopes allowed sky gazers to observe the heavens, European astronomers have known that our sun experiences regular cycles of intense magnetic storms—*sunspots*—followed by predictable periods of quiet. These cycles have been observed on a regular basis since 1610. Since the measurements began, 23 cycles of sunspots averaging 11 years each have occurred, with the last beginning in May of 1996. Precisely when cycle 23 would end remained a mystery until the spring of 2006 when NASA reported the event that astronomers had been waiting for. On March 10 of that year, the magnetic storms and solar flares suddenly stopped, and the sun became "quiet," signaling the end of the 23rd sunspot cycle. The quiet, however, is misleading.

The end of a cycle is an indication that a new one, with new storms, is beginning. What makes the coming cycle so different is that the strength of sunspots observed from 1986 to 1996 suggests that cycle 24 is going to be one of the most intense ever recorded. "The next sunspot cycle will be 30 percent to 50 percent stronger than the previous one," says Mausumi Dikpati of the National Center for Atmospheric Research (NCAR) in Boulder, Colorado.[10] David Hathaway of the National Space Science and Technology Center agrees, suggesting that the sunspots created in the previous cycle are expected to amplify themselves and "reappear as big sunspots" in the new cycle. [11]

An unexpected twist regarding when the new cycle will peak with its greatest intensity occurred in the spring of 2008. Even though cycle 24 had definitely started, three sunspots with the characteristics of the previous one appeared on the 28th of January. NASA's Hathaway explained what this means in a technical bulletin: "We have two solar cycles in progress at the same time. Solar Cycle 24 has begun (the first new-cycle spot appeared in January of 2008), but Solar Cycle 23 has not ended."[12] In other words, the cycles are overlapping! While such activity has occurred in the past, it is generally short-lived. This is important to us because the *peak* of the new cycle is directly related to the old one's activity.

Based upon the behavior of the present sunspots, and taking into consideration the observations of the 1986–1996 solar cycles, both NASA and NCAR team leader Mausumi Dikpati have calculated the same year for solar maximum: the time of solar cycle 24's greatest intensity. Perhaps it is no surprise that the projected time coincides with the Mayan calculations of our sun's alignment with the center of our galaxy: the year 2012.

If these predictions are accurate, the solar magnetic storms will be second in intensity only to those of 1958 when the aurora borealis lit up the night sky as far south as Mexico. At that time, however, we didn't have communications technology that could be disrupted by such storms.

Building the 2012 Template

The first known civilization is widely accepted by

scholars as occurring in Mesopotamia, sometimes called the "Cradle of Civilization," approximately 5000 B.C. While there were certainly people living well before this time, it's believed that organized hubs of human cities originated about 7,000 years ago.

Because this span of time starts *before* the beginning of our great cycle, the term *civilization* includes everything that has happened during our current world age, lasting from 3114 B.C. to the present. So when we apply the Time Code Calculator to investigate the effect of 2012 on human events and civilization, it makes sense to use the Mayan great cycle—our world age of 5,125 years—as the window of time considered.

When we use the Time Code Calculator to find patterns of Earth events, however, those patterns occur over periods that are much longer than the 5,125 years of the world age. They happen over spans of time that are studied on the geologic scale covering hundreds of thousands, and sometimes millions, of years. To answer the question of what Earth events we can expect for 2012, we must look to the larger "parent" cycle of which the current world age is part. This is the entire precessional cycle discussed in Chapter 2, which lasts for approximately 26,000 years. Because each cycle holds clues that give us a clearer picture of what we can expect, we will apply the Time Code Calculator to both.

With the broad categories of human events, Earth events, and celestial events, and keeping the 5,000- and 26,000-year cycles in mind, we can now build a bridge to the past that gives us a window to the future. Our bridge will identify five keys:

1. The cycle we are working with, as discussed on the preceding page

2. The target date of 2012

3. The seed date for the pattern that the Time Code Calculator computes

4. The seed date adjusted for the modern (Gregorian) calendar

5. The significant things that happened on that date shown as the three categories identified in the previous section

So let's begin. First, we will use the Time Code Calculator, as we have in previous chapters, to identify the key date within each cycle that tells us where we can find the patterns that will repeat in 2012. These dates are based upon our knowledge of the fractal nature of time and the ratio that governs so much of nature *within* time.

As we have done in the earlier chapters, I've placed the details of our calculations in the appendices (see Appendix C) for ease of reading. The results of the Time Code calculations are as follows:

For the world-age cycle of 5,125 years, the seed date for the conditions we can expect in 2012 occurred 3,164 years before that date, in the year 1155 B.C.

For the precessional cycle of 25,625 years, the seed date for the conditions we can expect in 2012 occurred 15,836 years before that date, in the year 13,824 B.C.

Before we get to the summary, I've included a simple legend to describe what the column headings for the comparisons mean. Briefly, they are as follows:

- **Previous cycle:** Indicates which of the cycles we are looking at.

- **Reference date:** Indicates the date calculated by the Time Code Calculator to tell us where to look in the past for the conditions that will repeat during 2012.

- **Magnetic strength:** Indicates the overall strength of Earth's magnetic field using the Virtual Axial Dipole Moment (VADM) method.[13] It's important here to focus on the numbers relative to one another. Are they very similar or very different? Are they rising or falling?

- **Solar output:** Indicates the strength of the sun's radiant energy reaching the earth, as a reading relative to an entire 90,000-year glacial cycle. It's important here to determine whether the radiant energy is increasing or decreasing.[14]

- **Climate status:** The effects of the changes in the magnetic strength and solar output.[15]

- **Civilization status**: The events occurring on a civilization-wide basis during the time of the reference date, correlated with the changes in magnetic strength and climate.

With these dates and our template in mind, we now have everything we need to know where and how to discover what we can expect for 2012. If you're like me, you like to know where you're going before you begin your journey. Here is a high-level summary of the events that occurred for our three categories between 13,824 B.C. and 1155 B.C.:

Figure 15 shows us at a glance what we can expect for the time before and immediately following the 2012 end date. Although there are more than 12,000 years between the reference dates for each of the two cycles, in general the conditions are remarkably similar. At the time of both dates, we find:

- Global magnetic-field strength was in the same general range as it is today.

- There was a sharp increase in the amount of the sun's energy reaching Earth.

- Global temperatures increased.

- Polar ice sheets melted and collapsed.

- Global sea levels rose.

What Can We Expect?
2012 Reference Dates and Their Conditions

	Magnetic Strength	Solar Output	Climate Status	Civilization Status
Present Time Early 2008 End of Cycle	~7.5 Units	Sharp Increase	*Warming +.6/-.2C *Polar-Ice Collapse *Sea-Level Rise	*Multiple Wars *Collapsing Economy *Overextended Military
Previous Cycle 5,125-Year Reference Date 1155 B.C.	~10.5 Units	Sharp Increase	*Warming +1C *Polar-Ice Collapse *Sea-Level Rise	*Collapse of Egypt's 20th Dynasty *Multiple Wars *Overextended Economy
Previous Cycle 26,000-Year Reference Date 13,824 B.C.	~5.25–7.25 Units	Sharp Increase	*Warming +2C	*No Civilization as We Now Know It

Figure 15. This summary shows the key conditions for the 2012 reference dates indicated by the Time Code Calculator for both the 5,125-year world age and the 26,000-year precessional cycle. The similarities in the conditions between these two vastly different times in our past are striking. If the cycles of nature follow the patterns of the past, these indicators give us a concrete idea of what we can expect in the 2012 transition between world ages.

The strength of Earth's magnetic fields is important to note here in light of the growing concern that we may experience a magnetic "flip-flop" near the time of the 2012 end date. Because so many of the changes we're discussing seem to hinge upon the planet's magnetic intensity, let's explore just a little more deeply what these readings are telling us.

The continuous records of Earth's magnetic fields made possible by the Antarctic ice cores have confirmed a very powerful piece of information. They show that the overall strength of our planet's magnetic intensity must drop to a certain level before the field can reverse. With the brief explanation for the column headings of Figure 15 in mind, this "threshold" appears to be a reading that registers below 2 units on the VADM scale.

If the historical patterns hold true, the numbers in Figure 15 show that we are nowhere near that threshold today. Additionally, it's unlikely that the years immediately before and after 2012 will change that . . . that is, unless something happens that's not part of the past cycle and that we're not expecting.

There are extenuating circumstances, for example, that could "shake up" the delicate balance of what scientists call Earth's "magnetic dynamo." If the balance were disturbed enough, it is entirely possible that the shake-up could throw the fields into a dramatic decline, followed by a 180-degree reversal, or the flip-flopping of the South and North poles. While there is no historical reason to believe that these scenarios are on the horizon for the immediate future, they are often cited as possibilities in popular 2012 literature, so I mention them here.

Recent discoveries regarding the way Earth's magnetic fields work suggest that rather than a single one, there are actually multiple fields that merge ("couple") to create the magnetic shield that protects us from the sun's high-energy effects. A portion of these fields appears to originate from within the earth itself, while another forms in the atmosphere that surrounds the planet.

Anything that creates a disturbance large enough within the earth itself or within the atmosphere could potentially disturb the balance that maintains the fields. In other words, anything packing enough of a wallop could send the system into a tailspin. Although there are a number of scenarios that *could* cause such an effect, the ones of greatest concern are among the following:

- A disruption of the fields due to the unusually strong burst of particles from a "super" solar flare

- A galactic "superwave" of high-energy cosmic rays and radiation that bolts through the universe every 15,000 years or so[16]

- A physical jolt to the planet itself from the impact of a meteor

- A physical jolt to the planet from inside the earth itself, such as the one we felt from the 2004 tsunami that affected the wobble of Earth's orbit

- The effects of a "near miss" from a large

orbiting body such as an asteroid, comet, or planet

- The push/pull effect of Earth's crossing of the galaxy's equator

Although these descriptions are simplified, they are enough to serve as a caveat about the possibility of a polar reversal in the 2012 window. They certainly *sound* ominous; however, the geological record that describes the same crossing of the Milky Way's equator during the last close of the precessional cycle 26,000 years ago gives us no reason to suspect that we will see any of these events happening immediately before or after the actual year 2012.

Time Code 17: There is nothing in the geological record to suggest that Earth's magnetic fields will reverse before or immediately following the 2012 cycle end date.

It's important to bear in mind that the world-age transition marked by 2012 is a process rather than an event. And it's one that is already well under way. According to the calculations described by John Major Jenkins (see the Introduction), Earth slipped into the zone of alignment that marks the cycle's end somewhere around 1980. This means that not only is the alignment already happening, but so are its *effects*—ones that we're experiencing as extremes in rainfall and temperature, as well as hurricanes, forest fires, and drought in certain places of the world. This tells us that we've been dealing with the most controversial effects of the shift for nearly 30 years, and doing so successfully.

The bottom line to what the historical records seem to show is that while the strength of the magnetic fields has definitely declined, it appears that by doing so, they are now in the same place that they've been at this time in past cycles—low enough to trigger the changes in climate and life, yet high enough to prevent them from going into a full reversal. In other words, the fields are just where they need to be, at just the right point in time, to close one world age and begin the next.

Time Code 18: The Time Code template shows that the human, Earth, and celestial conditions of today are in the same range as the key reference dates of the past. In other words, the changes happening now are just what we'd expect for the end of a world age.

Details for the 2012 Seed Dates of 1155 B.C. and 13,824 B.C.

Figure 15 gives us the opportunity to compare where we are in the world-age cycle today to the fractal dates for two cycles in the past. The following discussion provides a level of detail that we don't see in the chart. This is especially true when it comes to the human events of 1155 B.C. and what we can expect to see during the 2012 cycle. The findings are discussed in the same order as they're listed in the template described earlier in this chapter.

Human Events

The year 13,824 B.C. is before the time of "civilization" and large populations organized into nations recognized by scholars today. For this reason, we have no indications of how the changes affected human populations that may have existed during this time.

The year 1155 B.C., however, was pivotal for one of the greatest civilizations known in the history of our species: the superpower of Egypt. As shown in detail in the paragraphs that follow, it was in that year that many of the systems that were needed to maintain such a world power failed, and it was the convergence of so many failures that led to the collapse of the civilization. These events happened within the single year that is the fractal of the entire world age. They also appear to be repeating in large part during the 2012 window that leads to the end of the same world age.

— As with any world power, much of the **civilization** and **government** depended upon the way in which the empire was ruled. Egypt's last great pharaoh, Ramses III, died c. 1155 B.C. (possibly due to smallpox). His death and the chaos that followed began the decline of Egypt's 20th Dynasty. The Egyptian decline is attributed to a number of different factors that seemed to contribute to a prolonged war to fight off foreign invaders during this time.

These factors include the heavy costs of war itself and the depletion of Egypt's financial resources to fund it. Egyptian scholars also find accounts of the first recorded labor strikes during this time, possibly linked to food shortages due to abrupt changes in climate and the crop damage from natural disasters, including volcanic ash believed to be from an eruption of Iceland's Mount Hekla.

As we near the end of the present great cycle, in many ways it appears that we are following the dangerous pattern that we see in 1155 B.C. The changing climate and competition for dwindling resources, headed by the shortages of oil and food, has led to the violent competition that sparked many of the wars in the late 20th, and now in the early 21st, century. Recognizing this pattern and knowing where it led before brings us to a question today: *will we learn from the cycles of our past and avoid falling into the ancient trap that pits us against one another at the end of our cycle?* Time will reveal the answer.

Earth Events

As we saw previously, the strength of Earth's magnetic fields is the foundation for many of the systems that we depend upon to sustain life. The readings for global magnetic strength summarized in Figure 15 are based on two studies, both using the same method of determining past intensity,[17,18] both essentially telling the same story.

For the year 1155 B.C., they show a magnetic intensity in the range of 10.5 on the VADM scale; and for the year 13,824 B.C., the readings range from 5.25 to 7.25 on the same scale. These readings suggest that the present magnetic intensity of approximately 7.5 is right in line with what we would expect for where we are in the great cycle.

— The **global temperature readings** in the summary are from the Vostok Antarctic ice samples, the results of which were published in 1999. Both cores used in the study reveal the same trend. In 1155 B.C., there was a global warming that averaged approximately 1 degree Celsius (C), while the warming indicated for 13,824 B.C. was twice that, at about 2 degrees C. In general, it appears that the rise in global temperatures that we see today is precisely in the range of those that have occurred in the past at such key points in the cycle.

— The same studies used to determine global temperatures from the Antarctic ice cores also correlate those temperatures with the **polar ice conditions** at the core locations. The results for both the 1155 B.C. and 13,824 B.C. dates show the same trend of melting at the poles. The data seem to support what we intuitively know about the relationship between temperatures and ice: when Earth's temperature increases, the volume of ice decreases proportionally. This appears to be precisely the pattern that we are seeing in the early 21st century, with the breakup of the South Pole's ice sheet and the unprecedented melting of the North Pole's ice pack reported by top climate researchers at the National Snow and Ice Data Center in Boulder, Colorado, in 2008.

Celestial Events

By calculating the strength of Earth's magnetic fields in the past, scientists are now able to estimate how much of the sun's radiant energy was reaching the earth throughout the cycle. New models linking ocean temperatures with certain forms (isotopes) of oxygen (^{16}O and ^{18}O) found in the deep-sea core samples now provide a continuous record of how much solar energy has reached the earth over long periods of time.

The readings are relative (expressed in terms of less or more energy) and describe the sun's influence for 90,000 years, about the time of one complete cycle of glaciers. What's important here is that although the total amount of radiant energy reaching Earth was lower in 13,824 B.C. than during 1155 B.C., there was still a sharp increase for both dates. With the increased energy, a corresponding warming of the earth shows up in the ice-core records as well. Once again, this is the same pattern that we are seeing today with the decline in magnetic strength, and the same effect.

The End of Time Revisited: What Can We Expect?

While it's impossible to be certain exactly what the 2012 end of our world age has in store for us, now we can know the facts about what similar cycles and seed points within them have heralded in the past. Armed with information that our Time Code Calculator has provided, we can build a reasonable picture of what we can expect as we move through the 2012 end date and even beyond. We can do so with confidence because of the clear reference dates that the Maya designed into their calendar.

Based upon the dates indicated by the Time Code Calculator, the following summary describes what we can expect immediately before and after December 21, 2012.

The conditions for world-age reference dates of the past describe what we can expect for the years before and immediately following the 2012 Mayan end date. They include:

- A magnetic intensity for the earth between 5.5 and 10.5 on the VADM scale. (This places the present reading of 7.5 precisely in the range of past-world-age measurements.)

- No indication of a 180-degree polar reversal, barring the special circumstances described previously.

- An increase in global temperatures of 1–2 degrees C. (This places the warming that we see today in the same range as those of world-age cycles past.)

- A sharp increase in the amount of radiant energy that Earth receives from the sun. (The increase that we see today follows this pattern.)

- The melting of the polar ice and a collapse of the ice caps. (The geological record suggests that the warming we are seeing today will be quick, brief, and followed by a period of general cooling.)

With these conditions in mind, the rare alignment marked by the winter solstice of December 2012 appears to be the cosmic marker that the ancient Maya and others identified as the time of such great and cyclic change on Earth. But in addition to the physical changes to the planet itself, they foretold of the emotional and spiritual transformations that the people of Earth would undergo to come to terms with the new weather, land, ocean, and climate conditions that the changes bring.

From this perspective, our 2012 end date truly *is* the end of one kind of balance that we have grown accustomed to and feel comfortable with and the beginning of something brand-new. In other words, when we hear ourselves saying that we want things to get "back to normal," we may just discover that the world created by the changes has a *new* normal. The opportunity here is for us to benefit from our individual and collective experiences of the last 5,125 years and apply what we've learned as the foundation for the sixth world age of humankind.

It may be no coincidence that it's only now—in the last years of the darkest part of our cyclic journey through the heavens, just when we are faced with the greatest threats to our future and even our survival—that we have discovered we have the ability to cooperate with one another in a way that is unprecedented in the history of the world. It's as if we've pushed ourselves to the very edge of our limits and our beliefs. Now we must apply what we've learned in order to survive what we've created.

We find ourselves living at this rare moment in time when the motion of the universe is converging in just the right way to give us just the right conditions that lead to a shift in the way we think of our world and ourselves. In the same way that we would check the road signs throughout a cross-country trip to make sure that we're going in the right direction, 2012 is like an end-of-cycle reality check. It allows us to think about where we've been, evaluate the choices and direction of our past, and make any midcourse corrections necessary to complete our cosmic journey successfully. This possibility exists only when everything we need to make such a change appears in a single window of time. The 2012 "zone" of alignment appears to be just such a window.

※　※　※

CHAPTER SEVEN

CHOICE POINT 2012: ARMAGEDDON OR THE SECOND EDEN?

"The human race is at a unique turning point. Will we choose to create the best of all possible worlds?"

— *Scientific American* (September 2005)

"Once you have glimpsed the world as it might be, it is impossible to live anymore complacent in the world as it is."

— Anonymous

When we combine the consistent message from our ancestors for more than 5,000 years with the best insights of contemporary science, the uniqueness of our time in history becomes clear. As it does, the message of 2012 makes tremendous sense. If (1) the lessening of Earth's magnetic shield allows more of the sun's energy to create greater change, (2) the way we respond to that change is the catalyst for our spiritual growth, and (3) both are occurring at precisely the same time that a rare 5,000-year cycle combines with an even rarer alignment happening just once every 26,000 years, then it's as if the cosmos has somehow conspired to shower us with the influence of what José Argüelles calls the "galactic synchronization beam."

What a rare and precious gift! How we receive our cosmic offering is the choice that we're making individually and collectively today. We're doing so by the way we choose to live our lives in the presence of the greatest challenges of recorded human history.

The world is shifting before our eyes. Faster than we can teach about it in our textbooks or chronicle it in documentaries, the ice caps on the poles are disappearing; the sea levels are rising; food is disappearing; and "super storms" are wiping entire communities, villages, and cities from the face of the earth. These are precisely the weather changes that Antarctic and sea-floor records reveal and that the predictions, prophecies, and visionaries have seen and warned us about.

It's not that these things are "about to happen" or are "on the horizon." They're happening *now,* and the pace is quickening. While our ancestors warned that our lifetime would herald precisely such events, the heart of their message was less about the events themselves and more about our response to them. In other words, we were told that the changes in our world would become the catalyst for ones within *us.*

In the presence of dwindling resources, do we fight one another for what remains, or do we pull together and solve the problems that confront us? Do the nations with the most money, power, and leverage use them to grab the remaining deposits of oil, fertile valleys, and clean water, leaving others to fend for themselves? Or do we recognize that we're a family, Earth is our home, and we're much stronger when we solve the problems of a changing world together than when we try to do so as a fragmented civilization clutching at the last vestiges of an unsustainable way of life?

We may well discover that our answer to these questions is the great secret to understanding 2012 and the message of our past. Our ancestors went to tremendous lengths to preserve something that they wanted us to have today. The fruit of their labor is scattered across the face of the earth in the temples, tombs, and monuments that mark their legacy. Every one carries a message. As different as each message appears to be from the others, the common thread that weaves through them and binds them together is that they all tell us something about *ourselves*.

From the Mayan calendar that reminds us of our relationship, to time's cycles to the Buddhist message "Reality exists only where we create a focus"; from the Christian dictum that tells us our choices in this lifetime determine what happens beyond this life, to the Hopi tradition that carries the instructions to make powerful life choices . . . it's clear that our ancestors worked desperately in their times to preserve something that they knew we would need in ours.

That "something" is the message of renewal that

comes with the dawning of a new cycle, the new world age that allows us to succeed where others have failed and to assure nothing less than the future of our species by learning from our past. Today the changing landscape of the earth is forcing us to a new way of thinking, a new way of being, and a new way of life. Perhaps the greatest awakening that we are experiencing is the discovery of the fact that we have a choice!

Will You Change It?

One of the most unsettling revelations in Michael Drosnin's book *The Bible Code* is a sequence of words that relate directly to the Mayan 2012 end date. Located within the coded Torah at a point linking the text to the Hebrew year 5772 (2012 in the Gregorian calendar) are two ominous words that read: *Earth annihilated*. Without a doubt, to discover such words encoded into the Bible is a frightening experience. It certainly seems to play into the doom-and-gloom scenarios that suggest we're heading toward a time of Armageddon and the end of the world. A closer look at the code, however, reveals something quite unexpected: another sequence of words that describes a second possibility and offers a ray of hope for the same year.

In his discussion of just what such a message may be telling us, Drosnin first describes how the words *darkness* and *gloom* intersect with the word *comet* and appear with the 2012 date. He then calls our attention to a curious phrase located near the text describing the threat that seems to contradict it. The phrase offers the welcome news of another scenario. Translated, it reads: "It will be crumbled, driven out, I will tear it to pieces, 5772 [*author's note:* 5772 is the Hebrew notation for 2012]."[1] With these words, whoever or whatever is responsible for the Bible Code itself seems to be telling us that there is another, Earth-saving outcome possible for the time when the code states: "Earth annihilated." Rather than the planet being destroyed, in this scenario it's the threat itself that will be destroyed on that date.

So which is it? Does 2012 mark the end of the world or the end of the threat that may destroy it? How can both outcomes be possible for the identical moment in time? A third phrase, found in the same proximity of the code, seems to hold the key to this paradox and an answer our question. It's one that appears in other places throughout the Bible Code, especially when specific outcomes such as elections, wars, and assassinations are identified. Accompanying the sequence that describes the gravest outcome for our future are four words that offer hope, while asking the reader of the code a simple and direct question. Translated, they are: *Will you change it?*[2]

Mirroring the discoveries of modern physics and the beliefs of our most cherished spiritual traditions, these four words remind us of one of the greatest secrets of our existence: *we are part of our world rather than separate from it.* As a part of our experience, we play a powerful role in what happens in our lives for 2012 and beyond. In fact, if we're to believe the Bible Code, our role is so powerful that we can even alter the course of an event identified 3,000 years ago with the potential to end the world. The words *Will you change it?* appear to be a direct question to those who would be certain to read the ancient code maker's message. It is a question to *us*.

It's as if whoever created the code knew that the technology to understand the message would only become available at the time of the threat. *Because* we've now discovered it, we're also ready to participate in the end of time to transcend the darkest of possibilities. In this way, the Bible Code offers yet another example of an ancient message that identifies 2012 as a gateway of opportunity.

Almost universally, the darkness of our cycle is described as a brief but intense period of chaos and confusion. From the perspective of what we now know about our galactic alignment, this would seem to imply that the years between 1980 and 2016 (the entry and exit points for the sun's zone of alignment) mark the time of the greatest intensity. Just as we've always heard that the darkest part of the night is just before the dawn, the same traditions that carry the warnings also tell us that our time of darkness *is the very path* that leads to a time of light—the increase in physical and spiritual light accompanying the cosmic orbit that brings us closer to the core of the Milky Way.

It's during the darkness of the end-time that our faith, strength, beliefs, and true nature will be tested. One of the most important lessons of those who have lived through such cycles in the past is that the greatest challenge of such a time is to survive the darkness without succumbing to the fear that it brings. It's precisely this fear, they suggest, that destroys the world and the values we cherish. They believed that such a warning is necessary because this kind of loss appears to be what has led to the collapse of civilizations in the past.

New evidence of a highly advanced civilization between what is now India and Pakistan, for example, places its end eerily close to the close of the last great cycle, at the time when our current one began. Archaeological evidence now dates what appear to be the remnants of the ancient, massive, and high-tech war that destroyed the civilization at approximately 5,000 years old.[3,4]

In light of the changes that 2012 signals for our time, maybe our greatest test will be to find a way to adapt to them without betraying what philosopher Francis Bacon called our *fundamental character of goodness*. That test may also be our greatest opportunity to respond to the stress of a changing world by helping one another in cooperation, rather than turning against one another in fear.

The Hopi Path of Life

"The Prophecy says the Earth will shake three times."

With these words, author Robert Boissiere begins describing the large-scale events that serve as the time markers for the Hopi prophecy of the fourth world and the end of time. When we think of the defining events of the 20th century, the meaning of the signs is unmistakable.

> First the Great War, then the Second One, when
> the Swastika rose above the battlefields of Europe to
> end in the Rising Sun sinking in a sea of blood.[5]

The specifics of such a verbal time map leave little doubt as to what they describe. There have been only two world wars in the last 5,000 years, and the associations of Germany's swastika and Japan's rising sun have happened in only one of them. In the minds of Hopi elders, there is no question what this prophecy means or where the events of the last 100 years place us in history's timeline. Before his death in 1999 at the age of 108, for example, Chief Dan Evehema, the eldest elder of the Hopi nation at that time, clarified his tradition's perspective in his "Message to Mankind":

> Now we are at the very end of our trail. We are
> instructed in our ancient prophecy that this would
> occur. We were told that someone would try to go up
> to the moon; that they would bring something back
> from the moon; and that after that nature would show
> signs of losing its balance. Now we see that coming
> about. Floods, drought, earthquakes, and great storms
> are occurring and causing much suffering.[6]

The signs that were given to the Hopi people hundreds of years ago—such as the description of the swastika and two great wars—do, in fact, seem to point to things that can only be attributed to 20th-century events. From the Hopi perspective, the shift into the next world is already well under way. Of that they are certain.

What makes the prophecy especially intriguing,

however, is that it doesn't tell us *how* the fourth world will end. Just in the way a mystery novel leaves us hanging in anticipation of the next chapter, the Hopi prophecy stops short of describing how the earth will "shake" after the two great wars. It can't go that far because there's an unknown factor that prevents predicting any outcome with certainty. *We* are that factor. This is where our choice comes in.

Just as the Bible Code suggests that we are choosing the outcome for 2012, the Hopi prophecy states that we're the ones writing the last chapter of the fourth world story. We're doing so by the way we choose to live our lives today. Boissiere's translation states:

> . . . the Prophecy does not say [what the third shaking of the Earth will be]. For it depends upon which path humankind will walk: the greed, the comfort, and the profit, or the path of love, strength, and balance.[7]

Within this single statement, we find the Hopi message to our time in history: that while the change is inevitable, our response to it is a matter of choice. It's our *choice*, for example, as to how we respond to the shortage of food that "suddenly" appeared at a global level in 2008. It's our choice as to how we meet the needs of those who suddenly find a lifetime of work washed away by the waves of a record storm surge or tsunami. While the evidence shows that we are in a time of certain change, the message of our past reminds us that we're the ones who *choose* how we treat one another as we respond to the change.

What sets the Hopi prophecy apart from so many others is that the Hopi offer an action plan for our time of change. The instructions as to *how* we choose "love, strength, and balance" were left to their "eldest elders" in a way that assured they would be preserved until the end of time. With those instructions we are shown the path to prepare for and accommodate the shift into the next Great Age.

The Hopi Map of Choice

Almost universally, the creation stories describing the cycles of previous worlds explain how the collapse of one is the foundation for what comes next. From this perspective, the end of the cycle is not really *the* end of all endings. Clearly it's not that of the planet or all life on Earth. Rather, it's the end of a way of being that's a necessary step of growth and evolution. Although the ending is sometimes difficult, it's also as natural as the passing of night that becomes the new day.

To ease the transition that comes with the shift between worlds, the Hopi say the Creator gave them a life plan to share with those who would listen. The purpose and location of that plan is described in the prophecy itself.

> [After the great flood of the third world, Spider Woman, who weaves the web that unites all life, asked Massoua, guardian of the Earth:] "Can the people, the remnants of the Third World you destroyed by water come live with you?"

He answered, "If they pledge to live according to the life plan originally given them by Taiowa. . . . Although many have forgotten [the life plan], many will remember. . . . But it is written . . . on the face of the rock [my brackets]."[8]

The prophecy is telling us that the Creator's life plan exists as a simple map holding a profound message, and that it's preserved on a rock face in northern Arizona's Hopi village of Oraibi—a place called *Prophecy Rock*. What makes this map so unusual is that that it's not a conventional one of places. Instead, it's a map of "being," of consciousness. It tells us the state of consciousness that's required to survive the great changes that accompany the end of our world age.

Figure 16. Photograph of the Hopi prophecy etched into the stone at Old Oraibi, Arizona. In it, we see the two paths that lead to the new world age of the fifth world. (Photo used with permission, and taken by Bill Tenuto with permission of Hopi Elder Grandfather Martin on 6/4/2007. Martin used a chalk-like rock to highlight the ancient inscriptions for the camera. For additional images and interpretations of the Hopi prophecy, visit: **http://thenewhumanity.blogspot.com**)

No one knows how long the images on Prophecy Rock have existed or precisely who placed them there. But one thing is certain: the rock's message is central to the Hopi prophecy. Just in the way the tablets of Moses became the guidelines for an entire civilization, the Oraibi map holds the core of a life-affirming philosophy for the Hopi and all who recognize its truth. While there are multiple layers of meaning, in general the message has remained constant.

The code on Prophecy Rock centers around two parallel lines across the map, two possible paths that humankind may choose as a way of life. Each leads to a very different experience. The lower path shows people healthy and vital, living to advanced ages and harvest-ing corn from an abundant field. The upper one depicts people as well; a closer look, however, shows that their heads aren't attached to their bodies and are floating just above their shoulders. The line beneath them is rough and jagged.

Boissiere's translation states that the upper path shows what happens with "people who use their mind, instead of their faith in the spirit way." In place of the abundant crops seen on the lower path, there are storms over a rocky terrain. To those who can read the map, its message is clear: the lower path leads to a life of health and abundance; the upper leads to a difficult life of lack and suffering.

The good news is that the map also shows a third path, a vertical line that connects the jagged and the smooth ones. This line is said to represent the ladder of choice. It's because the ladder exists that those who have chosen either way of life in the past can change, and choose the other path. The Hopi say that as we approach the end of this world age, there will be a time of confusion during which many people will do just that. The conditions of the earth will move them from the comfort zone of the past and force them to choose a new path.

To the Hopi, this time of confusion is seen as the period of "purification" that occurs before Earth's cleansing. Just as the intense fires that roar through a forest make way for the growth of new and healthy trees, the traditions of our past have prepared us for the great clearing that comes with the end of each world age.

From their perspective, the clearing is necessary and it's inevitable. Because we're part of Earth's garden, it's an opportunity for us to sweep away the debris of 5,000 years of history and embrace the best of what we've learned. With that embrace comes the opportunity to choose what we value in the new world age and leave behind the things that have caused the pain and suffering of the past: the judgments, biases, and beliefs that have guided our choices.

If the conditions of such purification—extremes in climate, the failure of unsustainable economies, the largest shift in wealth in the history of the earth, and the growing competition for dwindling resources—are, in fact, triggered by astronomical alignments, as the evidence indicates, then modern science would seem to agree. The point here is that the changes do occur. They're happening now. The scientific evidence and indigenous signs suggest that our lifetime is part of such a clearing. Luckily, clearings like this one are few and far between.

While this sounds like a good thing, the key is that

before we can plant a new way of being in the garden of a new world age, we must first recognize what we need. Following the descriptions of global signs and imbalances that have now become commonplace in our world, the last part of the translation for the Hopi prophecy states: "So it seems we now are all at this point in our lives."

The Hopi also say that the way to choose the good path is as simple as the map itself: "When prayer and meditation are used rather than relying on new inventions to create more imbalance, they [the people of the Earth] will also find the true path." [9]

In addition, the key to staying on the path of life is equally simple: "Give love to all things, people, animals, plants, and mountains; for the spirit is one, if Catsinas [expressions of the spirit] are many." [10]

The Hopi traditions of Oraibi are a beautiful example of a complete worldview. They inform us of where we are in the cycle through the clarity of unmistakable signs. Then they guide us with a practice—*a way of being*—that is sustainable and one that we can easily follow. With that practice we are given the opportunity to choose how we experience the end of our great cycle and the transition to the next.

Choice Point 2012

So what do the Hopi map, the Mayan calendar, the Bible Code, and the other powerful messages from our past really tell us? Is it possible that by *choosing* a way of being, we can actually *change* the way we experience things, such as the frightening outcomes predicted for

2012? While there are a number of new discoveries that show us how consciousness directly affects our world, they are generally variations of the century-old experiment that was designed to find out how much our beliefs really affect our reality, answering this question.

※

In 1909, Geoffrey Ingram Taylor, a British physicist, devised the famous "double-slit" experiment and began a revolution in the way we view ourselves in the universe. The bottom line to his investigation was that the mere presence of consciousness in the room—*people*—affected the way the quantum particles (the stuff our world is made of) were behaving.

On February 26, 1998, scientists at Israel's Weizmann Institute of Science repeated Taylor's experiment. Not only did they confirm that our world is affected just by being watched, but they also discovered: "The greater the amount of 'watching,' the greater the observer's influence on what actually takes place."[11] In other words, the greater the focus upon the experiment by those present, the greater the influence their focus had upon the outcome.

Herein lies the key to understanding what quantum physics and the Mayan calendar may really be saying to us about our power in the universe. A growing number of scientists have arrived at an inescapable conclusion: There's a place where all things begin, and that place is the realm of quantum energy. It's the same realm that's influenced by our thoughts, feelings, emotions, and beliefs. In this "no-man's-land" where all things are possible, the laws of time and space seem to break down and what scientists call "quantum weirdness" takes over. It's also in this place that the atoms of matter are influenced by thought, feeling, emotion, and belief to become the reality of our world.

In 1957, Princeton University physicist Hugh Everett III carried these ideas a step further, devising the theory that describes *how* the focus of our awareness creates reality. In a landmark paper that included his *many-worlds interpretation,* Everett described simple moments in time when it becomes possible to "jump" from one reality to another by creating a quantum bridge between the two already-existing possibilities.[12]

He called these windows of opportunity "choice points" and described them as the time when conditions make it possible to begin one path of experience and then to change it by changing the focus of our awareness—our beliefs. From Everett's perspective of choice points, chaos, suffering, and destruction are certainly possible—and maybe even probable—*if* the course of human events remains on the same trajectory that it has been set on for the last two centuries or so. The discovery of choice points gives us the opportunity to change that trajectory.

This is good news in the face of the frightening scenarios of 2012. To the people who understand that the repeating patterns of a seed event also show us the best times to change unwanted patterns, the 2012 transition appears as a mixed blessing. They will be experiencing the birth of a beautiful new world, and at the same time they will be experiencing the death of everything that does not support that new world. While any time is a good one to make positive and life-affirming choices in our lives, it seems as if nature is conspiring to create the perfect conditions that make choice and change easier: the 2012 choice point of opportunity.

The key is that we tend to experience those things that we most identify with. In other words, while dis-ease and healing may both be happening at the same time, we will *feel* that the healing is dominant if this is where we place our focus. We've all been training to do this throughout our lives. We've all had the blessing of families, jobs, friendships, and romance; while simultaneously the suffering and tragedy of the world has raged on. From World War II and the Vietnam War to the more recent violence in Iraq and Afghanistan, those of us not directly in their midst have continued the daily routines of our lives while others were losing theirs in conflict. Both realities were happening at the same time. We were also aware of both.

However, in our everyday routines, when we get up in the morning and fix breakfast to prepare for the day, we generally identify most with what *our* day will bring, rather than what is happening in someone else's. This kind of focus appears to be the secret to surviving the greatest change in the history of humankind as well. If we can identify with the life-affirming changes locally, while doing what is in our power to help others globally, our individual choices become our collective focus for whatever 2012 brings our way.

Our "Bottleneck" of Change

In 2005, the journal *Scientific American* published a special edition entitled "Crossroads for Planet Earth," which identified a number of scenarios, including those described throughout this book, that, if left unchecked, hold the potential to end life as we know it on Earth today.[13] Through various essays and reports, the experts present a strong case for a single, simple fact: our civilization cannot sustain the same path of violent competition, ever-expanding economies, continued depletion of resources, and growing contribution to greenhouse gases and climate change that we've traveled for the last 100 years.

The convergence of so many problems compressed into such a brief period of time is what E. O. Wilson, a Harvard University biologist, calls "the bottleneck" in time. *Scientific American* editor George Musser characterizes Wilson's bottleneck as "a period of maximum stress on natural resources and human ingenuity." The point the journal makes is that while each of the scenarios alone is catastrophic, *all* are happening right now. And now is precisely the time of the 2012 shift.

Time Code 19: There is a consensus among the best minds of our time that the current depletion of natural resources, exponentially growing population, global poverty, and competition for the necessities of life are converging toward a "bottleneck" in time.

Even before we realized the magnitude of such problems, however, one of the great minds of the 20th century had already paved the way to doing so—and he did it with a warning. Recognizing that our global civilization was on a course of expansion, resource consumption, and vast differences of economies that were not sustainable in the long run, Albert Einstein stated the obvious in a single sentence. "We shall require a substantially new manner of thinking," he said, "if mankind is to survive." We'll never know if the conditions of the world of today are what Einstein had in mind when he made this prophetic remark.

Regardless, the sheer number of crises and the magnitude of their consequences are clear indications that we're heading to a convergence point where something must "give." If they are left unchecked, our world could possibly plunge into the time of collapse and suffering envisioned by so many prophecies and predictions. For those living in such a time, it could very possibly seem like the Armageddon described in biblical terms. But both the prophecies and the evidence suggest that none of these things need happen. Although the first Garden of Eden disappeared long ago, armed with our knowledge of what world-age cycles have meant for the past, we can turn the darkest of possibilities into the seeds of the second Eden.

Because of the scientific models and ancient prophecies, we now have the wisdom to see what's before us and to recognize the possibilities. Today we recognize the need for vast and sweeping change in our relationship to the earth, one another, and ourselves. We recognize that everything from the way we live each day to how we use the resources that are disappearing before our eyes must change for us to survive. It's *because* of our ability to recognize this path of destruction and to acknowledge that we do have a choice that the new movements based in holistic, sustainable living and green industries have gained such wide acceptance.

So what does all this mean for 2012? Are we headed into a time of catastrophe or 1,000 years of peace? Are we looking at Armageddon, Eden, or possibly both? The truth is that no one knows for sure.

While the solar eruptions and magnetic reversals of our past were real and our ancestors survived them before, such changes have never happened with 6.5 billion people living in the world. They've certainly never happened with so many dependent upon the technology of power grids, microwave communications, computers, and global-positioning satellites. No one truly knows the full extent of the consequences; how we would deal with them; or precisely what such a monumental experience may mean to life, our emotions, and our bodies.

We do know, however, that ancient humans did experience similar cycles. While the biblical and oral traditions suggest that such a time is certainly not business as usual, the fact is that they lived to record the story, and we're here to read it. New discoveries linking the physics of heart-based focus with what happens in the world tell us that how we experience the transition appears to be largely up to us. The results of the discoveries are conclusive. The way *we feel about* our experiences has a direct effect upon what *we actually* experience.

Time Code 20: The results are conclusive: heart-based focus and living will have a direct effect upon the way we experience 2012 and our time of change.

For our rendezvous with 2012, this suggests that if we live life focused upon all of the bad that could happen, we may miss the very life experiences that could actually *keep* those things from occurring. Conversely, if we recognize our individual power of heart-based focus and understand how that power may be pooled into a collective wave that directly influences the life-sustaining fields of the earth, we may well discover that the hopeful descriptions of what follows 2012 are more than a metaphor. We will have learned that we literally have the power to create a beautiful new world.

The key is that the only way to do so is by working together. A powerful new project, based upon an equally powerful discovery, now paves the way for us to do just that.

Linking Hearts Through Global Coherence

While there is a lot that we don't know about consciousness, there is one thing that we do know for certain: it is made of energy. That energy includes magnetism. While we can explore the magnetic nature of consciousness for another hundred years and still not solve all of its mysteries, we can apply what we've learned so far to help us meet the conditions of a changing world. A growing body of evidence now suggests that Earth's magnetic field plays a powerful role in connecting us with one another, as well as the planet.

In September 2001, two geostationary operational environmental satellites (GOES) orbiting the Earth detected a rise in global magnetism that forever changed the way scientists view our world and us. The GOES-8 and GOES-10 each showed a powerful spike of Earth's magnetic-field strength in the readings they broadcast every 30 minutes. It was the magnitude of the spikes and the time they occurred that first called them to the scientists' attention.

From a location of about 22,300 miles above the equator, GOES-8 detected the first surge, followed by an upward trend in the readings that topped out at nearly 50 units (nanoteslas) higher than any that had been typical for the same time previously. The time was 9 A.M. eastern standard time, 15 minutes after the first plane hit the World Trade Center and about 15 minutes before the second impact.

The correlation between the events and the readings was uncanny. And it was undeniable. In light of the data, two questions had to be asked: *Were the attacks on the World Trade Center and the satellite readings actually related? If so, what was the link?* It's the answer to the second question that sparked the research, and the ambitious initiative, that has followed.

Subsequent studies by Princeton University and the Institute of HeartMath, an innovative nonprofit institution formed in 1991 to pioneer research and development of heart-based technologies, have found that the correlation between the GOES readings and the events of 9/11 are more than coincidences.[14] Following the discovery that the satellites had recorded similar spikes during events of global focus in the past, such as the death of Princess Diana, the factor that seemed to connect the readings was clear: the indications pointed to the human heart.

Specifically, it's the heart-based emotion of the world's population that results from such events that seems to be influencing the magnetic fields of the earth. What makes this discovery so significant is that those fields are now linked to everything from the stability of the climate to the peace between nations.

Among the new findings are two discoveries that give new meaning to what the satellites showed us on September 11, 2001:

— **Discovery 1:** It is well documented that the human heart generates the strongest magnetic field in the body, nearly 5,000 times stronger than that of the brain. This field creates a doughnut-shaped pattern that extends well beyond the physical body and has been measured at distances of five to eight feet from the physical heart. Data suggest that this field may be so large that we end up measuring it in miles; however, it's beyond the scope of the equipment used to detect such fields.

Implication: The heart's magnetic field responds to the quality of emotion that we create in our lives. Just as the intuitive link between feelings and the body seems to suggest, positive emotions increase the physical balance of hormones and heart rhythms, as well as mental clarity and productivity. Just as intuitively, studies show that negative emotions can influence as many as 1,400 biochemical changes in the body that include hormonal imbalance, heart-rhythm chaos, mental "fogginess," and poor performance.[15]

— **Discovery 2:** Certain layers of Earth's atmosphere, along with the earth itself, generate what is now being called a "symphony" of frequencies (between .01 and 300 hertz), some of which overlap the same ones created by the heart in its communication with the brain. It's this apparently ancient and almost holistic relationship between the human heart and the shield that makes life possible on Earth that has led to a beautiful theory and the project exploring it. In the words of HeartMath researchers, the relationship between the human heart and Earth's magnetic field suggests that "strong collective emotion has a measurable impact on the earth's geomagnetic field."[16]

Implication: If we can learn the language of the heart—the same one that Earth's protective magnetic shield recognizes and responds to—then we can participate in the effects that the field has upon all life. This is where such a futuristic-sounding relationship becomes even more exciting. Changes in the magnetic fields that we access through our hearts have been associated with shifts that include the activity of the brain and nervous system, memory, and athletic performance; the ability of plants to create vital nutrients; human mortality from heart conditions; and the numbers of reported cases of depression and suicide, among others.

These two discoveries have opened the door to a new era of understanding our relationship with the earth. From their revelations the question has shifted from *Is there an effect between collective emotion and the earth?* to <u>*Why not?*</u> If a large enough portion of Earth's population were to focus the strongest magnetic field of the human body upon one emotion in the same period of time, it makes tremendous sense that such a focus would affect the portion of the planet that operates in the same range of frequencies as the emotions.

The relationship is clear: A change in the way we feel about ourselves and our world has the potential to affect the world itself. If the change is a positive one, then the effect of the emotions that result should be positive as well. Such a change is known to create coherence between the heart and the brain, and it now appears that the effect extends into the fields that support life on our planet. In the words of the HeartMath researchers, "Regulating emotions is the next frontier in human evolution."[17]

The discovery that we may choose to create more coherence between the magnetic fields of the earth and us has led to one of the most ambitious science-based initiatives in history. The magnitude of the project is profound, the implications epic. In light of the challenges posed by our time in history, this new project, "The Global Coherence Initiative," now makes it possible for anyone to learn the heart's language of coherence.[18] In doing so, it now becomes possible for more people than ever before to participate in the changes that are taking place on the planet.

The key to the Global Coherence project is twofold:

1. In partnership with internationally renowned astrophysicist and nuclear scientist Elizabeth Rauscher, Ph.D., the Institute of HeartMath is developing the Global Coherence Monitoring System, which uses a series of newly designed sensors deployed across the earth to specifically measure the changes in the magnetosphere. The goals of this system are to measure how Earth's magnetic field affects human heart rhythms, brain activity, stress levels, and emotions. Preliminary studies, such as those involving the GOES data, suggest that such effects are part of a two-way relationship. This is where the second part of the initiative comes in.

2. While we know that life on Earth is affected by changes in the planet's magnetic-field strength, the data suggest that life may actually influence the very fields that sustain us. Part two of the Global Coherence Initiative is the ambitious effort headed up by HeartMath to teach individuals how to achieve the coherence that enhances our daily lives and how to know when we are really in a coherent state. The idea is that when a large number of people respond to a potentially destructive global event, such as a hurricane or a tsunami, with a common emotional feeling, it can affect the quality of the common field that connects us.

Just as the human stress experienced by a natural disaster can create an incoherent global stress wave, a positive emotional wave could create a global coherence wave. This perspective is supported by the research at HeartMath, as well as other endeavors such as Princeton University's decadelong Global Consciousness Project.

The consistent data from Princeton have provided compelling evidence that mass human emotion creates global effects that can be documented through the activity of electronic devices.[19]

To put into context precisely what such a project means and why it's important, we need look no further than our understanding of cycles and our place at the close of a great world age. It may be no accident that the Global Coherence Initiative is being developed now, in the first years of the 21st century. It is *now,* at the end of a world age, that experts tell us that we're facing the greatest number and greatest magnitude of challenges in the 5,125 years of recorded human history.

Now we are finding that some of those challenges carry the potential to forever end life as we know it on Earth. But at precisely the same time, we are discovering that we are born with the power to harmonize our bodies with the life-sustaining fields of the earth in such a way that we can alleviate the potential suffering of those challenges. The way to do so is through the silent language of the heart.

Time Code 21: Faced with the greatest number and magnitude of potentially world-ending challenges in 5,125 years of human history, we now discover that the key to our transition lies in our collective feelings about the change.

What a powerful, beautiful, and awesome convergence of circumstances. The way to ease the 2012 world-age transition is to change the way we feel about the world and to do so together. Could we ask for a more perfect scenario?

The Global Coherence Initiative is vitally important to the health and future of our planet. For the first time, we have the ability, the reason, and the technology to transcend the ideas that have separated us in the past and to work together to inspire millions of people to participate in a pivotal moment of change. At the very least, the project holds the blueprint to transcend the traditional boundaries of geography, culture, religion, and belief to unify a global community around a new way of living: the heart-based choices that promote global coherence.

The Meaning of the Time Codes

Throughout the preceding chapters, we have explored the mystery of, and discoveries about, our relationship to time and reality. Within each section, I have highlighted the ideas that help anchor its message in our minds. Following is a summary of those ideas, offered in the order that they've appeared throughout the book. Individually, they are interesting and will serve as a reminder of the importance of each section. Collectively, they tell the story of our relationship to time, cycles, and the mystery of 2012.

Just as Appendix A describes the way an algorithm lays the foundation for a computer's code to do its work, the keys that follow may be thought of as the code that spells out our relationship with time in a way that's meaningful, practical, and easy to follow. As with any code, the keys are in a sequence for a reason. Simply put: just as the instructions to change the oil in a vehicle work only when they are followed in a precise order, our keys to time, cycles, and 2012 make sense only if each one is understood before moving to the next.

For this reason, I invite you to consider the following sequence of the Time Codes one at a time. Work with it until it becomes comfortable and makes sense to you. Together, these codes can become your personal guide to greet the change of 2012 and the years beyond.

The Time Codes

Time Code 1: We're living the completion of a 5,125-year-long cycle of time—a *world age*—that the ancient Maya calculated would end with the winter solstice on December 21, 2012.

Time Code 2: Our ancestors recorded their experience of the last "end of time," showing beyond a reasonable doubt that the close of one world age is the beginning of the next, and not the end of the world.

Time Code 3: New discoveries show that we can think of time as an essence that follows the same rhythms and cycles that govern everything from particles to galaxies.

Time Code 4: We can think of the *things* that happen in time as *places* within cycles—points that can be measured, calculated, and predicted.

Time Code 5: If we know where we are in a cycle, then we know what to expect when it repeats.

Time Code 6: The Time Code Calculator shows us when we can expect the *conditions* of the past to repeat, not the events themselves.

Time Code 7: Ancient traditions divide Earth's 25,625-year orbit through the 12 constellations of the zodiac—the precession of the equinoxes—into five world ages lasting 5,125 years each.

Time Code 8: The position of the earth within our galaxy creates powerful changes that signal the end of one world age and the beginning of the next. The knowledge of these cyclic changes is known as the doctrine of World Ages.

Time Code 9: The Vedic traditions describe an extended time of devotion, expressed in action (bhakti), that began around 1898 and lasts well beyond the 2012 Mayan end date.

Time Code 10: The present world age began on August 11, 3114 B.C. Its end is signaled by the rare alignment of our solar system with the core of the Milky Way galaxy on December 21, 2012—an event that last occurred approximately 26,000 years ago.

Time Code 11: Nature uses a few simple, self-similar, and repeating patterns—fractals—to build energy and atoms into the familiar forms of everything from roots, rivers, and trees to rocks, mountains, and us.

Time Code 12: Everything we need to understand the universe lives in the simplicity of each piece of it.

Time Code 13: Our knowledge of repeating cycles allows us to pinpoint times in the future when we can expect to see the repeating conditions of the past.

Time Code 14: The Time Code Calculator can pinpoint personal cycles of love and hurt, as well as global cycles of war and peace.

Time Code 15: Patterns identified for an earlier time in history tend to repeat themselves with greater intensity at later dates.

Time Code 16: Using a template of human events, Earth events, and celestial events gives us a consistent way to view the past as a realistic window to 2012.

Time Code 17: There is nothing in the geological record to suggest that Earth's magnetic fields will reverse before or immediately following the 2012 cycle end date.

Time Code 18: The Time Code template shows that the human, Earth, and celestial conditions of today are in the same range as the key reference dates of the past. In other words, the changes happening now are just what we'd expect for the end of a world age.

Time Code 19: There is a consensus among the best minds of our time that the current depletion of natural resources, exponentially growing population, global poverty, and competition for the necessities of life are converging toward a "bottleneck" in time.

Time Code 20: The results are conclusive: Heart-based focus and heart-based living will have a direct effect upon the way we experience 2012 and our time of change.

Time Code 21: Faced with the greatest number and magnitude of potentially world-ending challenges in 5,125 years of human history, we now discover that the key to our transition lies in our collective feelings about the change.

The Once-in-26,000-Years Opportunity

When you ask the descendants of the Maya why their ancestors disappeared long ago, they usually tell a story that sounds more like a plot from the science-fiction film and television series *Stargate* than an indigenous history. They will begin with an account of the mysterious timekeepers who tracked the cycles of the universe with unprecedented accuracy more than a thousand years ago. Then, for a reason that only the ancient prophet-scientists could know, they left their temples, observatories, and pyramids forever. Just as mysteriously as they appeared, they walked into the jungles of the Yucatán and returned to wherever it was that they had come from. Regardless of what their story means to us today, it's clear that whoever those original Maya were, they knew something in their time that we are just beginning to understand in ours.

The key to their message is that their secret was more than the precise representations of time on a slab of stone. The one element of their wisdom that they could not inscribe as a hieroglyphic message is precisely the piece that gives meaning to the end of our world age today. From their viewpoint of Earth as a mirror of the cosmos, they regarded the great cycle that ends on 2012 as the end of an incubation period, the fractal "gestation" of human consciousness that is so beautifully described by people like John Major Jenkins and José Argüelles. As any birth is the end of the pregnancy and the beginning of new life, the Maya viewed our emergence into a post-2012 world as the beginning of a new cycle of history, complete with all of the opportunities described in this book . . . and more.

From these perspectives, the solstice on December 21, 2012, becomes a powerful window for our collective emergence into our greatest potential. Such a moment is so rare that we have been preparing for it since the end of the last world age, and it will be another 26,000 years before the same opportunity cycles around again for our descendants.

Time Code 22: December 21, 2012, is a rare and powerful window of opportunity for our collective emergence into our greatest potential.

The possibilities of such an emergence bring to mind the ancient accounts of the Garden of Eden, a place that once held all of the possibilities of our greatest joys and heartfelt desires. If we're to believe the calendars, myths, and prophecies, it is just such a potential that awaits us following 2012. We could create a second Eden that picks up where the first one left off.

Biblical correlations do suggest, in fact, that the last time an Eden appeared upon the earth was about 5,000 years ago, at the end of the last great cycle. During that time, the planet's inhabitants had everything they needed to live in balance with the earth, enjoying vital, healthy lives. As the choices of our post-Eden ancestors planted the seed events for everything that would unfold as the cycle that followed, they set into motion the patterns that define our world today. Some, such as forgiveness and peace, serve as powerful reminders of what is possible in our lives; while others, such as betrayal and war, have become the great challenges that divide us as people, families, and nations.

From cycles of weather to the balance of carbon dioxide between the oceans and the atmosphere, nature shows us that a pattern will repeat until something new replaces it. The change that accompanies the 2012 convergence of cycles is a rare opportunity to wipe away the patterns that we've outgrown from the past. At the same time, it's also a precious choice point to set healthy, new patterns in place for our future and the future that belongs to our children . . . and to *theirs*.

It's an undeniable fact that in the presence of the greatest challenges to our world, we are also changed as people. Can we recognize that the greatest threats to our familiar way of life are really nature's "nudge" toward a new way of being? As we witness the chaos that accompanies the perfect alignment with our galaxy's core, are we ready to receive the greatest gift of all: the inner change that comes from responding to life's challenges with the cooperation and nurturing of a heart-based way of living? What instructions will we leave from our time to those who will go through the next world age and remember us as their ancestors?

We've already answered these questions in our hearts. Now is the time for us to live what we've chosen as we emerge from the mystery of 2012 into a new world age. The stage is set. The choice is ours. The cosmos is waiting.

$ $ $

*"Time is the substance I am made of.
Time is a river which sweeps me along, but I am the river;
it is a tiger that devours me, but I am the tiger;
it is a fire that consumes me, but I am the fire."*

— Jorge Luis Borges (1899–1986), writer

APPENDIX A

THE TIME CODE CALCULATOR

The Time Code Calculator is a user-friendly tool that gives us easy access to the patterns that unfold as nature's cycles—the same patterns that govern much of the universe and life. It allows us to peer into the timeline of history in a way that in many respects mimics the vision of prophets and remote viewers.

Just as such gifted seers can identify the events that are probable at a given time, the Time Code Calculator shows us when we can expect the *conditions* of the past to play out again as our present or our future. The reason the program works is because of the nature of cycles themselves. Because they *are* cycles, they repeat. And because those of history are made of space and time, when the time repeats, the conditions of the space that it carries do, also.

It's important to emphasize that just as the future vision of a prophet or remote viewer is subject to change based upon what happens within the timeline, the Time

Code Calculator cannot take into account the effect of consciousness and choice. It can only show us when the conditions of the past will appear again. The outcome depends on whether or not the conditions play out to completion. The choices that we make along the time-line of the cycle can create a new path and a new time-line with a new outcome. This is the beauty of knowing where we are in a cycle.

What makes the Time Code Calculator so useful is that in addition to giving us a "heads-up" so we know what to expect, it also shows us when our choices of change have the greatest potential for success. This is where the marriage of science and spirituality takes on a practical application that is unlike anything we've seen in the past.

If we can use the science of cycles to find the times that are ripe for change, and if we can use the spiritual traditions of our past to trigger peaceful and life-affirming outcomes, then we suddenly have a powerful new way to think of ourselves and our world. It's all based upon cycles and possibilities, nature's patterns that can be known and predicted.

Three Ways to Use the Calculator

Once we begin to think of time in terms of repeating cycles, the steps to find the key points of change become obvious. If we know (a) when the cycle begins, (b) when it ends, and (c) when the first event (seed event) that sets the pattern into motion within the cycle occurs, we can calculate the repeat points for the pattern that the event establishes for the portion of the cycle that remains. With a few simple calculations, we can use the Time Code Calculator as our window into such cycles in one of three ways: Mode 1, Mode 2, and Mode 3. With each mode, we can answer a different question.

Mode 1: When Can We Expect Something That Has Happened in the Past to Happen Again?

In this mode, we can identify a seed event in our personal or collective *past* and calculate when the conditions created by it will repeat in our future. It can be anything—good or bad—from the great joys of love, romance, success, and peace to the great tragedies of loss, suffering, and war.

What's important here is that the seed event begins the cycle. As cycles repeat in intervals that follow the rhythms of the mysterious ratio of phi (.618), we can apply this number to the events of the past to discover when we can expect to see the same conditions again. Whether the cycle lasts for a moment or for thousands of years, *because it is a cycle* the conditions that it carries will repeat within the larger one that spawned it—our present world age of 5,125 years.

Mode 2: What Date in the Past Holds the Conditions We Can Expect for the Future?

In this mode, we can identify a key event in our personal or collective *future* and look back into the past to find the last time the same conditions existed in the cycle. Chapter 6 illustrates this by using the Time Code Calculator to identify what we can realistically expect for 2012. By using the phi ratio described previously in Mode 1, we can pinpoint a concrete date in our past that is the seed for what we can expect in 2012.

The principles of cycles and time appear to be universal. For this reason, they apply to the things that happen in our personal lives as well as what occurs on a global scale. Mode 3 of the Time Code Calculator is a powerful aid to help us identify precisely such cycles and when we can expect the conditions that we experienced at one point in our lives to repeat at a later time.

For ease of reading in the main text, I placed the explanations and calculations for Mode 1 and Mode 2 in this section of the appendices. The calculations and application of Mode 3 are a little different—they aren't dealing with vast cycles of time like 5,000-year world ages. Instead, they are designed to find patterns that occur within the 100 or so years of a human lifetime. Because the calculations are briefer and simpler, and because many readers will want to apply them immediately to their own lives, I have left them in the text of Chapter 5. It's there that you will find the reasons for discovering personal cycles and instructions that describe how to use Time Code Calculator Mode 3. With these things in mind, a brief explanation of Mode 3 follows.

Mode 3: When Can We Expect the Conditions of a Personal Experience, Either Positive or Negative, to Repeat in Our Lives?

In Mode 3, we can calculate the times in our lives for the repeating conditions of an emotional experience that left a powerful imprint in our hearts. The conditions can range from the elation of an accomplishment to the hurt from a loss. The key in this mode is that the÷experiences that create the greatest magnitude of feeling tend to become the seed events for similar conditions, and similar patterns, to repeat at cyclic intervals. From our greatest loves to our deepest hurts, the experiences from one time in life impact other relationships after the seed is planted in ways that are amazing to see.

Building the Time Code Programs

The word *program* suggests that the calculations made by the Time Code Calculator are part of an automated system, a piece of software that makes everything easy and does all of the mathematics for us. And they are. While an automated and user-friendly version of the Time Code Calculator is available for your use on my Website (**www.greggbraden.com**), the calculations themselves are easy and may be done with a simple household calculator.

Just as any computer program may be described using an algorithm (the step-by-step procedure that tells the programmer how to build the software), so, too, can the Time Code Calculator. In the following sections, you will find:

- Step-by-step instructions (an algorithm) for each mode in words

- The instructions applied to actual examples discussed in the book, such as the events of September 11, 2001, which are described in Chapter 1

Note 1: Conversion to absolute dates. For ease of use, the "modern" dates (Gregorian dates) are converted to absolute dates in terms of the cycle itself. For dates after the year 0, this conversion is accomplished by adding 3113 (the number of years between the beginning of the Mayan great cycle in 3114 B.C. and the year 0) to the seed event (*example for the year 2012:* 3113 + 2012 = 5125).

Note 2: Conversion of decimals to months. Some of the calculated dates create numbers to the right of the decimal point. These are portions (fractions) of the year indicated and may be converted into the corresponding month for greater accuracy using the following formula.

- Number to right of decimal = (month ÷ 12) × 100

- (Percent of the year × 12) ÷ 100 = month of the year

Example: August of the year 2001 translates to (8 ÷ 12) × 100 = 66.66 percent of the year or 2001.67. The key here is to think of the decimal that is expressed in tenths as a portion of the 12 months that are possible. For convenience, I have included a reference chart of the decimal-to-month calculations for numbers 1 to 12 below:

Portion of Year	Equivalent Month
.08	January
.16	February
.25	March
.33	April
.42	May
.50	June
.58	July
.67	August
.75	September
.83	October
.91	November
.99	December

Note 3: These formulas calculate *zones of time* that make the events possible, rather than the specific date and time that an event will take place. So in our example of September 11, 2001, as a repeat of the cycle that began in 1941, the calculations show a lag between the Time Code calculation and the actual event. The key is that the calculator clearly pinpoints the time(s) of the repeating pattern within the greater 5,125-year cycle. As the discussion of choice points in Chapter 7 illustrates, human choices can alter the course of events, even when the conditions that support those events are present.

And this fact is precisely why the Time Code Calculator is so valuable. It gives us the heads-up as to when we can expect such conditions to be present.

Mode 1: When Can We Expect Something That Has Happened in the Past to Happen Again?

To answer this question, we need two pieces of information:

- *Input 1*: The target date in the past when an obvious pattern (the seed) occurred

- *Input 2*: The total length of the cycle that tells us where we are in present time

— *The Time Code algorithm described*: Always apply these same eight steps:

Step 1: Identify modern (Gregorian) date of seed event.

Step 2: Convert the Gregorian date to an "absolute" date in terms of the total cycle. This is an optional step and is done for ease of calculations.

Step 3: Calculate the lapsed portion of the cycle represented by the seed date (divide the absolute date by the years in the cycle).

Step 4: Calculate the phi ratio of the cycle's lapsed portion (multiply by .618).

Step 5: Calculate the cycle balance from the seed to the end.

Step 6: Apply phi ratio of lapsed cycle to the balance of the cycle to find the interval in years between the seed date and the next time it repeats.

Step 7: Add the interval to the absolute date to find next repeat (new seed date).

Step 8: Convert back to Gregorian date.

— *The Time Code algorithm applied to conditions:* We'll be using four examples to demonstrate Time Code calculations for repeated conditions.

Example 1—*Find:* When can we expect the *first* cyclic conditions of "surprise" and "attack" on America to repeat?

- *Input 1*: The target year and month in the past when the first obvious pattern of "surprise" and "attack" upon America (the seed) occurred: **1941.99 (December 1941)**

- *Input 2*: The total length of the cycle that tells us where we are in present time: **5,125 years**

Step 1: Identify modern (Gregorian) date of seed event (S_1).
1941.99

Step 2: Convert event (S_1) to absolute date (A_1).
1941.99 + 3113 = 5054.99 (A_1)

Step 3: Calculate lapsed portion of cycle (L_1) as a ratio of (A_1) / total cycle length 5125.
5054.99/5125 = .986 (L_1)

Step 4: Calculate phi (L_{1phi}) of lapsed cycle (L_1).
.618 × .986 = .609 (L_{1phi})

Step 5: Calculate cycle balance (B_1) as total cycle length (A_1).
5125 − 5054.99 = 70.01 years (B_1)

Step 6: Apply phi ratio of lapsed cycle (L_1) to the balance of the cycle (B_1) to find the interval in years between the seed date and the next time it repeats (I_1).
70.01 × .609 = 42.64 years (I_1)

Step 7: Add the interval (I_1) to the original seed date to find the next repeat (new seed date).
5054.99 + 42.64 = 5097.63

Step 8: Convert back to Gregorian date.
5097.63 − 3113 = 1984.63 (August 1984)

Meaning: This date translates to August 1984. The date for the destruction of KAL Flight 007 and the events described in Chapter 1 occurred in September 1983, less than a year earlier. The span *between* September 1983 and February 1984 is documented as one of the most tense periods of the war between the two superpowers. Post–Cold War documents reveal that it was precisely during this time frame, and within 30 days of the date predicted by the Time Code Calculator, that a preemptive nuclear strike was being planned against the United States.

The Time Code calculations demonstrate that the plans for a surprise attack on America—the *first fractal* of the pattern that was created in 1941—are part of the cyclic pattern that can be known and calculated. As described in the text and shown in the following example, the second fractal pattern occurred in September 2001.

Example 2—*Find:* Date when we can expect the *second* cyclic conditions of "surprise" and "attack" on America to repeat

- *Input 1*: The first target year following the seed of 1941 when an obvious pattern of "surprise" and "attack" upon America (the seed) occurred: **1984.63 (August 1984)**

- *Input 2*: The total length of the cycle that tells us where we are in present time: **5,125 years**

275

Step 1: Identify modern (Gregorian) date of seed event (S_1).
1984.63

Step 2: Convert event (S_1) to absolute date (A_1).
1984.63 + 3113 = 5097.63 (A_1)

Step 3: Calculate lapsed portion of cycle (L_1) as a ratio
of (A_1) / total cycle length 5125.
5097.63/5125 = .995 (L_1)

Step 4: Calculate phi (L_{1phi}) of lapsed cycle (L_1).
.618 × .995 = .615 (L_{1phi})

Step 5: Calculate cycle balance (B_1) as total cycle length (A_1).
5125 – 5097.63 = 27.37 years (B_1)

Step 6: Apply phi ratio of lapsed cycle (L_1) to the balance of the cycle (B_1) to find the interval between the seed date and the next time it repeats (I_1).
27.37 × .615 = 16.83 years (I_1)

Step 7: Add the interval (I_1) to the original seed date (S_1) to find the next repeat (new seed date).
5097.63 + 16.83 = 5114.46

Step 8: Convert back to Gregorian date.
5114.46 – 3113 = 2001.46 (June 2001)

Meaning: This date translates to June 2001. It falls well within the range of the time that the attack is believed to have been in the planning phase, and it is less than three months before the date that the World Trade Center and Pentagon attacks actually occurred. There is only a 1-in-61,500, or .0000162 percent, chance of determining that 2001 would be the year within the present world-age cycle of such an attack.

Example 3—*Find:* Date when we can expect the *third* cyclic conditions of "surprise" and "attack" on America to repeat

- *Input 1:* The first target year following the seed of 1941 when an obvious pattern of "surprise" and "attack" upon America (the seed) occurred: **2001.46 (June 2001)**

- *Input 2:* The total length of the cycle that tells us where we are in present time: **5,125 years**

Step 1: Identify modern (Gregorian) date of seed event (S_1).
2001.46

Step 2: Convert event (S_1) to absolute date (A_1).
2001.46 + 3113 = 5114.46 (A_1)

Step 3: Calculate lapsed portion of cycle (L_1) as a ratio of (A_1) / total cycle length 5125.
5114.46/5125 = .998 (L_1)

Step 4: Calculate phi (L_{1phi}) of lapsed cycle (L_1).
$.618 \times .998 = .617$ (L_{1phi})

Step 5: Calculate cycle balance (B_1) as total cycle length (A_1).
$5125 - 5114.46 = 10.54$ years (B_1)

Step 6: Apply phi ratio of lapsed cycle (L_1) to the balance of the cycle (B_1) to find the interval between the seed date and the next time it repeats (I_1).
$10.54 \times .617 = 6.50$ years (I_1)

Step 7: Add the interval (I_1) to the original seed date (S_1) to find the next repeat (new seed date).
$5114.46 + 6.50 = 5120.96$

Step 8: Convert back to Gregorian date.
$5120.96 - 3113 = 2007.96$ (December 2007)

Example 4—*Find:* Date when we can expect the *fourth* cyclic conditions of "surprise" and "attack" on America to repeat

- *Input 1:* The first target year following the seed of 1941 when an obvious pattern of "surprise" and "attack" upon America (the seed) occurred: **2007.96 (December 2007)**

- *Input 2*: The total length of the cycle that tells us where we are in present time: **5,125 years**

Step 1: Identify modern (Gregorian) date of seed event (S_1).
2007.96

Step 2: Convert event (S_1) to absolute date (A_1).
2007.96 + 3113 = 5120.96 (A_1)

Step 3: Calculate lapsed portion of cycle (L_1) as a ratio of (A_1) / total cycle length 5125.
5120.96/5125 = .999 (L_1)

Step 4: Calculate phi (L_{1phi}) of lapsed cycle (L_1).
.618 × .999 = .617 (L_{1phi})

Step 5: Calculate cycle balance (B_1) as total cycle length (A_1).
5125 – 5120.96 = 4.04 years (B_1)

Step 6: Apply phi ratio of lapsed cycle (L_1) to the balance of the cycle (B_1) to find the interval between the seed date and the next time it repeats (I_1).
4.04 × .617 = 2.49 years (I_1)

Step 7: Add the interval (I_1) to the original seed date (S_1) to find the next repeat (new seed date).
5120.96 + 2.49 = 5123.45

Step 8: Convert back to Gregorian date.
5123.45 – 3113 = 2010.45 (June 2010)

Meaning: This date translates to June 2010. It is the return of the seed cycle planted in 1941, so it also identifies the greatest opportunity to heal the conditions that led to the events of the original seed. The weeks and months preceding this date hold the greatest opportunity for the conscious easing of tension and creation of peace from the last repeat of 2007, until the next return.

Mode 2: What Date in the Past Holds the Conditions We Can Expect for a Date in the Future?

To answer this question we need two pieces of information:

- *Input 1*: The target date in the future that is in question

- *Input 2*: The total length of the cycle that tells us where we are in present time

— *The Time Code algorithm described:* Always apply these same five steps:

Step 1: Identify modern (Gregorian) date of target event.

Step 2: Convert the Gregorian date to an "absolute" date in terms of the total cycle for ease of calculations (optional).

Step 3: Calculate the phi ratio of the absolute date (multiply by .618).

Step 4: Subtract the phi ratio date from the target date.

Step 5: Convert back to Gregorian date.

— *The Time Code algorithm applied to the 2012 end date:* Here's an example of how to search backward through time for seed conditions.

Example 1—*Find:* Date in the past that holds the conditions can we expect for the 2012 end date

- *Input 1*: The target date in question: **2012**

- *Input 2*: The total length of the cycle that tells us where we are in present time: **5,125 years**

Step 1: Identify modern (Gregorian) date of target date (T_1).
2012

Step 2: Convert target date (T_1) to absolute date (A_1).
2012 + 3113 = 5125 (A_1)

Step 3:   Calculate phi (L_{1phi}) of absolute date (A_1).
.618 × 5125 = 3167.25 (L_{1phi})

Step 4:   Subtract the phi ratio date (L_{1phi}) from the target date (A_1).
5125 − 3167.25 = 1957.75

Step 5:   Convert back to Gregorian date.
1957.75 − 3113 = −1155.25 (1155 B.C.)

Meaning: The result of this calculation is a negative number, indicating that it is a date before the time of Christ (B.C.) in the historical notation. As noted in Chapter 6, this is precisely the year that witnessed the collapse of one of the greatest civilizations of the past, Egypt's 20th Dynasty. The parallels between the conditions of 1155 B.C. and the 2012 close of the present great cycle are unmistakable. By applying the nature's language of cycles, the Time Code Calculator identifies the single date in the past 5,125 years that holds the key to what we can expect for our near future.

� ✻ ✻ ✻

APPENDIX B

GLOBAL FLASH POINTS FOR THE FUTURE

We have seen how the cycles of time and events repeat in rhythmic intervals that follow the mysterious number phi (.618). Knowing this, we can apply the seed events that posed the greatest threats to our world in the 20th century to discover when we can expect the conditions they created to appear again. We can use our knowledge of such conditions as a window of opportunity to avoid in the present the outcomes of the past.

Knowing when the patterns of the last century's global wars are primed to repeat gives us the edge to avoid new conflicts based upon the old patterns. If we know that we're in a year when the cycle that led to World War II is repeating, for example, then we also know that we're in the time when it is wise to use a little extra care and sensitivity when dealing with the inevitable disagreements that arise between nations over resources, borders, and human rights.

Using Mode 1 of the Time Code Calculator, we can

identify when such a cycle begins in order to calculate when the conditions it created will repeat in our future. What's important here is that the seed event is what begins the cycle.

Mode 1: When Can We Expect Something That Has Happened in the Past to Happen Again?

To answer this question we need two pieces of information:

- *Input 1*: The target date in the past when an obvious pattern (the seed) occurred

- *Input 2*: The total length of the cycle that tells us where we are in present time

— *The Time Code algorithm described:* Always use the following eight steps:

Step 1: Identify modern (Gregorian) date of seed event.

Step 2: Convert the Gregorian date to an "absolute" date in terms of the total cycle. This is an optional step and is done for ease of calculations. For dates after the year 0, the conversion is accomplished by adding 3113 (the number of years in the 5,125-year world-age cycle before the year 0) to the seed event (*example for the year 2012:* 3113 + 2012 = 5125).

Step 3: Calculate the lapsed portion of the cycle represented by the seed date.

Step 4: Calculate the phi ratio of the cycle's lapsed portion.

Step 5: Calculate the cycle balance from the seed to the end.

Step 6: Apply phi ratio of lapsed cycle to the balance of the cycle to find the interval in years between the seed date and the next time it repeats.

Step 7: Add the interval to the absolute date to find next repeat (new seed date).

Step 8: Convert back to Gregorian date.

— *The Time Code algorithm applied to key dates:* We'll be using 13 examples to demonstrate Time Code calculations for future events.

Example 1—*Find:* First cycle-repeat date for the conditions of 1945 (atomic weapons and end of war)

- *Input 1*: The seed date for global war in the 20th century: **1945**

- *Input 2*: The total length of the cycle that tells us where we are in present time: **5,125 years**

Step 1:   Identify modern (Gregorian) date of seed event (S_1).
1945

Step 2:   Convert event (S_1) to absolute date (A_1).
1945 + 3113 = 5058 (A_1)

Step 3:   Calculate lapsed portion of cycle (L_1) as a ratio of (A_1) / total cycle length 5125.
5058/5125 = .987 (L_1)

Step 4:   Calculate phi (L_{1phi}) of lapsed cycle (L_1).
.618 × .987 = .610 (L_{1phi})

Step 5:   Calculate cycle balance (B_1) as total cycle length (A_1).
5125 − 5058 = 67 years (B_1)

Step 6:   Apply phi ratio of lapsed cycle (L_1) to the balance of the cycle (B_1) to find the interval in years between the seed date and the next time it repeats (I_1).
67 × .610 = 40.87 years (I_1)

Step 7:   Add the interval (I_1) to the original seed date to find the next repeat (new seed date).
5058 + 40.87 = 5098.87

Step 8: Convert back to Gregorian date.
5098.87 – 3113 = 1985.87 (November 1985)

Example 2—*Find:* Second cycle-repeat date for the conditions of 1945 (atomic weapons and end of war)

- *Input 1*: The seed date for global war in the 20th century: **1985.87**

- *Input 2*: The total length of the cycle that tells us where we are in present time: **5,125 years**

Step 1: Identify modern (Gregorian) date of seed event (S_1).
1985.87

Step 2: Convert event (S_1) to absolute date (A_1).
1985.87 + 3113 = 5098.87 (A_1)

Step 3: Calculate lapsed portion of cycle (L_1) as a ratio of (A_1) / total cycle length 5125.
5098.87/5125 = .995 (L_1)

Step 4: Calculate phi (L_{1phi}) of lapsed cycle (L_1).
.618 × .995 = .615 (L_{1phi})

Step 5: Calculate cycle balance (B_1) as total cycle length – (A_1).
5125 – 5098.87 = 26.13 years (B_1)

Step 6: Apply phi ratio of lapsed cycle (L_1) to the balance of the cycle (B_1) to find the interval in years between the seed date and the next time it repeats (I_1).
26.13 × .615 = 16.07 years (I_1)

Step 7: Add the interval (I_1) to the original seed date to find the next repeat (new seed date).
5098.87 + 16.07 = 5114.94

Step 8: Convert back to Gregorian date.
5114.94 – 3113 = 2001.94 (December 2001)

Example 3—*Find:* Third cycle-repeat date for the conditions of 1945 (atomic weapons and end of war)

- *Input 1*: The seed date for global war in the 20th century: **2001.94**

- *Input 2*: The total length of the cycle that tells us where we are in present time: **5,125 years**

Step 1: Identify modern (Gregorian) date of seed event (S_1).
2001.94

Step 2: Convert event (S_1) to absolute date (A_1).
2001.94 + 3113 = 5114.94 (A_1)

Step 3:   Calculate lapsed portion of cycle (L_1) as a ratio of (A_1) / total cycle length 5125.
5114.94/5125 = .998 (L_1)

Step 4:   Calculate phi (L_{1phi}) of lapsed cycle (L_1).
.618 × .998 = .617 (L_{1phi})

Step 5:   Calculate cycle balance (B_1) as total cycle length – (A_1).
5125 – 5114.94 = 10.06 years (B_1)

Step 6:   Apply phi ratio of lapsed cycle (L_1) to the balance of the cycle (B_1) to find the interval in years between the seed date and the next time it repeats (I_1).
10.06 × .617 = 6.21 years (I_1)

Step 7:   Add the interval (I_1) to the original seed date to find the next repeat (new seed date).
5114.94 + 6.21 = 5121.15

Step 8:   Convert back to Gregorian date.
5121.15 – 3113 = 2008.15 (February 2008)

Example 4—*Find:* Fourth cycle-repeat date for the conditions of 1945 (atomic weapons and end of war)

• *Input 1*: The seed date for global war in the 20th century: **2008.15**

- *Input 2*: The total length of the cycle that tells us where we are in present time: **5,125 years**

Step 1: Identify modern (Gregorian) date of seed event (S_1).
2008.15

Step 2: Convert event (S_1) to absolute date (A_1).
2008.15 + 3113 = 5121.15 (A_1)

Step 3: Calculate lapsed portion of cycle (L_1) as a ratio of (A_1) / total cycle length 5125.
5121.15/5125 = .999 (L_1)

Step 4: Calculate phi (L_{1phi}) of lapsed cycle (L_1).
.618 × .999 = .617 (L_{1phi})

Step 5: Calculate cycle balance (B_1) as total cycle length – (A_1).
5125 – 5121.15 = 3.85 years (B_1)

Step 6: Apply phi ratio of lapsed cycle (L_1) to the balance of the cycle (B_1) to find the interval in years between the seed date and the next time it repeats (I_1).
3.85 × .617 = 2.38 years (I_1)

Step 7: Add the interval (I_1) to the original seed date to find the next repeat (new seed date).
5121.15 + 2.38 = 5123.53

Step 8: Convert back to Gregorian date.
$$5123.53 - 3113 = 2010.53 \text{ (July 2010)}$$

Example 5—*Find:* First cycle-repeat date for the conditions of global war that began in 1914.

- *Input 1:* The seed date for global war in the 20th century: **1914**

- *Input 2:* The total length of the cycle that tells us where we are in present time: **5,125 years**

Step 1: Identify modern (Gregorian) date of seed event (S_1).
1914

Step 2: Convert event (S_1) to absolute date (A_1).
1914 + 3113 = 5027 (A_1)

Step 3: Calculate lapsed portion of cycle (L_1) as a ratio of (A_1) / total cycle length 5125.
5027/5125 = .981 (L_1)

Step 4: Calculate phi (L_{1phi}) of lapsed cycle (L_1).
.618 × .981 = .606 (L_{1phi})

Step 5: Calculate cycle balance (B_1) as total cycle length − (A_1).
5125 − 5027 = 98 years (B_1)

Step 6: Apply phi ratio of lapsed cycle (L_1) to the balance of the cycle (B_1) to find the interval in years between the seed date and the next time it repeats (I_1).
98 × .606 = 59.39 years (I_1)

Step 7: Add the interval (I_1) to the original seed date to find the next repeat (new seed date).
5027 + 59.39 = 5086.39

Step 8: Convert back to Gregorian date.
5086.39 – 3113 = 1973.39 (May 1973)

Example 6—*Find:* Second cycle-repeat date for the conditions of global war that began in 1914

- *Input 1:* The seed date for global war in the 20th century: **1973.39**

- *Input 2:* The total length of the cycle that tells us where we are in present time: **5,125 years**

Step 1: Identify modern (Gregorian) date of seed event (S_1).
1973.39

Step 2: Convert event (S_1) to absolute date (A_1).
1973.39 + 3113 = 5086.39 (A_1)

Step 3: Calculate lapsed portion of cycle (L_1) as a ratio of (A_1) / total cycle length 5125.
5086.39/5125 = .992 (L_1)

Step 4: Calculate phi (L_{1phi}) of lapsed cycle (L_1).
.618 × .992 = .613 (L_{1phi})

Step 5: Calculate cycle balance (B_1) as total cycle length − (A_1).
5125 − 5086.39 = 38.61 years (B_1)

Step 6: Apply phi ratio of lapsed cycle (L_1) to the balance of the cycle (B_1) to find the interval in years between the seed date and the next time it repeats (I_1).
38.61 × .613 = 23.67 years (I_1)

Step 7: Add the interval (I_1) to the original seed date to find the next repeat (new seed date).
5086.39 + 23.67 = 5110.06

Step 8: Convert back to Gregorian date.
5110.06 − 3113 = 1997.06 (January 1997)

Example 7—*Find:* Third cycle-repeat date for the conditions of global war that began in 1914

- *Input 1*: The seed date for global war in the 20th century: **1997.06**

- *Input 2*: The total length of the cycle that tells us where we are in present time: **5,125 years**

Step 1: Identify modern (Gregorian) date of seed event (S_1).
1997.06

Step 2: Convert event (S_1) to absolute date (A_1).
1997.06 + 3113 = 5110.06 (A_1)

Step 3: Calculate lapsed portion of cycle (L_1) as a ratio of (A_1) / total cycle length 5125.
5110.06/5125 = .997 (L_1)

Step 4: Calculate phi (L_{1phi}) of lapsed cycle (L_1).
.618 × .997 = .616 (L_{1phi})

Step 5: Calculate cycle balance (B_1) as total cycle length – (A_1).
5125 – 5110.06 = 14.94 years (B_1)

Step 6: Apply phi ratio of lapsed cycle (L_1) to the balance of the cycle (B_1) to find the interval in years between the seed date and the next time it repeats (I_1).
14.94 × .616 = 9.20 years (I_1)

Step 7: Add the interval (I_1) to the original seed date to find the next repeat (new seed date).
5110.06 + 9.20 = 5119.26

Step 8: Convert back to Gregorian date.
5119.26 − 3113 = 2006.26 (April 2006)

Example 8—*Find:* Fourth cycle-repeat date for the conditions of global war that began in 1914

- *Input 1:* The seed date for global war in the 20th century: **2006.26**

- *Input 2:* The total length of the cycle that tells us where we are in present time: **5,125 years**

Step 1: Identify modern (Gregorian) date of seed event (S_1).
2006.26

Step 2: Convert event (S_1) to absolute date (A_1).
2006.26 + 3113 = 5119.26 (A_1)

Step 3: Calculate lapsed portion of cycle (L_1) as a ratio of (A_1) / total cycle length 5125.
5119.26/5125 = .999 (L_1)

Step 4: Calculate phi (L_{1phi}) of lapsed cycle (L_1).
.618 × .999 = .617 (L_{1phi})

Step 5: Calculate cycle balance (B_1) as total cycle length − (A_1).
5125 − 5119.26 = 5.74 years (B_1)

Step 6: Apply phi ratio of lapsed cycle (L_1) to the balance of the cycle (B_1) to find the interval in years between the seed date and the next time it repeats (I_1).

5.74 × .617 = 3.54 years (I_1)

Step 7: Add the interval (I_1) to the original seed date to find the next repeat (new seed date).

5119.26 + 3.54 = 5122.80

Step 8: Convert back to Gregorian date.

5122.80 − 3113 = 2009.80 (October 2009)

Example 9—*Find:* Fifth cycle-repeat date for the conditions of global war that began in 1914

- *Input 1:* The seed date for global war in the 20th century: **2009.80**

- *Input 2:* The total length of the cycle that tells us where we are in present time: **5,125 years**

Step 1: Identify modern (Gregorian) date of seed event (S_1).

2009.80

Step 2: Convert event (S_1) to absolute date (A_1).

2009.80 + 3113 = 5122.80 (A_1)

Step 3: Calculate lapsed portion of cycle (L_1) as a ratio of (A_1) / total cycle length 5125.
5122.80/5125 = 1.00 (L_1)

Step 4: Calculate phi (L_{1phi}) of lapsed cycle (L_1).
.618 × 1.00 = .618 (L_{1phi})

Step 5: Calculate cycle balance (B_1) as total cycle length − (A_1).
5125 − 5122.80 = 2.20 years (B_1)

Step 6: Apply phi ratio of lapsed cycle (L_1) to the balance of the cycle (B_1) to find the interval in years between the seed date and the next time it repeats (I_1).
2.20 × .618 = 1.36 years (I_1)

Step 7: Add the interval (I_1) to the original seed date to find the next repeat (new seed date).
5122.80 + 1.36 = 5124.16

Step 8: Convert back to Gregorian date.
5124.16 − 3113 = 2011.16 (February 2011)

Example 10—*Find:* First cycle-repeat date for the conditions of economic collapse that began in 1929

- *Input 1:* The seed date for economic collapse in the 20th century: **1929.83**

- *Input 2:* The total length of the cycle that tells us where we are in present time: **5,125 years**

Step 1: Identify modern (Gregorian) date of seed event (S_1).
1929.83

Step 2: Convert event (S1) to absolute date (A_1).
1929.83 + 3113 = 5042.83 (A_1)

Step 3: Calculate lapsed portion of cycle (L_1) as a ratio of (A_1) / total cycle length 5125.
5042.83/5125 = .984 (L_1)

Step 4: Calculate phi (L_{1phi}) of lapsed cycle (L_1).
.618 × .984 = .608 (L_{1phi})

Step 5: Calculate cycle balance (B_1) as total cycle length − (A_1).
5125 − 5042.83 = 82.17 years (B_1)

Step 6: Apply phi ratio of lapsed cycle (L_1) to the balance of the cycle (B_1) to find the interval in years between the seed date and the next time it repeats (I_1).
82.17 × .608 = 49.96 years (I_1)

Step 7: Add the interval (I_1) to the original seed date to find the next repeat (new seed date).
5042.83 + 49.96 = 5092.79

Step 8: Convert back to Gregorian date.
5092.79 – 3113 = 1979.79 (October 1979)

Example 11—*Find:* Second cycle-repeat date for the conditions of economic collapse that began in 1929

- *Input 1:* The seed date for economic collapse in the 20th century: **1979.79**

- *Input 2:* The total length of the cycle that tells us where we are in present time: **5,125 years**

Step 1: Identify modern (Gregorian) date of seed event (S_1).
1979.79

Step 2: Convert event (S_1) to absolute date (A_1).
1979.79 + 3113 = 5092.79 (A_1)

Step 3: Calculate lapsed portion of cycle (L_1) as a ratio of (A_1) / total cycle length 5125.
5092.79/5125 = .994 (L_1)

Step 4: Calculate phi (L_{1phi}) of lapsed cycle (L_1).
.618 × .994 = .614 (L_{1phi})

Step 5: Calculate cycle balance (B_1) as total cycle length – (A_1).
5125 – 5092.79 = 32.21 years (B_1)

Step 6: Apply phi ratio of lapsed cycle (L_1) to the balance of the cycle (B_1) to find the interval in years between the seed date and the next time it repeats (I_1).
32.21 × .614 = 19.78 years (I_1)

Step 7: Add the interval (I_1) to the original seed date to find the next repeat (new seed date).
5092.79 + 19.78 = 5112.57

Step 8: Convert back to Gregorian date.
5112.57 – 3113 = 1999.57 (July 1999)

Example 12—*Find:* Third cycle-repeat date for the conditions of economic collapse that began in 1929

- *Input 1:* The seed date for economic collapse in the 20th century: **1999.57**

- *Input 2:* The total length of the cycle that tells us where we are in present time: **5,125 years**

Step 1: Identify modern (Gregorian) date of seed event (S_1).
1999.57

Step 2: Convert event (S_1) to absolute date (A_1).
1999.57 + 3113 = 5112.57 (A_1)

Step 3: Calculate lapsed portion of cycle (L_1) as a ratio of (A_1) / total cycle length 5125.
5112.57/5125 = .998 (L_1)

Step 4:   Calculate phi (L_{1phi}) of lapsed cycle (L_1).
$.618 \times .998 = .617$ (L_{1phi})

Step 5:   Calculate cycle balance (B_1) as total cycle length − (A_1).
$5125 − 5112.57 = 12.43$ years (B_1)

Step 6:   Apply phi ratio of lapsed cycle (L_1) to the balance of the cycle (B_1) to find the interval in years between the seed date and the next time it repeats (I_1).
$12.43 \times .617 = 7.67$ years (I_1)

Step 7:   Add the interval (I_1) to the original seed date to find the next repeat (new seed date).
$5112.57 + 7.67 = 5120.24$

Step 8:   Convert back to Gregorian date.
$5120.24 − 3113 = 2007.24$ (March 2007)

Example 13—*Find:* Fourth cycle-repeat date for the conditions of economic collapse that began in 1929

- *Input 1:* The seed date for economic collapse in the 20th century: **2007.24**

- *Input 2:* The total length of the cycle that tells us where we are in present time: **5,125 years**

Step 1:   Identify modern (Gregorian) date of seed event (S_1).
2007.24

Step 2: Convert event (S_1) to absolute date (A_1).
2007.24 + 3113 = 5120.24 (A_1)

Step 3: Calculate lapsed portion of cycle (L_1) as a ratio of (A_1) / total cycle length 5125.
5120.24/5125 = .999 (L_1)

Step 4: Calculate phi (L_{1phi}) of lapsed cycle (L_1).
.618 × .999 = .617 (L_{1phi})

Step 5: Calculate cycle balance (B_1) as total cycle length – (A_1).
5125 – 5120.24 = 4.76 years (B_1)

Step 6: Apply phi ratio of lapsed cycle (L_1) to the balance of the cycle (B_1) to find the interval in years between the seed date and the next time it repeats (I_1).
4.76 × .617 = 2.94 years (I_1)

Step 7: Add the interval (I_1) to the original seed date to find the next repeat (new seed date).
5120.24 + 2.94 = 5123.18

Step 8: Convert back to Gregorian date.
5123.18 – 3113 = 2010.18 (March 2010)

※ ※ ※

REFERENCE DATES FOR 2012 CONDITIONS

We will use Mode 2 of the Time Code Calculator to pinpoint the times in the past when the conditions of the 2012 end date last appeared. With these dates in mind, we can then use the template created in Chapter 6 to make a meaningful comparison of those times from two different cycles—the 5,125-year world-age cycle and the 25,625-year precessional cycle—to give us an idea of what we can expect for 2012. Following the examples of Appendices A and B, the steps of the process are described in words, followed by the calculations themselves.

Mode 2: What Date in the Past Holds the Conditions We Can Expect for the Future?

To answer this question we need two pieces of information:

- *Input 1*: The target date in the future that is in question.

- *Input 2*: The total length of the cycle that tells us where we are in present time.

— *The Time Code algorithm described*: Always use the following four steps:

Step 1: Identify modern (Gregorian) date of target event.

Step 2: Identify total length of cycle in absolute years.

Step 3: Calculate phi of total cycle.

Step 4: Subtract the cycle's phi point (L_{1phi}) from target date (T_1).

Example 1—*Find:* Date in the 5,125-year world-age cycle that holds the conditions we can expect for the 2012 end date

- *Input 1:* The target date in question: **2012**

- *Input 2*: The total length of the cycle that tells us where we are in present time: **5,125 years**

Step 1: Identify modern (Gregorian) date of target date (T_1).
2012

Step 2: Identify total length of cycle in absolute years (C_1).
5125

Step 3: Calculate phi (L_{1phi}) of total cycle (C_1).
.618 × 5125 = 3167.25 (L_{1phi})

Step 4: Subtract the cycle's phi point (L_{1phi}) from target date (T_1).
2012 – 3167.25 = –1155.25 (1155 B.C.)

Example 2—*Find:* Date in the 25,625-year precessional cycle that marks the conditions we can expect for the 2012 end date

- *Input 1*: The target date in question: **2012**

- *Input 2*: The total length of the cycle that tells us where we are in present time: **25,625 years**

Step 1: Identify modern (Gregorian) date of target date (T_1).
2012

Step 2: Identify total length of cycle in absolute years (C_1).
25,625

Step 3: Calculate phi (L_{1phi}) of total cycle (C_1).
.618 × 25625 = 15836.25 (L_{1phi})

Step 4: Subtract the cycle's phi point (L_{1phi}) from target date (T_1).
$$2012 - 15836.25 = -13824.25$$
(13,824 B.C.)

Meaning: The results of these calculations are negative numbers, indicating that the dates are before the time of Christ (B.C.) in the historical notation. The two dates from these calculations, 1155 B.C. and 13,824 B.C., are the reference dates in our past that tell us where to look in the existing cycles for the conditions that we can expect to repeat in 2012. The results of this comparison are summarized in Chapter 6, Figure 15.

❊ ❊ ❊

ACKNOWLEDGMENTS

The Secret of 2012 and a New World Age is the result of a 22-year search for meaning in the great changes of the world and life. Throughout that time, an incalculable number of people have contributed directly, and sometimes indirectly, to the understandings that have made this work possible. While it would take an additional volume to mention everyone by name, I take this opportunity to express my deepest appreciation to the following:

Each and every person of the Hay House family for all that you do so very well. I could not ask for a nicer group of people to work with or a more dedicated team to help me share a lifetime of work. I'm proud to be a part of all the good things that your effort brings to our world.

I am especially grateful to Louise Hay, founder and Chairperson, and Reid Tracy, President and CEO, for your vision and dedication to the truly extraordinary way of doing business that has become the hallmark of Hay House's success. Reid, once again please accept my heartfelt gratitude for your faith in me and your trust in my work. To Jill Kramer, Editorial Director, I send my many,

many thanks for the impeccable honesty and special attention that you bring to the creation of each of our books. With your very full schedules, I'm still amazed at the way you answer your phone every time I call, and make me feel like I'm the focus of the day!

Carina Sammartino, my publicist; Alex Freemon, my copy editor *extraordinaire;* Jacqui Clark, Publicity Director; Jeannie Liberati, Sales Director; Margarete Nielson, Marketing Director; Christy Salinas, Creative Director; Summer McStravick, Radio Director; Nancy Levin, Event Director *par excellence;* and Rocky George, our on-site audio engineer: my deepest gratitude to you, and each of the talented people who work with you, for all that you do so very, very well! To Georgene Cevasco, Hay House Audio Publishing Manager: a very special thanks for your patience with my schedules, your experience and professionalism, the expertise that you bring to each of our recordings, and especially for the gift of your friendship.

Ned Leavitt, my literary agent: To simply say "thank you" cannot express my immense gratitude for your support and guidance and the integrity that you bring to each milestone we cross together. While I deeply appreciate your always-right-on advice, I am especially grateful for your trust and friendship.

Stephanie Gunning, my frontline editor: Many thanks for your sharp eyes and patience with my ever-changing schedules, our late nights, and last-minute changes. I so appreciate your honest insights, our friendship, and all that you do to help me hone my words while honoring the integrity of my message.

Lauri Willmot, my office manager: Over 11 years ago we began this journey without knowing where it would lead. Now working from different time zones, and in a very different world, you have my continued admiration and deepest gratitude for your willingness to adapt to the changes in both of our lives. Many thanks for being there always, especially when it counts!

Robin and Jerry Miner, everyone at Source Books, and all of the affiliates that have become our spiritual family: My deep gratitude and heartfelt thanks for staying with me over the years. I love you all.

To Jonathan Goldman, my sacred brother in spirit and dear friend in life: As we embark upon the journey of our new work together, the love, wisdom, and support that you and Andi send my way is appreciated even more than ever! I love you both and count you among the great blessings in my life.

To my dear friend and spiritual brother Bruce Lipton: I am so very proud to tour with you and share the stages of the world together. Your words of encouragement mean more than you can know, and the precious moments with you and Margaret are treasured blessings in my life. I love you both, and I'm especially honored to call you my friends.

To Kennedy, my beloved wife and partner in life: I love you deeply and cherish your beautiful heart, our time together, and the joy that you bring to our lives. Thank you for your willingness to embrace each day as a new adventure, in whatever form it takes. Most of all, thank you for showing that you believe in me always, and doing so through the language of your heart.

A very special thanks to everyone who has supported our work, books, recordings, and live presentations over the years. I am honored by your trust and in awe of your vision for a better world. Through your presence, I have learned to become a better listener and heard the words that allow me to share our empowering message of hope and possibility. To all, I remain grateful always.

※　※　※

ENDNOTES

Introduction

1. John Major Jenkins, *Maya Cosmogenesis 2012* (Rochester, VT: Bear & Company, 1998): p. 21.

2. T. J. Lazio and T. N. LaRosa, "Astronomy: At the Heart of the Milky Way," *Science*, vol. 307 (February 4, 2005): pp. 686–7. View a summary online: **http://scienceweek.com/2005/sw050415-5.htm**.

3. The original article describing the cycle of approximately 62 million years was published in 2005. Robert A. Rohde and Richard A. Muller, "Cycles in Fossil Diversity," *Nature*, vol. 434 (March 10, 2005): pp. 208–10. A nontechnical online version is available at: **http://www.dailygalaxy.com/my_weblog/2007/07/the-milky-way-c.html**.

4. Serbian astronomer Milutin Milankovitch theorized that slow changes over vast periods of time in Earth's orbit, tilt, and wobble influence climate change on a cyclic basis. The National Oceanographic and Atmospheric Administration (NOAA) Website's "Astronomical Theory of Climate Change," hosted by the National Climatic Data Center in Asheville, North Carolina, explores these relationships from a number of perspectives: **http://www.ncdc.noaa.gov/paleo/milankovitch.html**.

5. New research suggests a direct link between the magnetic fields of the human heart and those of the earth. With her late husband, William Van Bise, Ph.D., astrophysicist and nuclear scientist Elizabeth Rauscher, Ph.D., researched and developed a sensitive magnetic-field detector capable of measuring the subtle fluctuations of magnetic fields in the earth's atmosphere. Data from the GOES satellites in 2001 demonstrated that these magnetic fields are influenced by changes in

mass human emotion. These discoveries have led to the hypothesis that the communication between the human heart and certain layers of the ionosphere is a two-way communication: the field influences us, and we may influence the field. The Institute of HeartMath (founded in 1991 as a nonprofit research organization to explore the potential of the human heart) has initiated a global project to explore this relationship: the Global Coherence Initiative. For more information, please visit: **http://www.glcoherence.org**.

6. There are a number of translations of the Mahabharata available. Due to its immense size (over 100,000 verses), translations are usually published in sections, of which the classic book the Bhagavad Gita is the most recognized. The quotes that I have used come from author and researcher David Hatcher Childress, referring to the translation of Charles Berlitz and his book *Mysteries from Forgotten Worlds* (New York: Doubleday, 1972). Childress, a lifelong researcher and explorer, has amassed an impressive body of evidence suggesting that advanced forms of technology have existed in the past, which is presented in his book *Technology of the Gods: The Incredible Sciences of the Ancients* (Kempton, IL: Adventures Unlimited Press, 2000).

For those interested in reading sections of the Mahabharata text itself, one of the better translations that I have found is through the work of Pratap Chandr Roy. A portion of his translations may be viewed electronically for academic and research (noncommercial) purposes (see specifically pages 446–7 and 489–91) at: **http://abob.libs. uga.edu/bobk/maha/tovmahab.html**.

7. *Maya Cosmogenesis 2012*, pp. 106–14.

8. John Major Jenkins beautifully describes the astronomy of the 2012 alignment in his online paper "What Is the Galactic Alignment?" located at: **http://alignment2012.com/whatisGA.htm**. In this paper, he references the mathematics of Belgian astronomer Jean Meeus, from his book *Mathematical Astronomy Morsels* (Richmond, VA: Willmann-Bell, 1997).

9. T. S. Eliot, "Little Gidding," *Four Quartets* (Orlando: Harcourt, 1943): p. 49. Read the full text online at: **http://tristan.icom43.net/ quartets/gidding.html**.

Chapter 1

1. C. W. Ceram, translated by E. B. Garside, *Gods, Graves & Scholars: The Story of Archaeology* (New York: Alfred A. Knopf: 1951).

2. Robert R. Prechter, ed. *The Major Works of R. N. Elliott* (New York: New Classics Library, 1980).

3. Since it was created in 1947, the face of the doomsday clock and the current "time" depicting the magnitude of global threats—nuclear, environmental, and technological—has appeared on every cover of the *Bulletin of Atomic Scientists*. As of 2008, the clock reads five minutes before the worst possible time of midnight. Website: **http://www.thebulletin.org/content/doomsday-clock/overview**.

4. Robert M. Oates, *Permanent Peace: How to Stop Terrorism and War—Now and Forever* (Fairfield, IA: Institute of Science, Technology, and Public Policy, 2002): p. 35. This book is a revised version of *Creating Heaven on Earth* (1988) from the same author and publisher.

Chapter 2

1. Robert Boissiere, *Meditations with the Hopi* (Santa Fe, NM: Bear & Company, 1986): p. 32.

2. Ibid., p. 34.

3. Ibid., p. 35.

4. Excerpted from "Some Astrological Intrigue," an article in Caroline Myss' online newsletter, *Caroline Myss* (February 22, 2007): **http://www.myss.com/news/archive/2007/060907.asp**.

5. Ibid.

6. John Anthony West, *The Traveler's Key to Ancient Egypt* (Wheaton, IL: Quest Books, 1985): pp. 402–5.

7. R. A. Schwaller de Lubicz, *Sacred Science: The King of Pharaonic Theocracy* (Rochester, VT: Inner Traditions, 1982): pp. 283–86.

8. *Maya Cosmogenesis 2012*, p. 330.

9. Richard L. Thompson, *Mysteries of the Sacred Universe: The Cosmology of the Bhagavata Purana* (Alachua, FL: Govardhan Hill Publishing, 2000): p. 225.

10. Ibid., pp. 229–30.

11. Ibid., p. 226.

12. Jnanavatar Swami Sri Yukteswar Giri, *The Holy Science* (Yogoda Satsanga Society of India, 1949).

13. David Frawley (Vamadeva Shastri), *Astrology of the Seers* (Twin Lakes, WI: Lotus Press, 2000).

14. Ibid.

15. Different versions of the Puranas list the symptoms of life during the Kali Yuga. These are taken from translations of the Bhagavata Purana, beginning with verse 12.2. An online version is available at: **http://www.veda.harekrsna.cz/encyclopedia/kaliyuga.htm**.

16. *Mysteries of the Sacred Universe*, p. 212

17. The Brahama Vaivarta Purana, one of the 18 major Puranas, describes this time of increased devotion that begins 5,000 years after the birth of the Kali Yuga. It is found in verse 4.129.50. This cycle is referenced online at: **http://en.wikipedia.org/wiki/Kali_Yuga**, and a PDF version of the original Sanskrit text may be found at: **http://is1. mum.edu/vedicreserve/puran.htm**.

18. Villanova University Astronomy and Astrophysics Department's Web page on SkyGlobe software: **http://astro4.ast.vill.edu/ skyglobe.htm**.

19. Graham Hancock, *Heaven's Mirror: Quest for the Lost Civilization* (New York: Three Rivers Press, 1999) p. 98.

Chapter 3

1. "Thousands Expect Apocalypse in 2012," online story referencing a report on **ABCnews.com** regarding doomsday cults gearing up for 2012. Website: **http://news.aol.com/story/_a/thousands-expect-apocalypse-in-2012/20080706152409990001**.

2. Ibid.

3. John Hogue, *Nostradamus: The Complete Prophecies* (Boston: Element Books, 1999): p. 798.

4. Ibid., p. 570.

5. Ibid.

6. Mark Thurston, Ph.D., *Millennium Prophecies: Predictions for the Coming Century from Edgar Cayce* (New York: Kensington Books, 1997): p. 35.

7. Ibid.

8. Ibid.

9. Ibid., p. 110.

10. Charles Gallenkamp, *Maya: The Riddle and Rediscovery of a Lost Civilization* (New York: Viking Penguin, 1999): p. 57.

11. Michael D. Coe, *The Maya* (New York: Thames & Hudson, 1966): p. 47.

12. *Maya: The Riddle and Rediscovery of a Lost Civilization,* p. 57.

13. Michael D. Coe, *Breaking the Maya Code* (New York: Thames & Hudson, 1999): p. 61.

14. Website: **www2.truman.edu/~marc/webpages/nativesp99/aztecs/aztec_template.html**.

15. Website: **www.astro.virginia.edu/class/oconnell/astr121/azcalImages.html**.

16. *Maya Cosmogenesis 2012,* p. 23. It was not until early in the 20th century that modern scholars were able to reconcile the dates indicated by the Mayan galactic calendar with those on our modern calendar. Even today, there is still some controversy as to precisely when the 5,125-year cycle of the Mayan calendar begins. After the exhaustive study described in this text, and after taking into account the shifts and adjustments made by the Romans and the early Christian church, the date that is most widely accepted as the start of the great Mayan cycle is 3114 B.C. This is the date that Jenkins references in his work and the one I use for consistency throughout this book.

17. Ibid., p. xxxix.

18. Ibid., p. 330.

19. E. C. Krupp, Ph.D., director of the Griffith Observatory in Los Angeles, quoted in an article written for **ABC30.com** by Gene Haagenson Online version at: **http://abclocal.go.com/kfsn/story?section=news/local&id=5928063**.

20. José Argüelles, *The Mayan Factor: Path Beyond Technology* (Santa Fe, NM: Bear & Company, 1987): p. 145.

21. "Computer Models Predict Magnetic Pole Reversal in Earth and Sun Can Bring End to Human Civilization in 2012," *India Daily* online: **http://www.india daily.com/editorial/1753.asp**.

22. Ricardo Duran, a retired California State University professor who lectures on the Mayan calendar, quoted in an article written for **ABC30.com** by Gene Haagenson. Online version at **http://abclocal.go.com/kfsn/story?section=news/local&id=5928063**.

Chapter 4

1. Terence McKenna, *The Invisible Landscape: Mind, Hallucinogens, and the I Ching* (New York: HarperOne, 1994) and *True Hallucinations: Being an Account of the Author's Extraordinary Adventures in the Devil's Paradise* (New York: HarperOne, 1994).

2. Blog site devoted to Terence McKenna's TimeWave Zero 2012: **http://timewave.wordpress.com/2007/12/26/terrence-mckenna-timewave-zero-2012**.

3. Ibid.

4. Before McKenna's death in 2000, he worked with British mathematician Matthew Watkins to identify the strengths and weaknesses of the timewave zero theory and calculations. With an introduction in McKenna's own words, this article, "Autopsy for a Mathematical Hallucination?" offers an honest assessment and the recommendations that lay the foundation for the later revisions by physicist John Sheliak: **http://www.fourmilab.ch/rpkp/autopsy.html**.

5. Web page: **http://www.valdostamuseum.org/hamsmith/2012.html**

6. Edward Teller, et al. *Conversations on the Dark Secrets of Physics* (Cambridge, MA: Perseus Publishing, 1991): p. 2.

7. Seth Lloyd, *Programming the Universe: A Quantum Computer Scientist Takes On the Cosmos* (New York: Alfred A. Knopf, 2006): p. 3.

8. Ibid.

9. From an interview with Seth Lloyd in which he describes the universe as a computer, on the *American Scientist* Website: **http://www.americanscientist.org/bookshelf/pub/seth-lloyd**.

10. Genealogy of Paul Dirac: **http://www.dirac.ch/PaulDirac.html**.

11. Benoit Mandelbrot, *The Fractal Geometry of Nature* (New York: W. H. Freeman, 1983).

12. "The Seed Salon: Benoit Mandelbrot and Paola Antonelli," *Seed* (April 2008): p. 46. Website: **http://www.seedmagazine.com/news/2008/03/paola_antonelli_benoit_mandelb.php**.

13. Dan Brown, *The Da Vinci Code* (New York: Anchor Books, 2003): p. 93.

14. The golden ratio falls into a curious class of numbers that are related as reciprocals of one another. So while the value of *Phi* with a

capital *P* is 1.618, its reciprocal is *phi* with a lowercase *p,* whose value is .618. You can demonstrate this relationship for yourself through the formula 1 ÷ P = p. Substituting the actual values, we find that 1 ÷ 1.618 = .618. Because of this relationship, phi is sometimes called the golden-ratio conjugate. For the mathematical properties of Phi and phi, please see the BBC Website: **http://www.bbc.co.uk/dna/h2g2/ A2346374**.

15. An irrational number is one that that cannot be expressed as a repeating decimal or a terminating decimal. The number pi, π (3.14 . . .), is an example of a decimal that is believed to continue infinitely without repeating.

16. Plato's model of the universe and the dodecahedron. View online at: **http://www.mlahanas.de/Greeks/PlatoSolid.htm**.

17. "Physics: Isaac Newton's Mechanics," from the On Truth & Reality Website: **http://www.spaceandmotion.com/physics-isaac- newtons-mechanics.htm**.

18. Herman Minkowski, *The Principle of Relativity: A Collection of Original Memoirs on the Special and General Theory of Relativity* (New York: Dover, 1952): pp. 75–91. Online excerpt at: **http://alcor. concordia.ca/~scol/seminars/conference/minkowski.html**.

19. Alice Calaprice, ed., *The Expanded Quotable Einstein,* (Princeton, NJ: Princeton University Press, 2000): p. 234.

20. Ibid., p. 238.

21. From an article written by Walter Isaacson (author of *Einstein: His Life and Universe*), "The World Needs More Rebels Like Einstein," *Wired,* issue 15.04 (March 2007). Website: **http://www.wired.com/ wired/archive/15.04/start.html**.

22. B. S. DeWitt, "Quantum Theory of Gravity. I. The Canonical Theory," *Physical Review,* vol. 160, issue 5 (August 1967): pp. 1113–48.

23. Tim Folger, "News Flash: Time May Not Exist," *Discover* (June 2007):p.78.Onlineversionavailableat:**http://www.discovermagazine. com/2007/jun/in-no-time/article_view?b_stgart:int=1&-C=**.

24. Benjamin Lee Whorf, *Language, Thought, and Reality,* John B. Carroll, ed. (Cambridge, MA: MIT Press, 1964): pp. 58–9.

25. Ibid., p. 262.

26. Ibid.

27. Ibid., p. 59.

28. *The Expanded Quotable Einstein*, p. 75.

29. Website: **http://lambda.gsfc.nasa.gov/product/cobe**.

30. Donald Reed, "Torsion Field Research," *New Energy News,* vol. 6, no. 1 (May 1998): pp. 22–4. Online version at: **http://www.padrak. com/ine/NEN_6_1_6.html**.

Chapter 5

1. Michael Drosnin, *The Bible Code* (New York: Simon & Schuster, 1997): pp. 13–18.

2. Ibid., pp. 15–17.

3. Ibid., p. 19.

4. Ibid., p. 174.

5. Eric Hobsbawm, "War and Peace in the 20th Century," *London Review of Books* (February 21, 2002). Hobsbawm's statistics show that by the end of the century, over 187 million people—*a number that represents more than 10 percent of the world's population in 1913*—had lost their lives to war.

6. Zbigniew Brzezinski, *Out of Control: Global Turmoil on the Eve of the Twenty-First Century* (New York: Simon and Schuster, 1995): p. 12.

7. Robert J. Hanyok, "Skunks, Bogies, Hounds, and the Flying Fish: The Gulf of Tonkin Mystery, 2–4 August, 1964," *Cryptologic Quarterly,* National Security Agency. Website: **http://www.nsa.gov/vietnam/ releases/relea00012.pdf**.

8. Ibid.

9. Richard C. Cook, "It's Official: The Crash of the U.S. Economy Has Begun," Centre for Research on Globalization Website (posted June 14, 2007): **http://www.globalresearch.ca/index. php?context=va&aid=5964**.

10. Ibid.

11. Preston J. Miller, Thomas H. Turner, and Thomas M. Supel, "The U.S. Economy in 1980: Shockwaves from 1979," *Quarterly Review 412* (Winter 1980). The Federal Reserve Bank of Minneapolis Website: **http://www.minneapolisfed.org/publications_papers/pub_ display.cfm?id=137**.

Chapter 6

1. Richard Laurence, LL.D., Archbishop of Cashel, trans., *The Book of Enoch the Prophet* (San Diego: Wizards Bookshelf, 1995): p. iv.

2. Ibid., p. 111.

3. *Meditations with the Hopi,* p. 113.

4. J. R. Petit, J. Jouzel, D. Raynaud, N. I. Barkov, J. M. Barnola, I. Basile, M. Bender, J. Chappellaz, J. Davis, G. Delaygue, M. Delmotte, V. M. Kotlyakov, M. Legrand, V. M. Lipenkov, C. Lorius, L. Pépin, C. Ritz, E. Saltzman, and M. Stievenard, "Climate and Atmospheric History of the Past 420,000 Years from the Vostok Ice Core, Antarctica," *Nature,* vol. 399, no. 6735 (June 3, 1999): pp. 429–36. Press release online at: **http://www.cnrs.fr/cw/en/pres/compress/mist030699.html**.

5. Raimund Muscheler, Jurg Beer, Peter W. Kubik, and H. A. Synal, "Geomagnetic Field Intensity During the Last 60,000 Years Based On ^{10}Be and ^{36}Cl from the Summit Ice Cores and ^{14}C," *Quaternary Science Reviews,* vol. 24, issues 16–17 (September 2005): pp. 1849–60. This article describes the correlation between the historical magnetic-field intensity of the earth and specific elements, such as ^{10}B, ^{36}Cl, and ^{14}C, found in the atmosphere captured in Antarctic ice cores.

6. Charles A. Perry and Kenneth J. Hsu, "Geophysical, Archaeological, and Historical Evidence Support a Solar-Output Model for Climate Change," *Proceedings of the National Academy of Sciences of the United States of America,* vol. 97, no. 23 (November 7, 2000): pp. 12433–8. An online version is available at: **http://www.pnas.org/cgi/content/full/97/23/12433**.

7. "Earth's Magnetic Field Reversals Illuminated By Lava Flows Study," *ScienceDaily* (September 26, 2008): **http://www.sciencedaily.com/releases/2008/09/080926105021.htm**.

8. R. A. Kerr, "Magnetism Triggers a Brain Response," *Science,* vol. 260, issue 5114 (June 11, 1993): pp. 1592–93.

9. A. Jackson, A. R. T. Jonkers, and M. R. Walker, "Four Centuries of Geomagnetic Secular Variation from Historical Records," *Philosophical Transactions of the Royal Society A,* vol. 358, no. 1768 (March 15, 2000): pp. 957–90. An online explanation may be seen at: **http://geomag.usgs.gov/intro.php#variation**.

10. Online version of NASA Solar Storm Warning, March 10, 2006: **http://www.science.nasa.gov/headlines/y2006/10mar_ stormwarning.htm**.

11. Ibid.

12. Online version of NASA's explanation for the overlap of solar cycles 23 and 24: **http://www.science.nasa.gov/headlines/ y2008/28mar_oldcycle.htm**.

13. For information regarding the technique of Virtual Axial Dipole Moment (VADM) measurements, please read: "Geomagnetic Field Intensity During the Last 60,000 Years Based on ^{10}Be and ^{36}Cl from the Summit Ice Cores and ^{14}C" (see Note 5). To give greater meaning to the charts in Chapter 6, the units of the magnetic intensity are shorthand for the reading multiplied by 10^{22} ampere meters (AM)^2. For example, the reference date of 1155 B.C. shows the magnetic strength as 10.5 units, or 10.5 × 10^{22} AM^2.

14. *Luminosity*—the output of energy from the sun—is measured as a relative reading of power in terms of photon emissions. The sun's luminosity has changed throughout history and is currently accepted as 3.839 × 10^{26} watts. The historical readings referenced in Chapter 6 are relative to the present luminosity. They were extracted by the author from data reported in "Geophysical, Archaeological, and Historical Evidence Support a Solar-Output Model for Climate Change" (see Note 6).

15. New techniques in correlating temperatures with ice core characteristics have provided an unprecedented record of global temperatures for the last 420,000 years. The data for Chapter 6 temperature comparisons is extrapolated by the author from "Climate and Atmospheric History of the Past 420,000 Years from the Vostok Ice Core, Antarctica" (see Note 4).

16. About Paul LaViolette: **http://www.etheric.com/LaViolette/ Predict.html**.

17. "Geomagnetic Field Intensity During the Last 60,000 Years Based on ^{10}Be and ^{36}Cl from the Summit Ice Cores and ^{14}C."

18. Jean-Pierre Valet, Laure Meynadier, and Yohan Guyodo, "Geomagnetic Dipole Strength and Reversal Rate Over the Past Two Million Years," *Nature*, vol. 435, no. 7043 (June 9, 2005): pp. 802–5.

Chapter 7

1. *The Bible Code*, p. 155.

2. Ibid., p. 177.

3. Sir John Hubert Marshall wrote a three-volume work on the findings of the Indian Archaeological Survey's excavation, *Mohenjo-Daro and the Indus Civilization* (1931).

4. A. Gorbovsky, *Riddles of Ancient History* (Moscow, Russia: Soviet Publishers, 1966): p. 28.

5. *Meditations with the Hopi*, p. 112.

6. Chief Dan Evehema's message to humankind may be read in its entirety at: **http://www.wolflodge.org/hopi.htm**.

7. *Meditations with the Hopi*, p. 112.

8. Ibid., p. 41.

9. Ibid., p. 113.

10. Ibid., p. 112.

11. The title of an article about the 1998 study from the Weizmann Institute of Science in Rehovot, Israel, says it all: "Quantum Theory Demonstrated: Observation Affects Reality." In terms that sound more a philosopher's hypothesis than a scientific conclusion, the paper describes how we affect reality just by watching it. Rather than being buffered from our world and the things that make life what it is, the studies prove that we are intimately connected with everything from the life inside of our bodies to the world beyond them. Our experience of consciousness expressed as feeling and belief is doing the connecting. In the act of simply looking at our world, the feelings and beliefs that we have as we focus our awareness upon the particles that the world is made of changes those particles while we're looking. E. Buks, R. Schuster, M. Heiblum, D. Mahalu, and V. Umansky, "Dephasing in Electron Interference by a 'Which-Path' Detector," *Nature*, vol. 391 (February 26, 1998): pp. 871–4. Summarized in the online article "Quantum Theory Demonstrated: Observation Affects Reality": **http://www.sciencedaily.com/releases/1998/02/980227055013.htm**.

12. Hugh Everett III was the physicist who pioneered the first insights into parallel realities and coined the "many worlds" theory of reality. In the 1957 paper cited here, he went so far as to give a name to the places in time where the course of events may be changed. He called such windows of opportunity *choice points*. Hugh Everett III,

"'Relative State' Formulation of Quantum Mechanics," *Reviews of Modern Physics*, vol. 29 (1957): pp. 454–62. Online version available at: http://www.univer.omsk.su/omsk/Sci/Everett/paper1957.html.

13. From "The Climax of Humanity," George Musser's introduction to the special edition of *Scientific American: Crossroads for Planet Earth*, printed in September 2005. Website: http://www.sciam.com/sciammag/?contents=2005-09.

14. The Global Consciousness Project began in 1998. At that time, a series of random number generators (RNGs) were installed around the world to detect changes in global consciousness. All of the RNGs sent their data over the Internet to a single computer located at Princeton University. The specific correlations between this date; the GOES satellite data; and September 11, 2001, is available online at the Website of the Boundary Institute, a nonprofit scientific research organization dedicated to the advancement of 21st-century science: http://www.boundaryinstitute.org/randomness.htm.

15. Studies conducted by the Institute of HeartMath confirm the biochemical changes in the human body in response to stress. The original findings are reported in: Glen Rein, Mike Atkinson, and Rollin McCraty, "The Physiological and Psychological Effects of Compassion and Anger," *Journal of Advancement in Medicine*, vol. 8, no. 2 (1995): pp. 87–105. The following Website contains a summary of these findings and recommendations regarding how to transform stress: http://www.prwebdirect.com/releases/2008/10/prweb1415844.htm.

16. For information regarding the hypothesis of the relationship between heart-based emotion and Earth's magnetic fields, visit: http://www.glcoherence.org/index.php?option=com_content&task=view&id=30&sectionid=4.

17. Quoted by Howard Martin, executive vice president for strategic development at HeartMath LLC, during his presentation on December 2, 2007, in San Francisco, California.

18. Coherence between the heart and brain is something that may be achieved as the result of a conscious shift of awareness into the heart followed by precise techniques of focus—a key element of global coherence. Information regarding heart-brain coherence may be found at: http://www.glcoherence.org/index.php?option=com_content&task=view&id=30&sectionid=4.

19. The Global Consciousness Project: **http://noosphere.princeton.edu**.

※ ※ ※

ACKNOWLEDGMENTS

Excerpt from "Little Gidding" in FOUR QUARTETS, copyright 1942 by T. S. Eliot and renewed 1970 by Esme Valerie Eliot, reprinted by permission of Houghton Mifflin Harcourt Publishing Company. Additional grateful acknowledgment is made for the illustrations licensed through Dreamstime stock images, member of P.A. and C.E.P.I.C.; to Martin Gray and www.sacredsites.com for permission to use his image of the astronomical observatory of Palenque, Mexico; and to the NASA / WMAP Science Team for permission to reproduce images of the Cosmic History of the Universe and the Diffuse Infrared Background Experiment (DIRBE) from the Cosmic Background Explorer (COBE) satellite. Photo of Prophecy Rock at Old Orabi used with permission, and taken by Bill Tenuto with permission of Hopi Elder Grandfather Martin on 6/4/2007. Out of respect for Grandfather Martin and in honor of this site that is sacred to the Hopi people, and under United States and international copyright laws, this photograph may not be duplicated, scanned, reproduced, manipulated, copied, distributed, sold, or otherwise used for any commercial purpose. Photo of the La Mojarra Stela 1, Copyright © 2000, 2001, 2002 and used with permission under the terms of the GNU Free Documentation License, Free Software Foundation, Inc.

ABOUT THE AUTHOR

Gregg Braden is a *New York Times* best-selling author, a former Senior Computer Systems Designer for Martin Marietta Aerospace and Computer Geologist for Phillips Petroleum, and the first Technical Operations Manager for Cisco Systems. For over 20 years he has searched the remote monasteries of Egypt, Peru, and Tibet for the life-giving secrets that were encoded in the language of our most cherished traditions. His work has led to such pioneering books as *The God Code*, *The Divine Matrix*, and *The Spontaneous Healing of Belief*. Gregg's work is published in 17 languages and 27 countries and shows beyond any reasonable doubt that the key to our future lies in the wisdom of our past.

For further information, please contact Gregg's office at:

Wisdom Traditions
P.O. Box 6003
Abilene, TX 79608
(325) 672-8862
Website: **www.greggbraden.com**
E-mail: info@greggbraden.com

325

Hay House Titles of Related Interest

YOU CAN HEAL YOUR LIFE, *the movie,*
starring Louise L. Hay & Friends
(available as a 1-DVD program and an expanded 2-DVD set)
Watch the trailer at: **www.LouiseHayMovie.com**

THE SHIFT, *the movie,*
starring Dr. Wayne W. Dyer
(available as a 1-DVD program and an expanded 2-DVD set)
Watch the trailer at: **www.DyerMovie.com**

Cosmos: A Co-creator's Guide to the Whole-World,
by Ervin Laszlo and Jude Currivan

*It's the Thought That Counts: Why Mind Over Matter
Really Works,* by David R. Hamilton, Ph.D.

*The Moses Code: The Most Powerful Manifestation Tool
in the History of the World,* by James F. Twyman

Repetition: Past Lives, Life, and Rebirth,
by Doris Eliana Cohen, Ph.D.

Return to The Sacred: Ancient Pathways to Spiritual Awakening,
by Jonathan H. Ellerby, Ph.D.

Transforming Fate into Destiny: A New Dialogue with Your Soul,
by Robert Ohotto

Your Immortal Reality: How to Break the Cycle of Birth and Death,
by Gary R. Renard

All of the above are available at your local bookstore,
or may be ordered by contacting Hay House (see next page).

We hope you enjoyed this Hay House book.
If you would like to receive a free catalogue featuring additional
Hay House books and products, or if you would like information
about the Hay Foundation, please contact:

Hay House UK Ltd
292B Kensal Road • London W10 5BE
Tel: (44) 20 8962 1230; Fax: (44) 20 8962 1239
www.hayhouse.co.uk

***

Published and distributed in the United States of America by:
Hay House, Inc. • PO Box 5100 • Carlsbad, CA 92018-5100
Tel: (1) 760 431 7695 or (1) 800 654 5126;
Fax: (1) 760 431 6948 or (1) 800 650 5115
www.hayhouse.com

***

Published and distributed in Australia by:
Hay House Australia Ltd • 18/36 Ralph Street • Alexandria, NSW 2015
Tel: (61) 2 9669 4299, Fax: (61) 2 9669 4144
www.hayhouse.com.au

***

Published and distributed in the Republic of South Africa by:
Hay House SA (Pty) Ltd • PO Box 990 • Witkoppen 2068
Tel/Fax: (27) 11 467 8904
www.hayhouse.co.za

***

Published and distributed in India by:
Hay House Publishers India • Muskaan Complex • Plot No.3
B-2• Vasant Kunj • New Delhi - 110 070
Tel: (91) 11 41761620; Fax: (91) 11 41761630
www.hayhouse.co.in

***

Distributed in Canada by:
Raincoast • 9050 Shaughnessy St • Vancouver, BC V6P 6E5
Tel: (1) 604 323 7100
Fax: (1) 604 323 2600

***

Sign up via the Hay House UK website to receive the Hay House
online newsletter and stay informed about what's going on with your
favourite authors. You'll receive bimonthly announcements
about discounts and offers, special events, product highlights,
free excerpts, giveaways, and more!
www.hayhouse.co.uk

JOIN THE HAY HOUSE FAMILY

As the leading self-help, mind, body and spirit publisher in the UK, we'd like to welcome you to our family so that you can enjoy all the benefits our website has to offer.

 EXTRACTS from a selection of your favourite author titles

 COMPETITIONS, PRIZES & SPECIAL OFFERS Win extracts, money off, downloads and so much more

 LISTEN to a range of radio interviews and our latest audio publications

 CELEBRATE YOUR BIRTHDAY An inspiring gift will be sent your way

 LATEST NEWS Keep up with the latest news from and about our authors

 ATTEND OUR AUTHOR EVENTS Be the first to hear about our author events

 iPHONE APPS Download your favourite app for your iPhone

 HAY HOUSE INFORMATION Ask us anything, all enquiries answered

join us online at **www.hayhouse.co.uk**

 292B Kensal Road, London W10 5BE
T: 020 8962 1230 E: info@hayhouse.co.uk